58-12997

P9-APA-662

Date Due

Date Due			
JUL 1 3 '63			
AUG 1 '63			
MAY 5 '65			
OCT 12 65			
OCT 1 9 66			
		PRINTED IN U. S. A.	

Music with Children

Music with Children

Alfred Ellison

ASSOCIATE PROFESSOR OF EDUCATION
NEW YORK UNIVERSITY

DISCARDED

McGRAW-HILL BOOK COMPANY, INC.

New York   Toronto   London

1959

45609

MUSIC WITH CHILDREN

Copyright © 1959 by the McGraw-Hill Book Company, Inc. Printed in the United States of America. All rights reserved. This book, or parts thereof, may not be reproduced in any form without permission of the publishers. *Library of Congress Catalog Card Number* 58-12997

II

19192

780.72
E11

McGraw-Hill Oct.'61 Gift

Preface

THIS BOOK proffers a basic music program for the elementary school. Intended primarily for classroom teachers, it assumes no technical background in music. Since music is within people, the primary role of the teacher is to release the music within children. Based on the developmental point of view, the music program suggested emerges from the total framework of modern conceptions of children's growth and development, and the contributions that music as a specific area of curriculum activity can make to fulfill children's total growth potential.

Many different kinds of musical experiences can be provided for and with children by all teachers, despite limitations in their knowledge of musical techniques. Musical expression and sensitivity are matters quite different from the accumulation of musical techniques and skills. Every classroom teacher can meet the needs of children for joyous musical activities, for deep and basic involvement in various types of musical experiences. Accordingly, this book makes specific suggestions for desirable activities that are possible in the typical classroom situation: singing, movement and music, playing music, listening to music, and creating music.

v

Whether or not to include music as part of the school's efforts, fortunately, no longer remains a major controversial issue. Man's historic need for and use of music have led to increasing emphasis on musical activities as part of the school program. The realization that increasing emphasis on science, technology, and material growth in our society needs balance through the creative and expressive arts leads to a search for increasingly effective means to release the powers of music more completely so that they may serve man. Music, a feeling thing, thus has many contributions to make to the lives of children and society.

Classroom teachers increasingly face the responsibility for teaching music. Although no national figures seem to be available about the number of classroom teachers completely responsible for teaching music, a spot check recently indicated that the range extended up to 70 per cent of all elementary teachers in some states. In addition, a number of classroom teachers who have some specialist assistance in music receive such assistance on a very limited basis. Many classroom teachers have thought themselves unable to teach music either because of lack of technical background or because of mistaken ideas about what makes a good music program. This book has been written primarily with the needs of the classroom teacher who has had little or no specialized training in music in mind, including both those who are preparing to become teachers and those who inevitably seek to improve their effectiveness after they become teachers. Although some specific kinds of musical activities depend on the acquisition of specific musical skills, a balanced, rich, and vital music program can be conducted without specialized training in musical techniques; the classroom teacher can provide many exciting, extending, and pleasurable musical activities for children.

Music educators, whether they work as special teachers, supervisors, or consultants, might be presumed to have developed the outlooks, attitudes, and procedures contained in these suggestions to classroom teachers. Certainly, if classroom teachers with no technical background in music can provide the musical experiences suggested, music educators with their greater specialized training in music should be able to do so readily. Unfortunately, this assumption is not always tenable, since specialized training in music is ordinarily not accompanied by corresponding emphasis on understanding children and curriculum.

The success of the music educator will ultimately be determined on the basis of how well he works together with and through the classroom teacher, collaborating to pool their mutual backgrounds in the best interests of children's musical growth. Music educators, both in service and in training, will find in this book a framework for the music program different from the one too often suggested by technical mastery alone. This basic approach should be part of the equipment of every music educator, both as he expands his own conceptual framework of the music program and as he attempts to expand the implementation of an exciting music program through the good offices of the classroom teacher.

Administrators, supervisors, curriculum coordinators and consultants, and helping teachers will all find this material of value to them, both as it sets a frame of reference for their work with teachers and as it provides specific recommendations and suggestions for teachers to use in their own classes.

The genesis of an idea is extremely difficult to trace, and I am sure that my debts are far greater than I can possibly acknowledge. To many, many classroom groups of children, I am deeply indebted for what they have taught me as I worked with them, sometimes as a music specialist and at other times as a classroom teacher. During those teaching years and also while I was an elementary school administrator, many classroom teachers—my colleagues in working with children—helped me further to clarify my ideas. Since joining the staff of New York University's School of Education, I have learned much from students and colleagues. Undergraduate and graduate students, both those preparing to become teachers and those already teaching, have challenged and stimulated many ideas, forcing their crystallization and modification. My colleagues, especially in the Department of Early Childhood and Elementary Education, have been a never-failing source of support and stimulus.

Two other sources deserve special mention. To my daughter, Dara, who in the sweetness of her being and the example of her growth has taught me much, I am deeply grateful. My wife, Gertrude, has held up wonderfully under the trials and tribulations of a writing husband and has been a source of constant aid of substance and spirit, although she insists that her major role has been that of sounding board.

Alfred Ellison

Contents

Appendix

Teaching Music

EVERY CLASSROOM TEACHER can teach music successfully. Every classroom teacher, no matter how limited his own background of technical training in music, can successfully help his children to a vivid experience with music. Through design or inadvertence, the adequacy of the music program frequently depends on the classroom teacher. His knowledge of the children in his class and his desire to provide suitable experiences in music are his most important assets.

WHY TEACH MUSIC?

Children need music. Their full growth and development depend in part on a vital experience in the area of the creative arts. Music provides one of the most important creative mediums for children's expression, playing an important role in the here-and-now development of children. With the fulfillment of this role, we see a continuous, ever-growing enjoyment of music, leading to fuller, happier, and continuous growth and development of the child, laying the groundwork for a fuller and happier adult life which should include music.

Music as a Tool

Music provides release, fulfillment, stimulus. Whatever the mood of an individual may be, its counterpart or opposite may be found in some musical composition. In the classroom, music serves many social as well as personal values for children. In its contribution to the growth and development of children, music serves as a tool of good teaching. Music is so much a part of human make-up that the primary role of the teacher is to release the music that is within children, to provide the kinds of experiences which will enable children to fulfill their musical nature.

Music serves to balance the school day, providing opportunities for children to engage in a variety of advantageous activities. The joyous singing of different types of songs, expressing feeling through body motion, playing various types of musical instruments, active listening to music, actually creating music both as an activity in itself and as an approach to all other aspects of the music program—all of these are tools available to the classroom teacher as he plans to meet the growth and developmental needs of his children.

Individual and Group

All teachers face the dual problem of helping children learn how to work with others and how to work independently. In a good learning situation both of these goals receive continuous attention from teachers. There are few activities in which the role of the individual in contributing to the work of the whole group has the same quality as in a group musical effort. A great symphony orchestra, for example, may contain upwards of a hundred people, each of whom contributes to the group effort. The final outcome, the performance of some musical composition, exemplifies one of the finest instances of cooperative endeavor. The oboist molds his melodic line as he feels it, having mastered the technical aspects of oboe playing so that his intellectual understanding and feeling are expressed without any handicap of inadequate technique. As he performs this highly personal task, however, he does it within the framework of the cooperative endeavors of all the other instrumentalists in the orchestra. All the players subject themselves to the discipline of molding their efforts within the conception of the musical work indicated by the person who coordinates all their efforts: the conductor.

The orchestra would be completely ineffectual, indeed chaotic, if any instrumentalist, deciding that his own interpretation was superior, went off on his own individual path of interpretation without regard to the balance, tempo, and total interpretation of the conductor.

In the classroom we have no intention of performing any work on the level of a symphony orchestra performance, or of emulating the authoritarian control exercised by some conductors. But on the children's own level, varying with their ages, the individual control of his own role by each child and the subordination of that individual role to the cooperative efforts of the whole group can be just as important. It might be in the singing of a group song. It might be in a group instrumental ensemble. It might be a dramatic, rhythmic pantomime. The individual performance must be on as high a level as the individual has reached in capability; yet his own role must be subordinated to the cooperative effort of the group, the interpretation or conception of the entire work held by the entire group.

In the classroom each child contributes to the development of the conception of the entire work, and he contributes to the performance of the entire work. He learns in the process how to work with others, how to maintain his individuality and yet contribute to cooperative efforts. He learns that the work of the whole can be greater than the work of an individual, yet the work of the whole depends on the work of many individuals as individuals.

Leadership and Followership

In a democratic society leadership shifts on occasion. We do not believe in developing a group of leaders, an elite, with the rest of the population relegated to the role of followers. Everyone has some leadership potential in certain situations. As situations change, leadership can change. The leader in one situation becomes a follower in another situation. Teachers accept the responsibility of helping individual children learn how to be both good leaders and good followers. Children learn what is involved in being a good leader and the situations in which they feel most comfortable as leaders. The elements of good followership are similarly learned by the children.

Musical activities offer many splendid opportunities for each child to be both leader and follower. He learns the elements of leadership through experience in a situation in which total results frequently may depend on good leadership. Similarly, as a follower, the child learns through direct experience how to subordinate his personal wishes and desires and to cooperate with a leader.

Other Social Values

The development of the ability to work and play with others grows over a period of years. At the age of two, children generally do not play with each other. They play *at* each other, *by* each other, *near* each other, but not *with* each other. They may look around to see if the other child is still there but do not reach out to include the other in their play.

At three, most children usually begin to play with each other. Ordinarily, at this age such play will be in groups of two or three children. Social activity in small groups continues through about six years of age. The peripheral group may be slightly larger as the child comes to his sixth year. That is, several more children may be included in the periphery, but the basic play groups still consist of very small numbers of children.

At six and seven, the child begins to encompass a larger group in his direct play relations. He is probably seven or eight before he includes a total class in his play potential. At about eight, he may begin to see himself as part of a peer group which is quite important to him. He may identify with this group quite vehemently and exclude from his playmate circle those who are not in this peer group. Frequently, these peer groups are exclusively of one sex. Such peer groups may remain crucially important in the child's life until he is about twelve and begins to look with interest at children of the opposite sex.

Any definition of activity or interest that relates to a specific age group must always be broadly interpreted. While any one factor may be true of many children at the particular age cited, it may be true quite normally for other children at different ages. Variations from generalizations about children are very frequent. Some factors about which generalizations are made are culturally conditioned, determined largely by the expectations of the family and the community. Variations from generalized patterns must not be interpreted as "not normal"; the children who vary may be merely different in pattern of development.

Through music, teachers find opportunities to provide social experiences for children on whatever level of development they have reached at any particular time, and may help children enlarge their focus from small groups to larger ones. Musical activities can include large or small groups at various times. A rhythmic pantomime may be developed by a small group of children or an entire class. A small group may work out an instrumental composition; the whole class may compose a song. Children, in their interaction, stimulate each other as they learn to work together, and modify, clarify, and amplify their own ideas in consequence of working together.

Man, a social being, has derived all of his peculiarly human characteristics in a social setting. Only as he interacts with other human beings does he acquire human traits. Music offers opportunities for the furtherance of ability to relate with others toward a common purpose and stimulates individual social development, the growth of both interdependence and independence.

Emotional Response

Music, however, serves many individual needs as well as social ones. The primary appeal of music is to the emotions. The language of music itself does not carry with it the specific kind of meaning that words convey. A group of people listening to a composition new to all of them would interpret the literal meaning of the composition quite differently. Indeed, unless the "meaning" has been previously established by specific words, there would probably be as many different interpretations of the composition as there were listeners. And no one individual can properly insist that his interpretation is correct and the other ones wrong.

By the same token, no one may properly insist that his feelings about any particular musical composition are the "right" ones and other feelings about that composition "wrong." Properly, any one individual may insist only that his feelings about any one composition are right for him. Similarly, other individuals may insist only that their individual reactions about any one composition are "right" for them as individuals.

Since the primary appeal of music is to the emotions, it seems strange that anyone would put himself in a position of saying that a particular composition should or should not appeal to you. When you listen to a musical composition, you may like it or not. Suppose you do like it. Something about the composition appeals to you. The music "feels" right to you. You are as much entitled to your feelings and they are just as right for you as are the negative feelings that someone else may get about the same composition. You are both equally right as long as your view of the composition is for yourself, as long as you do not attempt to impose your feeling about the music on someone else. And, of course, one's opinions about a composition can and do change.

Children bring different emotional needs to their participation in musical activities, and such participation helps to meet varying kinds of needs. The child who has difficulty verbalizing his feelings may be able to express them through bodily motion in rhythmic activity. The aggressive child may find satisfactions in venting his pent-up aggression on a drum. The shy, retiring child may discover his first fulfilling social experiences with others in the mutual activity of a rhythmic pantomime. All children find means of personal expression through various musical activities. The direct interaction of a child with music provides an outlet for the expression of his feelings, a stimulus to the communication of feeling, and an enriching factor in his life.

The meaning of music can be interpreted only in terms of its meaning to individuals. Different individuals bring to music differing backgrounds of experiences, needs, and growth potential. Consequently, the meaning of a musical composition will vary from person to person according to his own needs. The interaction of the emotional charge of a musical composition with the emotional charge of an individual creates the feeling that individual has about that music and determines the meaning of the music for him.

One of the wonderful things about music is that it can be all things to all men. Everyone takes from music what he wants to take from it. Children respond to music similarly. They like it or not according to whether or not it appeals to them. And each child is correct for himself, both he who likes and he who dislikes the same composition, according to its emotional appeal. Response to music remains a highly personal attribute. One of the great powers of music is its fulfillment of individual emotional needs.

Physical Response

Life is full of rhythm. From the basic rhythm of our heartbeats and breathing, through the periodic recurrence of night and day, to the periodicity of most of our undertakings throughout life, we find rhythm. Rhythm is one of the bases of music. From the basic underlying pulsations, through the variations in the melodies and the periodic recurrence and variation of the larger musical ideas, rhythm is an inseparable part of music.

We often sense and feel the rhythm of music physiologically

either with overt muscular reactions or with a kind of sub-muscular reaction. For children to react as fully as possible to music, they need many experiences in which they can use their muscles specifically to express their reactions to music: rhythmic bodily motion.

This need for response to music with their bodies coincides with children's muscular growth needs. Children need to use their large body muscles in order to aid in their growth and control. Responding to music with their whole bodies offers an excellent means of meeting both of these needs: the physiological, muscular growth need and the need to sensitize and express bodily response to music.

Children's growth pattern muscularly starts with large body muscles and through a process of gradual differentiation and growing control proceeds to the development of coordination and control of the small muscles. Not only does music provide opportunities for the development of control over the large body muscles, it also provides opportunities for the development of control and coordination of the small muscles. Playing instruments requires the use and control of small muscles of the hands, fingers, and arms. Instruments may be broadly conceived to include shaking, striking, plucking, blowing, and bowing instruments of all kinds. Physiological values extend from the mastery of control over the simplest kind of rhythm instruments to the complexity of band and orchestral instruments.

Music activities have many physical contributions to make to the growth and development of children.

Intellectual Response

Understanding, listening to, and performing music also require an intellectual component. The trained musician must apply a high level of intelligence to the accomplishment of his training. In classroom music the intellectual component is quite different from that required of the technically trained musician, although an intellectual response is included.

In the classroom this intellectual response may take the form of understanding the way musical effects are produced. It may include the verbalization of feelings about music. We also see intelligence at work in the production of musical effects. The development of critical standards genuinely reflecting children's own levels of development rather than imposed adult standards also requires the application of intelligence.

On the adult level one function of the application of intelligence is to heighten the emotional reaction to a composition; the emotional response is increased through intellectual insight into the composition. At the child's level of growth, as he begins to focus his listening and his reactions to music, his intelligence is also at work applying what he knows as he listens. Consequently, on his own level, an intellectual component may well add to the emotional response he has to music.

Creativity

Our world of today has great need of creative people. We face problems in our society that have no previous counterpart in man's history. The rate of change in society is accelerating rapidly. With the promulgation of new techniques in automation in industry and the development of the potential of atomic energy for peacetime applications, the rate of change must accelerate even more rapidly. New problems will face our society. The structure, organization, and philosophy as well as the material aspects of society will be constantly subjected to the stresses of rapidly accelerating change. To the twin eternal sureties of death and taxes we must add a third: change. We are unable to predict with assurance about the world in which our children will mature; we can predict only that it will be even more different from the world of today than the world of today is from the world of our childhood.

New problems demand new solutions. New solutions depend on the development of people with the creative potential to be able to tap internal resources to find them. Creativity is most difficult to define and to localize precisely. It is the ability to take existing elements and arrange them in new and satisfying patterns. The great creative artist rarely develops new basic components. He uses components that already exist, but he uses them in a new way. He sees ways of organizing these components that no other person has seen. Our society suffers at present from the kind of malfunctioning caused by forcing new components into old patterns of organization. We need the application of creative minds to find new patterns as solutions to the problems created by new developments.

The closest analogy to this new need of society is the work of the creative artist. We need the application of creativity to the work of the sociologist, the physicist, the economist, the political scientist, yes, the psychiatrist and the psychologist, too. And more than ever, we need creativity in teaching. Through the arts we can not only provide for the great fulfillment of individual human beings, but also by using the arts in their creative essence, we can help to develop children's innate creativity. We can help them grow in their ability to see new ways of ordering presently existing components. We can help sensitize them to ways of seeing new patterns and help them develop the skills necessary to translate their insights into actualities.

WHO TEACHES MUSIC?

Current trends in elementary education point to an increasing responsibility for children's music experiences on the part of the classroom teacher. No matter what the school organization may be in terms of assigning the responsibility for teaching music, the adequacy of the music program really depends on the classroom teacher.

Current Patterns

Four patterns characterize present organizational efforts in assigning responsibility for teaching music in the elementary school.

THE SPECIAL MUSIC TEACHER. In some schools music responsibilities are assigned to a specialist who has been trained specifically for the position of music teacher. Such schools usually operate on a semi-self-contained classroom basis. The classroom teacher may be responsible for the total growth and development of the children in his class, but certain special subjects are treated on a semidepartmentalized basis. Subjects often included within the province of specialist teachers are art, music, and physical education. Schedules developed for the specialist teachers in each of these areas provide meetings of every class in the school with the specialist a certain number of times per week. Ordinarily the music teacher may meet with each class two or three times each week, usually for periods of twenty minutes to half an hour depending on the age of the children.

THE MUSIC SUPERVISOR. In some school systems music supervisors, specially trained for the position, have responsibilities covering a number of schools. The major responsibility for teaching music presumably is in the hands of the classroom teacher, who is told what to teach and how to teach it by the music supervisor. The supervisor may visit each classroom periodically, sometimes to teach a "demonstration" lesson, sometimes to check up on what the teacher has taught. Responsibilities of music supervisors may vary greatly according to the organizational pattern within a specific school system. The supervisor may be responsible for one school or for many. In New York City four supervisors in music have responsibility for the music program in over six hundred elementary schools. Under such circumstances the music supervisor's role is of necessity limited to attempts to train some teachers in the possibilities of teaching music. In other systems the music supervisor's role may be closer to that of the special music teacher. Where only one or two schools are included in the supervisor's responsibilities, the supervisor may assume most of the teaching of music. In most systems, however, music supervisors' load assignments permit them to visit each classroom no more than once every month or two.

THE MUSIC CONSULTANT. A comparatively new approach to the problem of increasing the effectiveness of the music program is through the use of music consultants, sometimes called music resource persons or helping teachers, an approach still in its early stages of development and as yet not widely utilized. Responsibilities for the music program, as for all other aspects of the elementary school program, remain in the hands of the classroom teacher as the person in the best position to determine what his children need. But all teachers cannot be equally competent in all areas of the elementary school program. Teachers need trained professional assistance in various areas. Not every teacher needs the same assistance, but it is likely that every teacher might profit by some help in certain areas of the program. To meet this need for adequate professional assistance in specific areas, some leading school systems have begun to appoint resource or consultant personnel to their staffs. Psychological and psychiatric assistance have already been recognized as important. Teachers needing assistance with individual children whose behavior puzzles them can turn to the school psychologist or psychiatrist or other guidance person who has been specially trained for deep insight into such problems.

School systems have begun to appoint resource personnel in other areas such as science and reading. The science consultant and the reading consultant do not work as the former science teacher or remedial reading teacher did. They are not assigned a specific schedule of class visitation. They work on a schedule determined by the teachers who want their help.

A classroom teacher, uncovering an interest in his class in a specific science area, may feel that he needs help in order to achieve the maximum potential indicated by the interest of the children and the importance of the area. He may ask the science consultant for such help as he needs. What the consultant does will be determined by what the teacher wants and needs. Is it to find resource materials? Design experiments? Establish field trips? Develop explanations on the children's level? Teach the class? Work with a small group of children for a while? Any of these would be possible. The science consultant's time is at the disposal of the teaching staff. In a conference the classroom teacher and the science consultant mutually agree on what is desired. If classroom time is needed, it can be scheduled then and there to their mutual convenience.

Teachers do not feel threatened when they turn for aid to a resource person. Such resource consultants have no supervisory powers. They are professional personnel at the same status and professional level as the classroom teacher, but they have because of their training specific skills which have been placed at the beck and call of the classroom teacher who would avail himself of them.

A desirable trend at present seems clearly to be the appointment of music resource-consultant personnel. This would provide the classroom teacher, when he needs it, with the support and assistance of a person well qualified technically in music.

THE CLASSROOM TEACHER. In many school systems throughout the country the elementary school teacher has the responsibility for teaching music. In some situations he may have a music supervisor to turn to for help, or in a few instances he may be able to rely on a music resource person. In most situations, however, the actual supervision will depend on the local administrator of the school. If the school principal knows something about music and feels that it is important, the classroom teacher may have some help. If the school principal knows little or nothing about music, the classroom teacher may be completely dependent on his own resources to develop a music program.

At present a very large number of classroom teachers face a situation in which they are responsible for a proper music program without the support of technically trained music personnel. In addition, many classroom teachers are handicapped by fears and frustrations stemming from erroneous ideas of what makes up a good music program geared to children's developmental needs and erroneous ideas as to the possible handicap of a lack of technical knowledge of music.

Should Classroom Teachers Teach Music?

Current trends point to an increasing responsibility for children's music experiences on the part of the classroom teacher.

Many areas of the country eliminated music specialists in the days of the Great Depression for budgetary considerations. The war period with accompanying personnel problems delayed the reappointment of music specialists in large numbers. During the postwar period the budgetary shock of immediate needs for construction and expansion of the regular teaching staff precluded hiring the specialist personnel required in many areas of the program.

In those schools where music specialists carry their responsibilities as special teachers working on assignments to various classes, the time which any one specialist can devote to any one class is ordinarily comparatively small. One or two 20-minute to half-hour periods per week, usually all that can be managed with any individual class by a typical music specialist, provide at best insufficient time for an adequate program in music.

In these situations responsibility for the actual conduct of an adequate music program falls on the classroom teacher. Some classroom teachers have felt unable to handle these responsibilities because of their own limited technical training in music. Many teachers, however, have felt that to put the music program in the hands of the classroom teacher was to put it where it really belonged. No individual in the school setup can possibly know all the children in a class the way the classroom teacher does. The specialist teacher faces a real handicap in coming to know children intimately. The problem of sheer numbers poses an insuperable barrier to real knowledge of individual children. No specialist can possibly know all the children in a school when the only contact comes through a period or two of music scheduled each week. The task of the supervisor with responsibilities for several schools in coming to know children as individuals is even more impossible.

The classroom teacher lives with his children five hours each day for five days each week for a full school year. Consequently, his knowledge of his children comes from full, detailed, daily contact in situations broad enough in scope so that he knows how his children react to varying kinds of stimuli. He knows their academic prowess. He knows which of them need much support and which have grown to some independence. He knows the family background and the effect that background has on individual children. He knows the little quirks in the behavior of each child in his class. In brief, he understands the developmental pattern and growth level of each child in his class to an extent impossible for anyone else in the school picture.

Furthermore, the classroom teacher knows the group personality of his class. Each class differs from every other class, even when composed of children of the same age and grade level. The individuals in the class differ and their personalities differ. Consequently, the sum total of these personalities and their interactions with each other must differ. Only the classroom teacher can possibly know and understand fully the class personality of his group of children.

As a result many educators have come to believe that the only person adequately informed to make program decisions for a particular group of children is the classroom teacher. No one else knows them intimately enough. It is a sign of the increasing professionalization of teaching that such important decisions are centered in the person who knows individual children in all their strengths and weaknesses best: the classroom teacher.

This trend in the direction of localizing authority as well as responsibility for the growth and development of children in the classroom teacher is made more difficult by the increasingly complex pattern of the expectations of our society and the demands that society makes on our schools. The elementary school teacher is expected to be a paragon of all virtues, all skills, and all accomplishments. He must understand the whole pattern of how children grow and develop and the influence of what he does and how he does it on this growth and development. He must also understand our society and culture, the complex forces at work in it, and the role of the school in that society. He must know how to develop an integrated pattern of learning for his children and how best to stimulate the full and vital growth of each child to his maximum potential. He must also be master of the teaching of all the skills which our children need for living in a modern industrial society.

We not only expect teachers to be almost supermen in their insight and academic prowess, but we also burden them with oversized classes and a mountain of clerical work. We need to devise means of relieving teachers of their mountainous burdens of nonteaching tasks—attendance records, routine reports, inventories, and the like. The crucial issue, however, is that we have reached the point where we should provide needed professional assistance to our teachers if they are to fulfill our expectations of them and their expectations of themselves.

Since the classroom teacher is the one professional in the school who best knows all the children, he is the one who should make the decisions about the program best designed to help them grow and develop. Music should be included as part of the total program.

The reality of the situation existing in most schools shows that classroom teachers actually do determine the adequacy of the music program, whether or not the organizational pattern plans it that way. Music specialists, with their limited time per class and the large numbers of children they contact, cannot actually provide enough experience musically to meet the needs of the children. Under the specialist organizational pattern, unless the few music periods with the specialist are augmented by the classroom teacher, children do not receive an adequate music program. Music should be part of every school day. The burdens of music supervisors with many schools to cover do not permit much direct work with children in music. Again it is the classroom teacher who determines the adequacy of the music program by the experiences he provides. In the other organizational patterns previously described, the classroom teacher frankly is assigned the responsibility of providing adequate music programs.

The question, "Should classroom teachers teach music?"

therefore, has been answered in practice by the reality of the school organizational patterns. If children are to receive an adequate music program, the classroom teacher must teach music, no matter what the organizational pattern.

Can Classroom Teachers Teach Music?

While the basic problem sketched previously indicates that the classroom teacher must in actuality face the problem of teaching music, many classroom teachers feel quite inadequate to provide a substantial music program for children.

For some teachers, their own experiences with music when they themselves were in elementary school have left a residue of dislike, a general feeling of inadequacy or almost helplessness about their competency in this field. Somehow many teachers have come to look at music as an area with an aura of magic about it. They have come to feel that only the initiated can really enjoy music; that one must possess a peculiar talent for it to pass through the magic doors of enjoyment. If they have come to enjoy music without having a technical background, somehow they have the feeling that their own love and enjoyment of music are not adequate as a base to help children learn to love and enjoy it.

Frequently bewildered by the mass of technical details with which the music periods they remember were filled, many teachers reacted quite normally with a sense of frustration. Music for them came to consist of "syllables," and the major purpose of the music period was felt to be mastery of the problem of reading notes. The music specialist had such glib facility in all these technical details. He was a person set apart by his skill and apparent competence.

Many of our present group of elementary teachers, influenced by attitudes created when they were children in elementary school, still look at music with the feelings engendered at that time. Little wonder then that many classroom teachers figuratively throw up their hands in horror at the idea of teaching music. They call for a music specialist to take over their classes. They "trade off" with the teacher down the hall. He had some piano lessons, an asset looked at with particular respect by teachers who did not have them. A frantic search of one's own special talents ensues in an effort to find one in which the "pianist" may be shy. Is it cooking? Or arts and crafts? "Let's trade classes. I'll teach your class arts and crafts if you will only take mine for music!" is the comment too frequently heard.

Unfortunately, the teacher who has taken some piano lessons may actually not be in a position to do a much better job with a real music program than the teacher with whom he is trading. Yes, he may read notes. But this skill alone does not ensure a good music program. The teacher who had no piano lessons may in fact do more to lead his children to full enjoyment of music. Certainly, ability to play an instrument would be a valuable asset to any teacher. The teacher who plays the piano may achieve a fine music program. It is also possible, however, for the teacher with no technical background to achieve a fine music program.

A balanced music program for children includes five major aspects: singing, listening, moving, playing, and creating. During their elementary school years children should have fine experiences in all of these areas, and it would be desirable for them to have experiences in all of these areas during each year. Actually, however, the real necessity is that children have these experiences during their whole elementary school progression. Some teachers may provide experiences in none of these areas because of their own feeling of frustration and lack of technical knowledge about music. It would be far better for each classroom teacher to discover those areas in which he might feel comfortable working with children. He might then provide musical experiences in those areas. The chances are good that all teachers would not feel equally comfortable in exactly the same areas. Consequently, over a period of several years children would have a much better chance of having a balanced music program than many have at present. Classroom teachers without special training in music need to keep in mind that it is very possible to help children have vital experiences in each of these areas, even though the teacher himself has had no technical training in any of them.

The world of music is available to the classroom teacher and through him to children. The classroom teacher need not feel inadequate because he has not had an opportunity to study the techniques of music. While such study can be an important asset, technical knowledge in itself does not guarantee the development of a good music program. There remain many experiences to which the classroom teacher can expose his children for a vital, exciting, stimulating, growth-provoking music program, experiences which require no technical training in music in a teacher's background.

The remainder of this book is devoted to helping teachers understand how they may proceed in developing a balanced music program. It has been written with the needs of the teacher with no technical facility in music in mind. Technical verbiage has been avoided so that this group will not be handicapped. The book will be helpful to all teachers who want to understand how they can develop a music program for children which will help them grow and develop more fully in the potential richness of their total emotional, social, physical, and intellectual well-being. The book will also be helpful to music specialists, especially those who work as supervisors and resource consultants, and to those who would like gradually to shift their role from that of special teacher to resource consultant. It will help them solve the problem of helping teachers, including those who have no technical facility in music, achieve a vital music program with children.

KEEP IN MIND

The following items summarize the major content of this chapter. Individual items may be used for debate, discussion, report, or research topics.

1. Music is a vitally important part of the school program. Not a frill, it is essential to the full development of children.
2. Music provides a splendid tool to be utilized during the entire school day, aiding program development in many ways.
3. Music aids teachers in helping children learn to work both independently and in groups.
4. Music offers opportunities for children to develop skills in both leadership and followership.
5. Music provides opportunities to help in the developing socialization of children according to their growth level.
6. Music serves many personal needs as well as social ones.
7. The primary appeal of music is to the emotions.
8. Music truly can be all things to all men.
9. Music provides opportunities to meet the physical needs of children for both large and small muscular activity.
10. In music the intellect may increase the emotional reaction.
11. Music offers many opportunities for the development of personal creativity.
12. In schools, responsibility for music ordinarily is assigned to a music specialist, a music supervisor, a music consultant or resource person, the classroom teacher, or to a combination of these.
13. Neither music specialists nor music supervisors can possibly know children as well as does the classroom teacher. They see too many children too infrequently.
14. The classroom teacher is the professional best equipped by reason of his detailed knowledge of his children to determine program.
15. Music should be part of every school day.
16. If children are to receive an adequate music program, the classroom teacher must teach music.
17. Many classroom teachers needlessly feel handicapped in the teaching of music because they have no technical training in music.
18. Other classroom teachers needlessly feel handicapped in the teaching of music because of the residue of unfortunate

attitudes created by poor music programs when they themselves were in elementary school.

19. A balanced music program for children includes singing, listening, moving, playing, and creating.

20. Every classroom teacher, no matter how inadequate his own technical knowledge of music, can offer vital music experiences to provide for the growth of his children.

CHAPTER TWO

Clearing the Air
for Singing

BEFORE WE GO into a detailed explanation of possibilities in each of the areas of musical experience for children, it would be well to explore the background and clear the air of some prevalent misconceptions about the nature of good music programs. This will serve two purposes. It will help some teachers understand better how their own feelings of frustration and inadequacy about music have come to be. It will also help all teachers understand when we teach music now how far we have come in leaving behind the unfortunate approaches which created frustration and feelings of inadequacy.

In this chapter we will discuss some of the major handicaps to the development of an expressive singing program. Many of the barriers to the development of adequate music programs are related to false emphases in those parts of the program connected in some way with singing. Later chapters will include discussions of handicaps related to other aspects of the music program.

ATTITUDES ABOUT SINGING

Our feelings about our singing voice usually determine the extent to which we use it. The development of attitudes about our voices, the factors which influence the development of these attitudes, and the implications of these factors for music programs with children need our attention first.

Vocal Cripples

A sizable proportion of the adult population today consists of "vocal cripples." A vocal cripple is a person afraid to use his singing voice. He may sing lustily in the confines of the shower or when he can hide his own voice within the massed singing of a group of people. But he cringes internally if asked to sing alone where others may hear him. Panic takes hold and a thousand rational excuses spring to mind to help him avoid the necessity of exposing his voice naked to others. Asked why he feels unwilling to sing alone, the usual answer of the vocal cripple will be akin to, "I can't sing in tune."

We attach the label vocal cripple to those of our adult population who have this feeling about their voices. It does not signify that the person actually cannot "sing in tune," merely that he thinks he cannot. For all practical purposes, thinking that he cannot serves just as effectively to block him from successful experience as actual physical handicap would.

Just as we find that a very sizable proportion of the general population falls into the category of vocal cripples, so do we find a similar proportion of classroom teachers. Unfortunate as it might be for anyone to be a vocal cripple, the results are far more devastating when the classroom teacher is. The individual of the general population who thinks of himself in this way has lost much pleasure that might come from greater confidence in using his singing voice. His loss is a personal one and affects others only to the extent that he is not as well rounded a person as he might be.

When the classroom teacher falls into the category of a

vocal cripple, however, each year his influence over another group of children is limited by his feeling about his voice. The teaching vocal cripple has little confidence in his ability to help children sing and too often lets this influence his whole approach to music. He thinks of music in terms of the things which caused him to become a vocal cripple. His ideas tend to stagnate because of the pervasive influence of his supposed handicap. Frequently he realizes how unfortunate his situation really is and determines that he will not let his self-felt "affliction" be imposed on his children.

In most cases "vocal cripple" is a state of mind or a feeling engendered by the kind of music experiences the individual had when he was in elementary school. While the practices that created vocal cripples have ceased throughout most of the country, they do linger on in some measure here and there. The most damaging legacy of these unfortunate practices lies not so much in their widespread prevalence and continuation. The damage and the danger remain in the pernicious influence on the people who were exposed to these practices when they were children. Our purpose is to try to overcome that influence.

Singers and Nonsingers

Let us think back to some of the things that happened to many of us when we were in elementary school—things that happened in the name of music.

Do you recall how the sheep were separated from the goats? The "crows" from the "nightingales"? The "singers" from the "nonsingers"? In any group of young children we usually find a few who have not as yet found their singing voices to the extent of being able to reproduce a given melody vocally. The unfortunate label of "monotone" was sometimes attached to such children. Much attention was directed toward helping them find their singing voices. Music specialists were concerned with this problem, and various devices were utilized to help solve it.

One of the early objectives of music programs included an emphasis on the product of group singing: the song should sound well. Those children who had not found their singing voices for reproductive purposes might not sing "in tune." Therefore, it seemed essential that these children be separated from the group at large so as not to spoil the lovely effect of the singing of the rest of the class. The "nonsingers" were directed not to sing with the other children of the group but to listen to the group singing. Often they were seated in the front of the room so that the clear "bell-like tones" of the rest of the class would waft over their heads, presumably bathing their ears in the kind of sound they should be reproducing. This made a convenient placement for the teacher. Since the children were not participating in the activity, it seemed quite likely that they would become restless and attempt to relieve their boredom by the kind of activity that could disrupt proceedings. At the front of the room they were under the immediate and direct view of the teacher and less likely to make trouble.

At times the group of nonsingers was seated together off to the side. In other schools the nonsingers were carefully paired off, each one located next to a child who had good control of his singing voice. However, in these situations the nonsinger was usually still instructed not to sing. This was carried so far in some (fortunately few) situations that the nonsingers were told that they might mouth the words of the song but must never, never *really* sing. The visitor to the classroom might be treated with the lovely sound of what appeared to be the entire class singing, little knowing that among the class were some who just seemed to be singing, some who were already beginning to form the feeling somewhere inside themselves that something was wrong with their singing voices.

"Monotones"

Good practice had it that these nonsingers needed special work. This idea of special work to help nonsingers improve should have effectively exploded that monotone label.

Let us make clear immediately that practically none of these young children having difficulty reproducing a given melody are truly monotones. The word *monotone* probably stems from the Greek. A good analytic look at the word shows that it means "one tone." A true monotone would be a person unable to differentiate one tone from another tone, either vocally or aurally. He would be unable to speak or sing on different pitches, and he would be unable to hear differences in pitches. His speaking voice would reflect this limitation and would largely consist of a single pitch level without variation. Aurally, the true monotone would be unable to differentiate between any different tones. These difficulties in a true monotone are rarely correctable, but the number of true monotones in the world is extremely small.

After the word *monotone* became disreputable, other labels were used. The children who had not yet developed control over their singing voices sufficient to enable them to reproduce a given melody were sometimes labeled listeners, nonsingers, uncertain singers, out-of-tune, or untuned, singers.

No matter what label was attached, many music educators felt that children who were unable to reproduce a given melody needed special help. Many devices, "gimmicks," little song plays, and games developed. "Too-too-too" on a high tone sang the teacher, and "too-too-too" in a matching tone the child was to sing back.

Many of these devices were quite ingenious and did serve to help some children develop control over the vocal apparatus more quickly. More frequently, in their zeal, many teachers forgot that a device is simply a tool and not an end. Where such devices were solely used with the nonsingers and no one else, the nonsingers quickly developed the idea that there was something wrong with their singing voices. The very existence of the idea that something is wrong with the voice can be the determining factor in delaying the development of control of the voice.

SINGING—A DEVELOPMENTAL APPROACH

Customarily young children were classified into two groups for school music purposes: those who could reproduce a given melody, the singers, and those who could not, the nonsingers. Actually, however, such a classification contains two misconceptions. In the first place, categorizing this way and the teaching approaches which accompany it do not take into account the factor of readiness and ignore the idea that increasing control of the singing voice is a developmental process and not solely a skill achieved through training. Secondly, these categories miscast a group of children who do not fall into either category, but who in the classroom were usually grouped with the nonsingers. A sizable number of children can sing quite well and yet are unable to reproduce a given melody.

Spontaneous Singers

Does it seem impossible to you that there would be such children who can sing, but who cannot reproduce someone else's song? Think for a moment. There are an infinite number of possible combinations of tones which when strung after each other become melodies. Sing a few of them—any that come to mind. Just let your voice "play around" with a few tones. Now think back to the last group of five-year-olds you saw at play. There were probably a few children who spontaneously sang as they played. They made up little tunes with appropriate words that occurred to them as they played. These were not necessarily songs in our adult sense of what a song must be. They were nevertheless songs to the children.

Much of this type of spontaneous singing is not truly song at all, but rather a snatch of song. The words may very well be merely a repetition of a phrase or a name or a group of words which caught the child's fancy at the moment. Free of misconceptions of what singing is and what a song is, he bursts forth in melody. He may be unable to repeat his song again with the same tones, or he may repeat the same group of tones endlessly. If he has not been made to feel inadequate about his singing voice, this process of spontaneous singing will continue. He will burst forth into song spontaneously whenever the spirit moves him. Frequently, it will be the repetition of some rhythmic motion in spontaneous dramatic play that will

stimulate him to accompany his motions with song. Loading
a truck with sand, throwing a ball, any of the countless actions
of a young child may be the stimulus for a musical accompaniment.

Such a child may contain within this spontaneous outburst
of melody many, many different tones. Some of these children
are also able to reproduce melodies which they hear others
sing. Some of them, however, have not as yet achieved this
control. Their vocal control may reach the stage of spontaneous singing of songs of their own without accompanying
control in reproducing songs of others. Schools, unfortunately,
have recognized no such category of children. Children were
either singers or nonsingers. The nonsinger appellation is
clearly a misnomer. These children are able to sing. They have
difficulty in reproducing songs of others, not in singing. But
what happens to them when they are classified as nonsingers?
They gradually begin to realize that something is wrong with
their singing voices in the teacher's estimation. They begin to
feel inadequate about their singing voices. Soon all that is left
is the feeling that they truly are nonsingers. The spontaneous
bursts of song disappear. They are still unable to reproduce the
songs of others. Consequently, they now do truly fit the category of nonsinger. This does not have to happen.

Readiness

Let us turn now to the other factor that categorizing children
as singers or nonsingers overlooks—the idea that the growth of
control over the singing voice is a developmental process involving readiness.

All growth is dependent on the interaction of the potential
of an individual with the environment. Some factors of growth,
however, are clearly not subject to modification by the environment except negatively. These facets of growth may be
slowed down by environmental factors but may not be speeded
up. For example, the time at which a young child walks is directly connected with the rate of development of his physiological self, his musculature, his skeletal and neural pattern

of growth. Poor nutrition may delay the full blossoming of the individual and delay such growth processes as walking. However, assuming good nutrition, no amount of training in how to walk will help a child learn to walk before his body is physiologically ready. Learning to walk depends on the readiness of the organism for walking and not on any factors of skill training. Putting a child up on his feet before he is ready for it will not serve to help him learn to walk sooner.

Similarly, the eruption of first teeth is a function of the growth pattern of the particular child. It comes, as does walking, to different children at different chronological ages. The time of eruption of first teeth, like the time of first learning to walk, has no aspect of innate value. One child is not superior to another because his teeth erupt earlier; his pattern of growth is merely different.

Normally children learn to talk at different ages. This, too, seems to be a developmental process. The age at which children first begin to speak may vary normally from about nine months of age to as much as three years. This variation carries no connotation of merit. There is some evidence that many bright children speak early. However, many bright children also speak later. The young speaker may be no brighter and in no way superior to the child who learns to speak at a later date. Their patterns of growth are merely different. No amount of direct teaching or training will help the later speaker to talk earlier, assuming that he has no physiological defect that prevents him from speaking.

Readiness, however, may involve factors other than physiological maturity, although without the physiological maturity, these other factors may have little significance. Readiness to read language depends on a complex of factors which includes physiological readiness but also includes mental age, social and emotional maturity, and facets such as attitude and experience. These readiness factors are subject to biological and environmental influences. The very young child is farsighted. As he matures, the muscles of the eye which control focusing also mature, and the child is more able to focus on near objects.

Research indicates that a physiological age of about six years and three months is the time when this focusing mechanism has reached the point of readiness for reading purposes. Chronologically the child may be younger or older than six years and three months when he achieves such an age physiologically. There is some evidence pointing to a later maturation of the eye muscles of some children, as late as nine years of age. Third- and fourth-grade teachers have frequently had children who, previously unable to read, suddenly seemed to catch on and from then on read voraciously. There well could be a relationship to later maturation of the focusing mechanism of the eye.

We also know that a mental age of about six and a half years offers the optimum point for the beginning of the teaching of reading. Aspects such as home environment, emotional stability, social maturation, and the experiences a child has had all play a role in readiness to learn to read.

But why has all this work been done attempting to find out when children were most ready to learn to read? First, there is the matter of efficiency. There is little point in struggling to teach something to a child at one particular age if by deferring the teaching a short time the child will learn that material much more readily. It is simply inefficient to attempt to teach the child before he is ready. Such attempts frequently end in failure anyway. The teacher pays a tremendous price in wasted energy and frustration. The child, attempting to do something that he may well be unable to do through no fault of his own, must fail and pay the price of failure.

The matter of the frustration and the penalty involved is the second point to be made. Is it not completely unfair to present anyone with tasks that he is unable to accomplish through no fault of his own? This becomes particularly appropriate to keep in mind when we face children with tasks for which they are not ready. At one time the nonpromotion rates from first to second grades were extremely high. The largest proportion of these nonpromotions (for which you may want to read "failures") was due to reading disability. The child had simply not learned to read adequately during the first grade. Later studies point rather directly to the fact that most of these children simply were not ready to read during the first grade. We know now that retaining a child in a grade for a second year can have lasting effects on his feelings about himself, affecting his whole emotional tone and stability. Constant pressure to accomplish a task he is unable to accomplish can do much to create a lasting feeling of inability to achieve that task. A child pushed to read before he is ready to learn can build up lasting attitudes against school, against teachers, against reading. This creates many reading disabilities and is one of the reasons for necessary remedial-reading teaching in the higher grades.

Reading specialists have come more and more to recognize the extreme importance of the readiness factor in learning to read. The complex interplay of the factors involved in reading readiness has led many educators to recognize that children will not all be ready to read at the same chronological age any more than they are ready to walk or talk at the same chronological age. Many teachers have come to recognize that while a good number of children will begin to read during the first grade, a sizable number will not be ready to read until the second and some children will not be ready until the third grade.

The control of the singing voice must now be recognized as a developmental problem. In many instances we have been attempting to push young children into a reproductive role that they are simply unable to accomplish. They may be singers who are able to reproduce a given melody. They may be singers who are able to produce their own melodies, but have difficulty in reproducing a melody given them by someone else. Or they may be among those who have not developed control of the singing voice to the extent that they even sing spontaneously, although this group is quite small in number.

Communication

Both the hearing and vocalization processes exist in human infants long before a relationship is established between these

two. The very young infant has an instinctive fear of loud
sounds. They startle him. He may cry as a result of a sudden
loud noise. Yet we could not say that hearing here is related
directly to the crying, since the crying is really an expression of
the child's fear reaction and triggered by his fear. He has no
conscious knowledge of the loud sound or of his crying. Another instance of his crying may be for food. Here, at first,
there is no connection between hearing and crying. Nor does
he cry consciously to direct attention to the fact that he wants
food. He cries because this is his generalized reaction to im-
balances in his body. He cries. His mother knows that he is
hungry and feeds him. This process could not be termed communicating.

Communication includes a conscious effort to send a signal
to someone else, with a conscious recognition that the other
person may recognize the signal. Actual communication does
not take place until the person sending the signal realizes that
the other person has received and recognized the signal as the
sender intended. Much communication takes place before language development grows into communication with words. We
often hear mothers say about their very young children, "He
can't talk, but he understands everything I say." These mothers
can demonstrate the truth of this comment, too. Very young
children are able to communicate, make their wants known,
and respond to the spoken wants of others before language
facility has developed.

The young baby in his crib will gurgle with glee when his
mother leans over and speaks quietly to him. He will amuse
himself endlessly repeating all kinds of nonsense syllables and
sounds. In this babbling and gurgling he repeats many of the
letter sounds common to languages of all kinds. From this undifferentiated repetition of a multitude of possible human sounds,
he gradually learns that certain combinations of sounds have
significance to the people around him. This recognition grows
both as he hears them speak and as they respond to his accidental repetition of certain syllables which have specific meaning in the native language. The baby may say "ga-ga-ga" and

"ba-ba-ba" repeatedly and get merely an amused smile from mother. But let him hit on "da-da" or "ma-ma" and she responds immediately with great pleasure. Her baby is now talking! Her response of pleasure encourages him again to repeat the accidental touchstone. Sometime after that, he realizes that the "ma-ma" and "da-da" have specific connotations to those around him. When, after such realization, he consciously uses those same syllables, expecting them to be understood as he meant them, and recognizes that they have been so understood, then verbal communication has begun. From such small beginnings verbalization grows until at the first-grade level children may have a vocabulary ranging up to over 40,000 words.[1]

Probably at every step of his development through the elementary school years, the child will continue to understand more words than he uses: his listening vocabulary will be larger than his spoken vocabulary. Both of these will be larger for quite a while than his reading vocabulary, although somewhere along the line his reading vocabulary will surpass all other vocabularies over which he may have control. During much of his elementary school career his writing vocabulary will be his smallest.

Beginnings of Singing

Let us return to the baby babbling in his crib. His cooings and gurglings are never on a single tone. They vary in pitch just as they vary in intensity or loudness and in their use of various vowel and consonant sounds. In a very real sense this may be classified broadly as singing. These cooings and gurglings and babblings vary in pitch, tone, rhythm, and type of sound. They might not be classified as singing in our adult sense of what a song is. Nevertheless we would be justified in pointing to these expressive reactions of the young baby as being closely allied to what we call singing. In this sense we may say that our young children sing before they speak.

[1] Mary K. Smith, "Measurement of the Size of General English Vocabulary through the Elementary Grades and High School," *Genetic Psychology Monographs*, vol. 24, no. 2, pp. 311–345, 1941.

The total content of a child's vocal production achieves tremendous variety and expressive power before he learns to talk. As he learns to communicate through the medium of words, he continues his expression of varying sounds with tonal and rhythmic variations. Frequently this expression has as its content the experimentation with all the varying sound possibilities of the human vocal apparatus. As he begins to learn words, he frequently includes these words in his tonal and rhythmic experimentations. A particular phrase may catch his fancy, and he will repeat the words over and over, not merely speaking them, but singing them. A word may be used this way long before the baby has any real notion of the adult meaning of the word. "Giggle, giggle, giggle, giggle," the baby sings with sheer joy at the sound of the word and the feeling of the word on the tongue, mouth, and larynx as it is sung repeatedly. Yet he may have no notion of the meaning of the word. To our adult ears quite inappropriate words may be the stimulus for this kind of rhythmic and melodic repetition. New Jersey Turnpike, merely the name of a fine, fast highway to us, may catch the fancy of a two-year-old and be the stimulus for a continuous song, whose melody goes on and on, but whose words consist merely of repetition of "New Jersey Turnpike, New Jersey Turnpike," pronounced by a two-year-old, perhaps, as "New Joisey Toinpike." Unlikely possibilities spark the spontaneous outburst in song, and many words not ordinarily considered a likely topic of conversation have a fine rhythmic quality that might serve as the vehicle of spontaneous song.

Countless incidents in the very young child's life and play offer these stimuli for spontaneous singing and practically all children respond during the play that is so much of a young child's life with song. As adults our ears have not usually been attuned to this particular response and frequently we do not hear it. The good nursery school and kindergarten situations provide continuous opportunities for the kind of experiences which stimulate such spontaneous singing.

The major musical focus of the school experience of children in kindergarten and the early elementary grades should be to encourage the growth of this facility for self-expression in spontaneous song.

Controlling the Voice

During the first five years of life some children develop the knack of singing melodies they hear. We do not know too much about how the voice itself is controlled. We do know that the vocal cords must be stretched tighter or made shorter in order to produce a higher pitch. But we also know that we consciously and directly have no control over the tautness or length of our vocal cords. As we grow and develop and have many experiences with language, both hearing and speaking, and with music, both hearing and singing, we develop facility in reproducing desired tones with our voices. We can assume that the control we develop over our voices at young ages is quite closely related to our hearing. We have no evidence at all that control over the singing voice in the sense of facility in reproducing a given melody can be hurried any more than the ability to walk can be hurried. It is quite likely that such control is a developmental process depending in part on growth and maturation of the individual. The most significant single factor influencing the development of control of the singing voice is the desire to sing. Attitudes about one's voice and about singing then become two important conditioning factors in the development of skill in reproducing a given melody.

Three Categories

In terms of control over the singing voice, children may be grouped in three categories:
1. Those children who are able to sing melodies of their own in spontaneous song and also have developed facility in reproducing melodies of others
2. Those children who are able to sing melodies of their own in spontaneous song, but who may be unable to reproduce melodies of others
3. Those children who are unable to reproduce the melodies

of others and have not developed facility in spontaneous
singing of their own melodies

These three categories are not sharply delimited; they shade
off into each other. We find no specific point at which an individual child suddenly achieves control of his voice for spontaneous singing. Similarly there is no specific point at which a
child develops control of his voice in reproducing melodies of
others. An individual child could be categorized by placing
him, in terms of his control, at a point on a continuum. This

Figure 1. OUTMODED CLASSIFICATION OF CHIL-
DREN AS SINGERS OR NONSINGERS

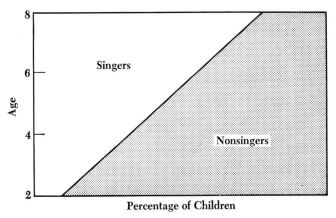

continuum would extend from one extreme of no control, mere
experimentation with sound, to the other extreme of complete
control for both spontaneous singing and reproduction of melodies, passing intermediately through the stage of control for
spontaneous singing but not for reproducing melodies. Each

Figure 2. DEVELOPMENTAL STAGES IN SINGING

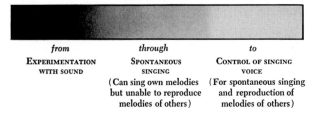

from	*through*	*to*
EXPERIMENTATION WITH SOUND	SPONTANEOUS SINGING	CONTROL OF SINGING VOICE
	(Can sing own melodies but unable to reproduce melodies of others)	(For spontaneous singing and reproduction of melodies of others)

category, however, includes variation in the degree of control which has developed to then. Figures 1, 2, and 3 should be interpreted with this in mind.

As the old categories of "singers" and "nonsingers" are replaced with the three categories described above, we can avoid misplacing those children who actually belong in the category of spontaneous singers. This changed conception of the development of powers of control over the singing voice can help us avoid creating new vocal cripples.

Figure 1 illustrates the old categories; Figures 2 and 3 illustrate the concept described here.

Figure 3. AS CHILDREN DEVELOP CONTROL OF THE SINGING VOICE

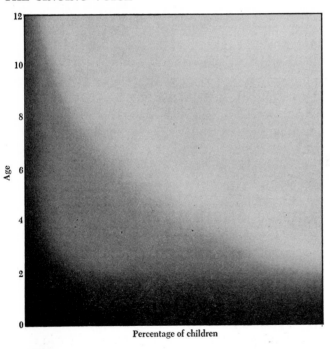

Percentage of children

Experimentation with sound

Control of voice for spontaneous singing but *not* for reproducing melodies of others

Control of voice for spontaneous singing *and* for reproducing melodies of others

Attitude

How important it becomes, then, for us to channelize our efforts to help children develop their singing voices by emphasizing the development of healthy attitudes. Beautiful group singing as an immediate goal and individual drill with "nonsingers" must give way to an approach based squarely on the developmental needs of children and our desire to help each child have the kind of experience in music that will be satisfying and fulfilling to him. Our objective must be to have the individual children in a group *want* to sing and *try* to sing. The resulting sound of a group's singing may not meet our adult standards of beautiful tone quality. No child in the group, however, should develop feelings of inadequacy about his singing voice. At all times, he must be encouraged to sing along with the group and alone when the spirit moves him.

Our classroom atmosphere must include the attitude that children properly sing at their work spontaneously as they feel the urge. Obviously this could not go on all day long, and that is not being advocated. But in those activities where children work in small groups, in constructive-manipulative activities, in "free" work periods, we no longer consider it possible or even desirable that children not talk with each other. Let us expand that to include the growth of spontaneous song. In a happy classroom atmosphere where children busily work on activities that stem from their own needs and concerns, an underlying background of spontaneous singing from individual children would be a splendid indication of one aspect of their emotional involvement in their work.

In group singing every child will be encouraged to sing along with the group. No child will be stigmatized by being asked always to listen while the others sing, merely because he may not be reproducing the song as well as some others in the class. His attitude about singing will be the prime concern of the teacher, who will try to help him develop confidence in his singing voice and will see that nothing she does gives him the idea that he cannot sing.

In kindergarten and the lower grades a large proportion of children will fall in the category of those who have control of the singing voice in spontaneous singing even though they have no control in reproducing melodies or songs of others. Consequently, we should see much more spontaneous singing at these levels than we ordinarily do. The teacher should be alert for those children who do react spontaneously with song, and encourage through various techniques both the development of the individual child and the spreading of such efforts to the other children. Recognition and praise by the teacher can encourage children who sing spontaneously to continue to do so, and can entice other children to try.

READING MUSIC

In many schools a disproportionate emphasis has been placed on attempts to teach children to read notes using the singing voice as the medium. This has been largely unsuccessful and accounts for many of the poor attitudes about music in schools both on the part of children and teachers.

Comparatively little research has been done in the area of readiness for reading in music. We can, however, turn to the vast body of research in readiness for reading in language for many cues. We know, for example, that there is little point in attempting to teach a child to read language until he has developed quite some facility in communicating with language. The teacher in the first grade will ask himself as he determines the readiness of individual children for reading activities, "Does this child speak easily and fluently? Can he express his ideas? Does he ask questions well? Does he speak in whole sentences?" In the classroom he will provide an atmosphere that encourages individual children to speak. He helps build a feeling on the part of the children that what they have to say is important— as important as anything anyone else has to say. He builds an atmosphere of respect in each child for the ideas and expression of every other child. He, himself, is accepting and encouraging in his own attitude as he helps children learn to take turns in speaking and in respecting each other's ideas. Just as important as this atmosphere supporting free and independent speaking is the content of what is spoken. Children need not only a feeling of freedom about expressing their ideas; they need something to talk about. The good teacher will try to make sure that the children's school day is rich in firsthand experiences so that the children will have matters ripe for discussion, analysis, and decision.

When children come to school, they already have a rich background of using language as a medium of communication. As previously indicated, their vocabulary may reach the surprising level of over 40,000 words by the time they are six. Many children have recognized that reading is a remarkable process of extracting meaning from printed "squibbles." Some have already achieved a small amount of skill in reading signs. Stop signs on street corners, their names, various brand names of items frequently advertised have become part of the reading vocabulary of some children. Through the constant repetition of commercials on television programs, children have become familiar with the appearance of printed symbols of one type. Other types of printed symbols become familiar as they see others read and as they watch the pages when they are read to. Some children are part of a reading family. Parents and older brothers and sisters read books and enjoy reading. Newspapers, magazines, and books are part of their home background. Children have been read to and have enjoyed "reading" the pictures in books. The good nursery school and kindergarten program specifically attempts to make children feel at ease handling books, but makes no attempt to teach reading directly. Teachers constantly read stories to children. The good classroom has a library corner or table where books are easily accessible to children and where they may browse as the feeling prompts them.

All these contacts with books and reading and talking and listening contribute to the child's readiness to learn to read himself. The child who has had rich experiences of these kinds will be more ready to learn to read than another youngster who comes from a nonreading home, where books and magazines and newspapers are not part of everyday life, who has not had a rich experience in nursery school or kindergarten, who has not had opportunities to speak and be heard and have his spoken ideas respected.

Music Reading Readiness

Comparable musical experiences should precede efforts to teach the child to read music. He must have many singing experiences that leave him with positive attitudes. He should be encouraged in individual spontaneous singing and in joining in group singing. Listening, creative, and rhythmic activities should be part of his experiential background prior to the time he is asked to learn to read music.

One of the ways classroom teachers can tell that a child is ready to learn to read language is that he begins to read. He is full of questions about reading. His interest and concern about developing this skill are apparent. In music we need to reach the point where we are willing to wait for such cues. When the child feels the need for learning any skill or technique, he makes such needs known. The perceptive teacher can always spot the youngster who has need for any skill. In music we must learn to hold off our efforts to teach skills until the child has had enough experience with different aspects of music so that his need becomes apparent to himself. The best time to teach any skill, including reading music, is the time when the child wants to learn that skill to achieve his own purposes. There is certainly little point in attempting to teach a child to read music until he has had a rich background of experience in music.

Schools would do well to eliminate any consideration of teaching music reading below the fourth grade even in situations where a wealth of experience in music is provided in the primary grades. In schools where such rich experiences cannot be provided in the primary grades, reading music should probably be postponed for the junior high school.

Vocal versus Instrumental Approaches

It is time we faced the fact, too, that very few children learn to read music when the traditional approaches are used. Ask any lay group of adults how many can read music to any degree. Then ask those who say they can read how many of them play or at one time played some musical instrument, no matter what it was. You will find that those able to read music almost invariably are those who have learned through the medium of some instrument rather than through the medium of the voice. In schools, by and large, the children who learn to read music are the ones who are learning it as they learn to play some instrument. Very few children who are not learning to play an instrument ever learn to read music. By "instrument" we mean the piano, a band or orchestral instrument, or some simple, easy-to-play instrument, such as the ocarina, tonette, recorder, harmonica, xylophone. The kind of instrument seems to make no difference. Any instrument, even the so-called "toy instruments," provides a medium for learning notation that far surpasses the voice.

Let us examine the reasons for this superiority of the instrumental to the vocal approach to learning music reading. We have already pointed out that the voice is not directly responsive to conscious physical manipulation. We control the voice largely through mental organization of what we hear. A deaf child has real difficulty learning to speak. Ordinarily when he does learn to speak, it is with a monotone quality; there is little variation in pitch level such as ordinarily accompanies the speech patterns of people with no hearing disability. Recent developments in speech therapy for deaf children have been encouraging in the new techniques which help these children vary the pitch of the speaking voice.

The movements of the vocal cords and the larynx cannot be specifically described in terms of the reproduction of a single tone or of a group of tones. We know that to produce a higher tone the vocal cords must be tightened or made shorter. How tight or how short are impossible to describe or prescribe or reproduce. Consider then the tremendous difficulty of relating a specific staff location of a tone to this imprecise and indeterminable physical control of the vocal apparatus. Consider, too, how simple it is to describe and reproduce any single tone or group of tones on a musical instrument. When we cover such and such a hole, or push down this particular key, we are playing a tone which has this name; on the musical staff it looks like this. In this process we use a specific muscular reaction to produce a given tone which has a specific staff location. This is rational and subject to individual understanding and control.

It is possible, indeed usual, to spend six years in school music attempting to teach children to read notes using the voice as a medium and not achieve the success in this skill that can accompany six months of instruction on an instrument.

The classroom teacher who has attempted to teach note reading by means of the vocal approach must not blame himself for his failure to achieve this goal. His own skill in teaching and his own ability to read music have nothing to do with it. The problem involved is far more acute, having to do with nothing less than the whole approach to music reading that has commonly been used in our schools.

There are additional reasons for not teaching music reading in the traditional manner using the voice as a medium. We will discuss each of these so that as we change from the vocal approach to the instrumental approach in teaching music reading, we will not leave a residue of bad practices that have as their major justification the learning of music notation.

Rote to Note

The usual pattern of teaching children to read music has included a "rote-to-note" process which employed the teaching of three types of songs, each one serving a specific purpose. The rote song was meant to provide a pleasurable experience for the children, who were not asked to read the music to this song. The observation song was also taught by rote; but after the children had learned it, they were led to follow the song on the printed page and to focus on the appearance of the music notes of this song which they already knew. The song usually contained a particular brief phrase or series of tones which received particular emphasis; the teacher had the children pay particular attention to the appearance of this group of tones as part of the song which they learned. The reading song was related to the observation song and presented some of the same phrases or groups of tones in the observation song, but in a different order. Presumably, since the children had learned the observation song by rote, knew it well, and then focused on the appearance of it on the printed score, they were to recognize the familiar phrases in the new context and thereby read them —sing them at sight. While this approach sounds reasonable and logical, *children not learning to play instruments very rarely learn to read music this way.*

Inferior Song Material

We must recognize that there was difficulty in finding good song materials that had already been composed that fit these particular patterns of rote-observation-reading songs. It is comparatively easy, however, for any trained musician to write dittylike material according to any formula. Unfortunately, the values of the note-reading process tended to supersede all other values, and the song materials that were created for some music text series included many potboilers. Such songs were not composed because of any great urge for creative expression on the part of the composer; they were composed to fit a logical, sequentially organized pattern of predetermined combinations of notes which were to form the framework for children to learn to read music. As a result much of this material was inferior musically. Such songs were used not because they provided a rich and happy musical experience but to teach children to read music.

Frequently lacking the spark of genuine creativity, these songs are often cute, dittylike imitations of a pseudo eighteenth-century melodic style, or pseudo folk song. Practically always, these songs scan regularly, in monotonous metrical format. Harmonically primitive, melodically uninteresting, they often fail to capture the interest of children, whose ears, through radio and television, are conditioned to sophisticated harmonic structures and interesting melodies.

Those teaching music were handicapped by the song material on which this approach to teaching music reading was based. The procedure was doomed to failure in part because of the inferior quality of the material.

Syllables

Other factors were involved in the failure, however. In traditional Western music, tones are related to each other in families called keys. Arranged in successive order, a family of tones forms a scale. There are two types of scales, depending on the mode, major or minor. These two modes descend from the ancient Greeks, who had eight modes. Guido of Arezzo, who lived from about 980 to 1050, developed two important contributions to the history of Western music. Before his time there was no written musical notation. Melodies were passed on in person and learned always by rote. While various aids to the memory, called neumes, were devised, they were imprecise, and the various pitches indicated were only approximations. Guido invented a system of using four lines and the intervening spaces to determine pitches precisely. These lines and spaces later developed into our present-day staff or clef.

Guido also adapted the first syllables of the first six lines of an old hymn, each line of which started on a successively higher tone of the scale:

> *Ut* queant laxis
> *Re*sonare fibris,
> *Mi*ra gestorum,
> *Fa*muli tuorum,
> *Sol*ve polluti
> *La*bii reatum
> Sancte Joannes

Taken successively, these first syllables give us *ut-re-mi-fa-sol-la*. Later *ut* was changed to *do* as more euphoneous, and *ti* as the seventh scale step was added.[2]

---

[2] Paul Henry Lang, *Music in Western Civilization*, W. W. Norton & Company, Inc., New York, 1941, pp. 84–85.

Two systems of using these syllables have grown over the years—usually called the *fixed-do* and *movable-do* systems. In the *fixed-do* system the syllables were related to specific tones and remained the same in all keys and scales. This system, used widely in France, receives little attention in our country outside of a few specialized music schools or conservatories. The *movable-do* system calls the first scale step *do,* the second scale step *re,* the third scale step *mi,* and so on through the scale in every major key or family of tones. Thus, the various scale steps would have the same syllable label and the same relationship to other scale steps no matter what the key or family of tones.

The basic purpose in using syllables in the teaching of music was to create a feeling for the family of tones and their relationship to each other. The original purpose was to help develop this feeling for *tonality.* Even this original purpose breaks down on two counts. First, a song which moves from key to key, or from one family of tones to another through a process musicians call modulation, creates real difficulties when the *movable-do* system is used: the same tone may be *do* in one key and *sol* in another key in the same song. Secondly, when tones in a family are changed from the usual ones, chromatically altered, the whole system with its *do-di, re-ri, fa-fi,* etc., for sharps and another pattern for flats becomes so complicated that it falls of its own weight.

Furthermore, let us turn from the intent to the practice. Rarely are syllables actually taught for the primary purpose of developing a feeling of tonality. They ordinarily find their use as the way to teach a song to children, presumably as an aid in learning to read notes. They are taught as another stanza of the song. Children are given to understand that this is a way to read music. Indeed, some few adults claim that the only way they can read music is by using the syllables. The vast majority of children do not learn to read notes using the syllables at all. They rarely understand the purpose of learning the syllables. Often they come to hate them because they do not understand their function. The syllables become the great tug of war between the music teacher and the children. The teacher has been taught that children must learn syllables. He finds himself in difficulty since the children do not learn them. Blaming himself, he drives harder and harder, alienating more and more children. Too often children leave the music session feeling that if this is music they want no part of it.

To most children, *do-re-mi* syllables are merely nonsense syllables. Although most young children love nonsense songs, there is no justification for teaching syllables under this guise. The classroom teacher as well as the music specialist would be well advised to forget syllables altogether as a teaching value.

Numbers

Because of the difficulties teachers had in using syllables, the suggestion that scale steps be numbered and the numbers used instead of syllables gained many adherents. Instead of the scale being represented by *do-re-mi-fa-sol-la-ti-do*, it would be represented by *1-2-3-4-5-6-7-8*. This process has the advantage that children more readily recognize the logic of it when sung from the lowest tone upward. The difficulties presented by changing keys within a song remain, however. The use of tones within the key which are raised or lowered, sharped or flatted, becomes nearly impossible.

While this numbering system has some advantage over the syllables, it, too, presents a barrier between the direct enjoyment of a song and the children who learn it. Since numbers also offer many of the same disadvantages as syllables, teachers would be well advised to eliminate them also from the scope of important musical activities for children.

OTHER BARRIERS

A few additional hurdles should be examined carefully as we clear the air of some of the outmoded practices in music programs. Some of these barriers have also played their part in destroying the effectiveness of teachers earnestly striving to develop good music experiences for their children.

Tone Quality

Improper emphasis has been placed on having children sing with a light head tone. The usual result of such emphasis is a hushed, devitalized half voice. Advocates of the light head tone as the proper singing voice for children base their stand on these points. They offer as evidence of its desirability the lovely, bell-like, "angelic" tones that characterize the singing of groups of young children when they use this type of tone quality. They insist that the young child's voice is a delicate mechanism that must be protected from misuse, and that the only way to protect the child's voice is by having him employ this light head tone.

Anyone who has heard a group of youngsters in lively play on a playground may well question the delicacy of a child's voice. There it sounds like a pretty rugged mechanism. It is difficult to reconcile the claim that singing enthusiastically may injure the child's voice with the reality of his out-of-school experiences, which so frequently include far more violent use of the voice that results in no damage. One of the real challenges facing the teacher is to get enthusiastic singing from his children. Too early an insistence on adult standards of good tone quality, particularly such a limiting one as the light head tone, may effectively block any enthusiastic response to singing on the part of the children. Enthusiastic singing does not have to be equated with shouting. We can encourage children to sing enthusiastically by our selection of songs which children really enjoy. Their normal singing voices, not the light head tone, are the proper vehicles with which children respond in joyous song.

Artificial Standards

To insist that the lovely, bell-like, angelic quality as the product of group singing of young children is the altar before which all other aspects must bow is to create an artificial standard for young children to achieve. Indeed, this standard can be reached only by sacrificing those children who have not reached the stage in their development at which they have learned to reproduce a given melody. These children would have to be "listeners" again in order not to "spoil" the results of the group effort. Even a few children who have not yet found their singing voices will be heard if they sing along with the group, perhaps not as individuals, but certainly as having voices that do not quite come up to the clear, bell-like, angelic standard. To the extent that this artificial standard is held up as a goal, teachers will feel impelled to eliminate such children from the group singing. We have already pointed out the dangers in that procedure; in this direction lies another generation of vocal cripples.

The achievement of the light-head-tone quality in group singing is a clear case of the application of adult standards to children's work. We have learned in other creative areas of the school program to avoid approaching children's work from the standpoint of the adult's critical standards. In the graphic and plastic arts we know better than to apply adult standards of form and color and representation to children's work. We know that such application will stifle creative imagination. This same principle applies to music. The prime objective of group singing is to provide a joyous musical experience for children. Overemphasis on fine tone quality as the product of group singing before children are ready to evolve their own standards will effectively stifle what might otherwise be a joyous musical experience.

Higher and Lower

As adults we readily use the terms *higher* and *lower* and *up* and *down* in music with an easy comprehension of our meaning. To sing "higher," we understand that we want to "raise" the pitch of the tones; to sing "lower," we want to "drop" the pitch of the tones. In terms of the piano we *know* that the keys toward the right end of the keyboard are "higher" and the keys toward the left end of the keyboard are "lower."

These labels have become so much a part of us that we tend
to forget that this knowledge is not inborn and that they are
labels of convenience and convention only.

To young children the terms *up* and *down* have their main
significance in the realm of space. A seesaw goes up and down.
An elevator goes up and down. Stairs lead up and down. The
fifth floor of a building is higher than the second floor. The
basement is lower than the first floor. These are spatial con-
cepts that have no specific transfer to the realm of music, except for those who have already learned to read notation. On
the musical staff, "higher" tones are located physically "higher"
on the staff, and "lower" tones are located "lower" on the staff.
But notation is not music; it stems from music and merely
represents music.

Actually, there is no good reason for calling the tones with
faster vibration rates "high" and those with slower vibration
rates "low." In Western music we have agreed to these labels
so that we would know what we mean. On the piano the only
actual high and low in the spatial sense is the difference between the black and white keys. When a cellist moves his left
hand "down" the fingerboard, stopping a string in successively
"lower" spots, he produces "higher" pitches, since by shorten-
ing the string length he makes it vibrate faster. Here the physical reality spatially is exactly opposite to the conventional
musical label. On the harp we would have considerable justification for calling the various tones "near" and "far" ones,
since the short strings, "higher" in pitch, are "near" the harpist
as he sits at his instrument, and the longer strings, "lower" in
pitch, are "farther" away. Consider the physical reality of
"higher" and "lower" in the brass instruments. We might with
real justification call the "higher" tones the "tight" ones, since
the player tightens his lips in order to produce them. On the
piano we would have real justification for speaking of "righter"
and "lefter" tones for our usual "higher" and "lower."

The ancient Greeks labeled their tones just the reverse from
our own labels. What we call "high" tones were "low" tones
to them, and our "low" tones were labeled "high" ones by them.

These Greek labels, exactly opposite to our own, may well have stemmed from some ancient stringed instrument whose longest strings were at the top. These long strings would have a slow vibration rate, and we would call them "low." The physical location at the top of the instrument might well have led the Greeks to label these tones "high."

We must not assume, then, that children automatically will understand our meaning when we speak of "high" and "low" tones. They must specifically be taught which are the "higher" sounding ones and which are the "lower" sounding ones. As they develop control over their singing voices, both through spontaneous song and through reproducing given melodies, we gradually call their attention to the kinds of tones we mean when we speak of "high" and "low" in music. As we begin to play various types of instruments, even rhythm instruments, we can grossly classify the tones we hear. Keep in mind that these labels are conventions and conveniences and that they must be specifically learned.

Pitch Level of Songs

The pitch level of songs as recommended by some music specialists, reflected in the range used by most music graded song texts, is too high for the comfortable and enthusiastic singing of children. While the upper notes may not be beyond the range of many children in the lower grades, these upper tones do not represent the most comfortable ones for them. Most children would respond better in singing if the songs were pitched lower.

The usual recommendation for the range of children's songs is "on the staff": from first-line E to top-line F on the treble staff. A better, more comfortable range for children would be from about middle C to fourth-space E-flat on the treble staff. While there is little factual evidence one way or another on this matter, long experience with children and their singing responses indicates clearly that the lower pitch range indicated is superior in eliciting responsive and enthusiastic singing.

Hattwick studied the pitch levels selected by children in

45609

comparison with the pitch levels of songs in songbooks intended for children of the same age. He found that "of 95 children aged 4½ to 8, mean pitch used by children when singing tones of their own choosing was significantly lower than the pitch level of the same songs printed in songbooks printed for this age child." [3]

Jersild and Bienstock in a study of the tones sung by children of different ages presented a chart of those tones sung by half or more of the children from two to ten years of age. They found that the range of this group included the five tones from D to A above middle C at the age of two and gradually expanded to include the range from F below middle C to G an octave and a half above middle C at the age of ten. [4]

We may conjecture that the tone F is the central tone in the range of most children. At the age of two the range may extend two tones above and below this central F. This range gradually expands for most children until at the age of ten the outermost limits are approximately one octave above and below this central F. Most songs in children's graded song texts are pitched too high. The upper pitch level of these songs is acceptable only if we accept the uppermost reaches of children's vocal range. No one is comfortable singing at the extreme limits of his natural range. Consequently, for most singing the upper range of songs should be about fourth-space E flat. The lower range suggested, middle C, could be expanded downward a bit beginning at the age of eight.

Most children, and their teachers too, will find themselves responding more readily to songs they like when those songs are pitched most comfortably. You may want to experiment with your own children to find the pitch level most comfortable for your group for a particular song.

[3] M. S. Hattwick, "The Role of Pitch Level and Pitch Range in the Singing of Preschool, First Grade, and Second Grade Children," *Child Development,* vol. 4, pp. 281–291, 1933.

[4] A. G. Jersild and S. F. Bienstock, "A Study of the Development of Children's Ability to Sing," *Journal of Educational Psychology,* vol. 25, no. 7, pp. 481–503, October, 1934.

Accompaniments

Some music specialists have in the past urged teachers not to use the piano or other instrument to accompany their teaching of a song to children. Accompaniments were not to be added until the children knew the song quite well, as shown by their ability to sing it alone. In large areas of the country we find no issue simply because most classrooms do not provide pianos and many teachers are unable to play the piano, even if one were provided. However, what about those situations where a piano may be available and you, as teacher, have enough facility to manage simple accompaniments, even if only a few chords? Also, what about the growing number of schools which have been turning to instruments such as the autoharp for both teacher and children to play?

If in your situation you have a piano or autoharp available and can play it at all, do not hesitate to use it to every possible extent. It seems rather ludicrous to fuss with a pitch pipe to get the right starting pitch when a few chords on the piano or autoharp could set the start of the song far better. Starting a song with a single pitch cannot possibly set the feeling for the family of tones, the key or tonality, of the song. A series of chords can do that much better. Furthermore, if you are at all shaky about your knowledge of the song or your ability to sing it alone, having the instrument at hand to support your voice can be of great aid. Many men will find the piano or any other instrument valuable in presenting the exact pitch of the melody, since men's voices naturally sing about an octave, eight tones, lower than children's voices. If you use the piano, do not sit with your back to the children. Arrange the piano so that the class is either at your right or left, not behind you.

No actual research proves that children learn songs faster or better without accompaniments than with them. Consequently, it seems reasonable for you to do whichever makes most sense in your situation. If you are more comfortable accompanying your singing with some instrument that you play, by all means do it. If you are comfortable singing with your children with-

NAZARETH COLLEGE
LIBRARY

out an accompanying instrument even if you can play one, try teaching new songs both ways.

Accompaniments to children's singing should usually be simple. A few chords on the guitar or ukelele or autoharp or, of course, the piano are frequently better accompaniments to children's singing than elaborate contrapuntal musical devices.

The dominant factor in deciding on the appropriateness of accompaniments basically belongs in the realm of the teacher's feelings. Anything which adds to his feeling of comfort and "rightness" about the situation should be broadly interpreted as good. Teachers' attitudes about singing and about songs will probably be the major determinants of children's attitudes about singing and about songs.

Children can provide their own accompaniments.

Edison School, Eugene, Oregon.

KEEP IN MIND

The following items summarize the major content of this chapter. Individual items may be used for debate, discussion, report, or research topics.

1. The term *vocal cripple* refers to people who *think* they cannot sing.
2. Vocal cripples are not born that way; they are created by poor teaching.
3. Children sing before they talk.
4. In using their singing voices children fall into three categories:
    a. Those children who sing spontaneously and can reproduce a given melody
    b. Those children who can sing spontaneously, but who cannot yet reproduce a given melody
    c. Those children who do not sing spontaneously and cannot reproduce a given melody
5. Learning to reproduce a given melody is a developmental process, often dependent on growth, maturation, and musical experiences.
6. Growth and maturation in this respect are frequently dependent on attitude—the feeling the child has about his voice.
7. Reading music depends on readiness for learning this skill as much as learning to read language depends on readiness.
8. Reading music is not as important to musical growth and enjoyment as has been emphasized.
9. The instrumental approach to teaching notation is by far superior to the vocal approach. If reading music is to be taught at all in the elementary school, it should be based on an instrumental rather than a vocal approach.
10. Ordinarily, music reading could well be postponed until the junior high school. If the primary grades have provided a rich musical background, music reading may be introduced in the fourth grade through the instrumental approach.

11. Syllables should be eliminated from consideration as an undesirable and unnecessary school music experience.
12. Numbers, while probably better than syllables, should also be eliminated from the singing program.
13. The light head tone so often recommended usually degenerates into a devitalized half voice. Children should be encouraged to sing enthusiastically.
14. Adult standards of good tone quality should not be applied to children's group singing.
15. "Higher" and "lower," "up" and "down" in music refer to conventional usage only. The meaning of these terms must be learned.
16. Most graded song textbooks have songs pitched too high for comfort and enthusiastic response.
17. Songs should be pitched comfortably for best response— probably from middle C to E flat over an octave above.
18. Simple accompaniments to group singing are always appropriate.

꧂ CHAPTER THREE

Singing

WHEN WE SING, we sing with our whole bodies; the human organism becomes an instrument for making music. Not only is the entire physical structure involved, but we also sing with our feelings, our attitudes, our emotional tone, and with our intellect or understanding. Consequently, singing offers one of the most rewarding of all musical experiences, one in which all children should participate.

Singing should be a joyous experience for children, which can serve to release their tensions and provide a deep-seated feeling of keen satisfaction through musical expression. Attitude provides the keynote to a successful singing program with children: if they are to sing well, they must *like* to sing and *want* to sing. A healthy attitude about singing will be reflected in children's enthusiastic response to song. If they respond to opportunities to sing with enthusiasm, we are on the right track as teachers. If their response to song is lackadaisical, dull, and lethargic, we have failed. Our problem boils down to finding the touchstone to enthusiastic response from children in joyous singing.

FACTORS IN GOOD SINGING

The factors involved in achieving such enthusiasm about singing from children are neither complicated nor difficult. Indeed, as we free ourselves from some misconceptions about a good singing program, these factors seem quite reasonable and based on common sense.

Classroom Atmosphere

Every classroom has an atmosphere or feeling tone or emotional climate. Elusive in precise definition, it nevertheless is apparent on any visitation to a classroom. The quality of this classroom atmosphere largely depends on the teacher who creates it, consciously or not. In effect it reflects the level of

Joyous participation in group singing utilizes the most natural and universal musical instrument—the human voice.

P.S. 5, Queens, New York City.

interpersonal relations which go on in that room. Classroom atmosphere is one of the most important aspects on which the growth of healthy attitudes about singing depends.

The classroom atmosphere most conducive to good singing and other musical responses does not differ from the good classroom atmosphere that provides for any other phase of healthy growth and development of children. In the room that provides such an atmosphere we find a warm, friendly climate that holds supreme the ideal of respect for individual human personality. In this classroom we see each child recognized as an individual in himself. He differs from every other child, and insofar as possible his particular needs and concerns are met. The teacher encompasses all children with the warmth of his own personality. Children look to him as a friend, a counselor, and a guide. They fear neither him nor his reactions to what they do. The disciplinary goal has become self-discipline, rather than ruthlessly imposed discipline. Mutual consideration dominates the scene. Because the teacher respects them, the children respect the teacher. A healthy give-and-take, representing a high level of interaction among the children and between teacher and children, has replaced teacher domination. The teacher leads and forms rather than dictates. The teacher finds his cues for program in the normal curiosity which is so much a part of the fiber and being of normal children. He formulates the program with the children as well as for them. The teacher believes in a democratic rather than a totalitarian classroom, but recognizes that a democratic process depends for its success not on the superficial trappings and outward forms of democratic action, such as voting and elections, but on mutual respect, interaction, and consensus. He recognizes the dangers of failing to see that functioning democracy depends on good leadership. He does not confuse truly democratic action with pseudo democratic action which may take the form of coercion ("You may do whatever you want, as long as you want to do what I want you to") or *laissez faire* ("Now do whatever you want, children").

While the tendency of all people is to do best those things

that they like to do, this has special significance for music. Since music has such a great potential contribution to make to the well-being and good living of everyone, we have a great responsibility to ensure that children like music. They cannot come to really love music until they know it. They cannot come to know music unless the experiences they have with music bring pleasure. Insistence that children perform musical tasks which they do not enjoy, overemphasis on skills before children recognize the importance of those skills, and the false application of adult standards to children's aesthetic expression can and usually do drive children away from the potential pleasure and fulfillment of musical experience. A good illustration of this may be seen in the countless numbers of children who have been forced to take piano lessons that were couched in the accumulation of technical skills. These children, forced to practice, soon rebel. We have many, many adults today who took piano lessons for a year or two, then rebelled, and gave up for a considerable period of time all interest in music. There are countless others who misinterpreted the school music program as one of learning to read notes, or as one of learning *do-re-mi*. They, too, rebelled, although our schools have the power to enforce their physical attendance in music class. Their rebellion often took the form of rejecting music, which never really became an important part of their lives.

All this points up the crucial importance of the basic factor mentioned before: children must really enjoy the music session. To achieve a successful singing program, children must really like to sing. The classroom atmosphere must encourage this attitude. Our choice of songs, our presentation, our method of teaching, our approach to skills, our application of standards should be selected on this primary basis: Will the particular aspect under consideration enhance our goal of providing a truly pleasurable experience in singing for children? Our goal must constantly be a focus on children, on their growth and development musically, on their feelings and attitudes about music.

Choice of Materials

The songs selected for classroom use provide an opportunity to build the kind of attitudes we have spoken of. One measure of children's response to songs and their attitudes about them is the way they sing these songs out of school. When children come home from summer camps, they are often full of a variety of songs they learned that summer, songs they sing to themselves and to others at a moment's notice. In a growing number of classrooms children learn songs that stay with them out of school.

The essence of what makes a good song that children like is just as difficult to define precisely as the essence of what makes any good song good. Children like songs with a definite rhythmic quality, such as "Erie Canal" and "Won't You Sit Down." They also like songs that flow gently, such as "Sweet and Low" and Brahms' "Lullaby." They love nonsense and silly songs, such as "Kemo, Kimo" and "Old Tante Kobe," and love just as much serious songs, such as "America, the Beautiful" and "Dona Nobis Pacem." In short, the range of types of songs that children love stretches as broadly as the range of types of songs that adults love. Children have a kind of natural good taste. They respond to genuineness in a song. They seem to recognize the aesthetic message a composer projects and to know instinctively if he wrote it as a result of a sincere need and desire to communicate through music. Children seem to sense very quickly when a song has been written down to them, when a song writer writes a song that is childish and not childlike, when a hack presents a potboiler, when a specialist puts together a supposed song which is intended primarily to teach note reading.

Our objective in selecting a song will be to find one that, in our best judgment, the children in a particular class under consideration will like and enjoy singing. All other criteria must be secondary to our primary objective of providing a joyous musical experience in singing. We do not plan to use this song for other purposes; we will not divert our energies or dilute the pleasure of singing by trying to teach children to read music through the song.[1]

Folk Songs

In recent years we seem to have had a folk-song renaissance. A wealth of material has been uncovered that has its roots deep in the feelings of people all over the world. American folk songs have come into their own. Efforts have been made to search out and record on tape and phonograph records the songs that people have sung. In these recordings the researchers have attempted to find people in all sections of the country who remembered and could reproduce old songs authentically. The materials collected have still to achieve widespread use. Generally, however, we have come to recognize our own folk songs as genuine musical expressions of our people. While some of these songs may possibly not be suitable for use with children, many of them are.

We do not know with assurance the origins of folk songs. Two theories are usually offered. One theory long held folk songs to be a spontaneous musical expression of a people. The more likely theory is that the original composer of the folk song is no longer known. Some creative musical personality, in response to a deep feeling about something that happened, expresses this feeling in a song which he makes up. Others, hearing his song, repeat it. In the process of moving from person to person, the song may gradually become modified. Indeed these modifications of the original song may vary in different areas, accounting for some of the different versions of folk songs we hear. The original composer, however, is not remembered for as long a time as his song is remembered. His identity is lost. The song now truly belongs to the people who remember it and sing it as they know it, according to their own needs.

This theory does account for the popularity of most folk songs. To have survived at all, the song must have contained an essence of almost universal appeal. When we use folk songs in our schools, we can usually count on that appeal to reach

[1] For discussion of reading music see Chap. 2.

our children. Folk songs ordinarily sing of some of the elements of living that are common to all of us. The joy and happiness, the trials and tribulations, the small triumphs, the petty disasters, the labors, the pains, the successes, the failures come to all of us with a ring of truth, a kind of remembrance of similar happenings in our own experience, or a reflection that it must be so, that it must have been like that, that it will be like that. The wedding of words and melody is quite close; ordinarily the composition of both must have taken place simultaneously.

Folk songs are universal, and peoples everywhere in the world have expressed their feelings through song. One of the indications of the brotherhood of man is the easy acceptance of each other's folk songs. Cultures and environmental influences may vary widely, but certain feelings apparently transcend those differences. These common feelings, captured and expressed through song, are readily accessible to all peoples. To the extent that the cultural influences on various peoples differ, the mode of folk-song expression may vary. These variations add a piquancy and special flavor to the song for people of other cultures.

As Americans we stem from a tremendous variety of sources. The migrants who came to America invariably brought their native songs with them. The first generation born here, their children, too often fell victim to a false notion of Americanization and rejected the native culture of their parents' origins. In this rejection they sometimes included the parents' songs. Somehow, the songs that the parents sang when these children were young became part of them anyway. Even though they might have ostensibly rejected the parental culture, the songs were still part of the environmental influences on that newer generation. In later years hearing such songs often brings back nostalgic feelings. Any proper definition of the process of Americanization should include the maintenance of the precious and the valuable in the culture of the migrant groups so that all of us may benefit. Our schools should properly seek out those folk songs native to any part of its school population and endeavor to keep them alive and vibrant. We need to help children to be proud of our American culture and show them that such pride does not include the necessity of rejecting the cultural heritage of their origins.

Primarily, the purpose of using the folk songs of those nationalities which may be represented in the school population is to widen the horizons of all children. By sharing songs we know, by recognizing that all peoples sing and express their feelings in music, we help all children grow in the depth of their own understandings of America, of the world, and in feeling the power of music.

A second consideration is in terms of the adjustment of the children, and indeed the children's children, of the migrant group. A vivid illustration may be seen in the most recent large-scale migration: the Puerto Rican migration. The Puerto Rican comes to the mainland for many of the same reasons that have brought others to the United States over the years—usually to provide a better life for his family. The Puerto Rican migration is the first one in which the migrants have been citizens of the United States. Puerto Ricans, however, stem from a culture different from that on the mainland, and they do speak a different language. Many classroom teachers miss the tremendous opportunity this presents for the native continental children to learn about the culture of Puerto Rico. Puerto Rican songs are lovely. Our children would love them, as they do lovely songs of any culture, if they had an opportunity to learn them. Perhaps the Puerto Rican children could teach their favorite songs to the other children. Perhaps some of the parents could be involved and induced to come to the classroom to sing their favorite Puerto Rican songs. Language would not be a barrier in such an activity. The power of music transcends limitations of language. Our children love to learn songs in a foreign language, and here we would have an opportunity to have the song taught by one who spoke the language truly "like a native." This activity would make real contributions to the continental children and would at the same time make the Puerto Rican youngster and his family feel wanted, feel that they, too, were making a contribution, that they had some status, that they were not rejected for what they were, but accepted as people of worth, with a real contribution to make to the general growth of all.

We do not mean, however, to limit folk songs to those native to the United States or to those nations which happen to be represented as the country of national origin of some part of the school population. Actually there is no limit to the widespread utilization of folk songs, or to the countries of their origin. Folk songs act as a kind of key to a culture. They capture the flavor of a people. Indeed those who claim to know a people but do not know their songs really delude themselves. The rhythm and tempo of their life, their aspirations and values, their successes and failures, their humor and tragedy are all reflected through their songs.

The Negro spirituals form one of the most indigenous American folk resources. They are frequently classified in a category of their own, since they are so distinctive. Through several centuries of slavery, the Negro spirit found its main outlet through music. Deprived of instrumental resources, the music poured out in song. Into this music went all the fervency of the Negro's make-up. His trouble, his hardship, his faith, his hope for the future, and his vision of that future molded his unique musical expression.

Spirituals are among the greatest native American musical contributions. They include some of our most beautiful music. Anyone who has not had opportunities to become familiar with these songs has been deprived of an outstanding experience. They are authentic folk material and properly belong in this large category of folk songs.

Folk songs, then, provide an inexhaustible source of good song materials for use with children. Start with ones you know and love. If you play the piano, browse through some collections of folk songs to find the ones you like. No one knows your children as well as you do. Think about the kinds of things that interest and intrigue them. You will find many folk songs that will reach your class. If you do not play the piano, listen to some of the many records of folk songs until you find some that you like and that you believe your children will like. A selected list of recommended folk-song books and a selected list of folk-song records will be found at the end of this book. There are many others. The lists in this book are to get you started, not to provide a complete bibliography of good materials.

As you meet the parents of the children in your class, try to find out if they know any songs that they might be willing to share with your group. If they are shy about singing for your children, perhaps they have taught a particular song to their own child already, or would do so. The child can then teach it to the others in your class. Ways of teaching any song are suggested later in this chapter.

Songs of the Great Composers

A number of the great composers have written songs suitable for use with children. We must realize, however, that the majority of songs by the great composers have not been written for children. These are usually not suitable, because the expressed sentiment is frequently too sophisticated to hold the interest of children for a sustained period of time, and the range of the song is too wide.

Songs of the great composers should be used when they meet the following criteria:

1. The range of the song does not present great difficulties to children.
2. The sentiments expressed are within the experience background of the children.
3. The translation of originally foreign texts makes sense in English.

Many of the great composers specifically wrote music for children; but few specifically wrote songs for children. Where song materials are appropriate, they can make a fine contribution to children's feeling for the music of a particular composer. Songs of the great composers should not, however, be used with children merely because of the status of the composer. Each song should be considered on its own merits. Indeed the utilization of composers' songs which are beyond the comprehension of children may serve negatively to create feelings of antagonism in children about the music of a particular composer.

We are somewhat skeptical of the use of instrumental melodies that are extracted from the symphonies and other works of the great composers to which words are later written and the whole presented as a song. With a few rare exceptions, these do not often present valuable song materials for children. One of the elements that makes a great composer great is his feeling for appropriateness of material. When he writes a melody for instruments, it is with the sound, tone color, and peculiar nature of the instruments in mind. When he writes for the voice, he takes the particular attributes of the human voice into account as he molds the melody. Consequently, while many instrumental melodies are eminently singable, that is not the same as saying they are particularly suitable as songs. There may be real values in having children sing a melodic excerpt from an orchestral composition when they become familiar with it through listening. Such an activity may make a real contribution to their familiarity with the symphonic work. Let us not, however, consider this as part of the singing program.

When we find a suitable song of a great composer, a song with satisfactory range, suitable text, good translation, let us cherish it for the valuable contribution it may make to children's growth. Children, as frank and honest as they are, will not be particularly impressed with the composer's name, and the song will have to stand or fall with them on its own merits. We can hope that our contemporary composers will turn more and more to children and write songs for them, about them, and perhaps even with them. When we find such material of contemporary composers, perhaps we have an obligation to encourage them so they will continue to write for children. Only in this way will we really be able to reach children with contemporary music, the music of our own times.

Songs of the Great Tradition

Part of the cultural heritage of everyone comes from those songs composed some time ago, but so well known that many of us assume that everyone knows them. A number of folk songs fall into this category, but in this section emphasis will be placed on songs that have been composed by someone identifiable. Frequently, we tend to think of many of these songs as folk songs and are surprised to learn that we know the names of the persons who composed them. A song may be so much a part of our tradition that we assume it has always been there. A song such as "Sweet and Low" seems part of many people's backgrounds; few know it was written by Joseph Barnby. It is more important to know the song than to remember Barnby's name. We all know and love many of Stephen Foster's songs, and his name is certainly well known. This category of songs grows out of and forms part of our Great Tradition.

These songs join with our folk songs to become the warp and woof of our cultural heritage. Many different types of songs are represented here, just as in the tremendous variety of folk songs. Through our entire history, songs have accompanied our efforts. We can turn to patriotic songs, to work songs, to comic songs, to descriptive songs, to story songs, to cowboy songs, to Indian songs, and to historical songs. Many of these songs are so familiar to us that we do not remember when or where we learned them. But learn them we did. Some children learn them in the home, and others learn some of these songs in camps. As teachers, let us turn to this rich storehouse of songs to see that each child becomes familiar with the music of our Great Tradition.

Other Types of Songs

In any kind of classification of songs there will be much overlapping. Our purpose now is to call your attention to types of songs which might be classified as folk songs or songs of the Great Tradition, and yet which might also be included under some other heading.

History abounds with many songs particularly reminiscent of a special event. "Yankee Doodle" and "John Brown's Body" immediately call forth a whole series of historical associations. The "Erie Canal" and "I've Been Workin' on the Railroad" may call forth just as vivid historical associations connected with the growth and expansion of our country as related to transportation. These might be labeled historical songs, and serve functions in the classroom above and beyond the joy of singing. They create a flavor of the times and help to create in the minds of children an association with an event that forever fixes that event more vividly for them. Songs may be used, then, for enrichment of other aspects of the school program.

Some songs are just good fun. Nonsense songs, such as "Kemo, Kimo," catch the fancy of children just as they do of adults. Children particularly seem to like to sing songs with nonsense syllables. Story songs, such as "Abdullah Bulbul Ameer," have a fascination all their own. Motion songs, such as "Under the Spreading Chestnut Tree," and silly songs, like "Old Tante Kobe," also are attractive to children. Similarly, cumulative songs, like "A Tree in the Wood," catch children's fancy. Each of these types of songs has a place in the singing program designed to further the primary objective of joy in singing.

Balance

The question may well be raised as to whether or not there might be a formula to be followed in the selection of songs from among these varied types. The answer would be an unqualified "no." There is no one order of progression in which the teacher must cover these varied types. The selection of songs must depend on two factors only. The most important one is the children in the class. No two groups, even of the same age children, are exactly alike. Every group has a total personality which differs from the group personality of every other class. The songs that would hold one group might not be as effective with another. The teacher's knowledge of his own children provides the guide to the selection of songs. The other important factor is the feelings of the teacher. Do not teach a song to your class that you do not like. Your feeling about the song will of necessity seep through, and your attitude about the song may become the attitude of the class. If you limit the songs which you offer to your children to the ones you really like and enjoy as a person yourself, you have a much greater chance of similarly infecting your children.

The ultimate goal, of course, would be to achieve a healthy balance among the various types of songs. Just what a good balance would be has no abstract existence. Balance should be sought in terms of the needs of a particular group of children. Try to find those songs which have an immediate appeal. Any song which you might try which does not get an immediately favorable reaction from the group, discard for the time being. Find songs which your children like to sing, and concentrate on those types until they respond in song freely and easily. After that begin to consider ways of expanding their horizons to include other types of songs they may have previously rejected. This kind of approach is particularly important with those groups of children who have previously had an unfortunate experience with music. With any group, however, seek the route with greatest appeal to the children. Doing this will not only serve to help you reach your children with music, but if you have any feelings of insecurity about teaching music, the children's enthusiasm will help you.

Grade Placement of Songs

Do not take too seriously the attempts that have been made to "grade" songs. There are practically no good songs suitable for one grade that are not just as suitable for other grades. "Sweetly Sings the Donkey" can be just as much fun at the sixth-grade level as at the first. Once again the teacher who knows his children is the best one to judge whether or not his children can "take" a particular song. Discarding the notion of using the singing voice as a medium for learning to read music eliminates the concern with the children's ability to read quarter notes or sixteenth notes as a basis for selecting a song.

Many song texts have selected songs on the basis of simple rhythms for young children. Yet we have all heard how quickly quite young children pick up complicated rhythms of songs they hear on radio and television.

A valid criterion for age placement of a song would be the meaning of the words. When the words of a song have a meaning beyond the experience level of the children in your class, question the use of that song. To sing a song well, children must understand it. A song is not just a melody, although the melody is a crucial part of the song. A good song welds words and music together in a single entity. If children do not understand the words of the song, if the meaning is beyond their level of comprehension, if their experiences in living have not been broad enough to encompass the significance of the words, then the song is usually not right for that group of children.

A song may not be suitable for a fourth grade and yet be quite appropriate for a second grade, not in terms of the difficulty or simplicity of the song, but in terms of the experiences of that particular fourth-grade and that particular second-grade group.

The professional judgment of the teacher who knows his own children is the best authority in evaluating the suitability of any particular song. Since the music of a good song is appropriate to the words, it is unlikely that a song with words within the comprehension level of any particular age level would have music that would make the song unsuitable.

SPONTANEOUS SINGING

In the development of favorable attitudes about singing and the growth of enjoyment of music, all children should be encouraged to sing with the group. No children should ever be left out because they might not be singing "in tune." No child should ever be made to feel inadequate because of his singing voice, or that he might be unable to sing. Children learn to walk, run, and skip at different ages. We would probably be properly horrified if anyone ever made a child feel inadequate simply because his body had not developed to the stage where he was able to do things in which other children had already developed some skill. The growth of control over the singing voice similarly is a developmental process which depends in part on readiness.

As pointed out in the previous chapter, children may be grouped into three categories according to the degree of control they have developed over their singing voices. For ease of reference, we might label these groups as follows:

1. Reproducing singers: children who have developed control over their singing voices, who can both sing spontaneously and reproduce a given melody
2. Spontaneous singers: children who have developed enough control over their singing voices to sing spontaneously, but not enough to be able to reproduce a given melody
3. Experimental singers: children whose control over their singing voices has not developed to the extent that they sing spontaneously and who are also unable to reproduce a given melody

The spontaneous singers have been much maligned in the past. Labeled "nonsingers" or "listeners" or even more cruelly "monotones," they soon came to feel that something was wrong with their singing voices. Since the development of control of the singing voice depends on one's feelings about the voice—the voice as a function of the whole organism can never be separated from feelings—these children quickly became nonsingers or listeners.

Most children who have not been handicapped by the creation of unfavorable attitudes develop control over the singing voice, become reproducing singers, sometime between the ages of three and eight. Some children develop this control past the age of eight. Young nursery school age children appear largely as spontaneous singers. A small group at this age will have developed power as reproducing singers, and a small group may still be experimental singers. At the age of eight, most children will have developed as reproducing singers. Of the others, most will have facility as good spontaneous singers, with varying facility in reproduction of given melodies. A very small group may still be experimental singers.

Developmental Stages in Singing

The developmental stages have not been precisely measured as children gradually increase their control over their singing voices. Let us, however, trace the process by which the first fumbling experimentation with vocal sounds gradually grows into the flexible and highly complex, automatically controlled mechanism of speech and song.

At first, the very young child produces only vague sounds, different in pitch, different in duration. Sometimes these sounds are not held long enough to be more than a kind of *Sprechstimme*, or speech-song. At other times, babies produce well-defined identifiable tones, in a specific pattern or sequence. For the most part the actual tones produced are accidental rather than conscious. The sequence of tones seems to have no significance to the child. Later in his development, the sounds he produces may be focalized in specific sequences or patterns which are consciously uttered by the child. He sings not accidentally in the wandering, hit-or-miss manner of the baby, but with the idea of expressing some feeling in song, or at least in tone. He, of course, does not know what a song is. Nevertheless, the sequence of tones now has shape and form and specificity.

It is unlikely that in the beginning of the random production of tones he hears them consciously and specifically. He may come to the point where he creates them so without being able to hear them so. For some children this stage may last for several years. The child sings often if even mildly encouraged, and develops quite a bit of skill in varying melodies, rhythms, patterns, and words when he uses them. If no negative developments occur, such as getting the idea from some misguided person, parent, teacher, or child that he cannot sing, he sooner or later hears specifically what he sings. It is only as he begins to hear definitely and concretely what he spontaneously sings that he can reproduce what he spontaneously sings. He will not be able to reproduce the songs of others until he has reached the stage at which he is able to reproduce his own spontaneous songs.

The ability to reproduce given tones and melodies is inextricably interwoven between powers of vocalizing and powers of hearing. Ability to control vocalization is related to ability to hear. Hearing at first is undifferentiated, just as first attempts at producing of any vocal sound are undifferentiated. In terms of control of the singing voice, the vocalization powers first need to develop through spontaneous song. The continuation of spontaneous singing leads to a gradual identification of hearing with singing. Thus, vocalization through spontaneous song is essential to the development of differentiation and discrimination in hearing. The growing powers of discrimination vocally and aurally ultimately merge. At this point of merger the child develops the ability to reproduce his own spontaneous songs. He now controls his singing voice to *produce* the spontaneous song he wants, hears this spontaneous song he has produced, and with the aural-vocal mechanism subject to control, he can *reproduce* the same song he sang spontaneously. Then, as the child gains in his ability to reproduce his own spontaneous songs, he develops with but a slight time lag the ability to reproduce the melodies of others.

Developing Spontaneous Singing

The development of skill in spontaneous singing, then, precedes the development of skill in reproducing a given melody. Consequently, as we work with children we should ensure an atmosphere conducive to the development of spontaneous singing. Just about everyone sings spontaneously at some time or other. For adults it might be only in the shower. For children, however, it might be almost any time. Spontaneous singing accompanies most activities of children. When they play, when they wash, when they go to bed, they often accompany their activities with song or a snatch of song. Perhaps someone may object to dignifying this kind of spontaneous singing with the label of "song." Call it what you will, we need only to open our ears to children when they do things they like to do, and we hear spontaneous singing with true melodic lines, definite pitches in sequence, rhythmic patterns, and often, quite appropriate words. Somehow this tremendously valuable activity has often been overlooked in terms of school use. However, if our objective is to help all children develop control over their singing voices so that eventually they may all be able to reproduce songs successfully, that they may sing "in tune," if you will, our primary aid will be the development of this skill in spontaneous singing.

The first and foremost asset in the development of spontaneous singing is, of course, the classroom atmosphere. The warm, friendly, accepting atmosphere, with an absence of tension and hostility, is a prime essential for any kind of good singing. No one who is tense feels like singing.

The Continuous Melodic Story

We need more than merely a good atmosphere, however, as important as that is. A number of techniques are available to the teacher which aid in the stimulation of spontaneous singing. One of them is the continuous story in music. The musical continuous story is analogous to the story game many of us have played. One person begins a story with a sentence or two, breaking off at some point along the way. At this point another person picks up the story and spontaneously develops the story line a bit further with another sentence or two. When the second person stops, a third person extemporizes. This process continues on and on, sometimes with hilarious results, often with the development of an interesting story. It might go something like this:

STARTER: "One day I was walking along the street minding my own business. All of a sudden . . ." Starter stops.

SECOND PERSON (*trying to pick up the sentence with a hardly perceptible break*): ". . . I felt a tap on my shoulder. I quickly turned around. To my amazement . . ." Second person stops.

THIRD PERSON: "...I saw a wizened old man looking at me strangely. I had never seen him before. He whispered..." Third person stops.

On and on it goes, with each person in the game taking his turn molding the story.

The continuous melodic story develops in much the same fashion. It may be done both with words and without words, although it will probably be more satisfactory at first without words. It would probably be preferable for the teacher to act as starter at first. Sing a short melody which you make up. If you are comfortable with your voice and confident of yourself, you will be able to make up the starting phrase spontaneously. However, if you feel at all inadequate about your ability to do this spontaneously, make up your starting phrase ahead of time. The night before, perhaps in the quiet of your own room, or even in the shower, try a few melodic snatches that will come to your mind. Sing them over to yourself a number of times until they come out the same way each time. Try them again sometime later to see if you remember them. Do not worry about not being able to reproduce them exactly the same way each time at first. Since you make up these bits of melody, no one will know if you are "right" or not, for what is "right" is what you want it to be. The next day in class, get some volunteers from the children. Set the progression; determine together who will follow you and the order of those to come next. Start them off by explaining briefly what the idea of the game is. Then sing your melodic bit. Thereupon a child picks up the melody where you left off and spontaneously continues it. The next child then starts where the first child stopped his extemporaneous contribution. And so, on and on your snatch of melody develops through the group of volunteers. As soon as the children understand the idea, they usually all want to participate. At this time, you may continue as starter yourself, or you may have different children act as starters. It is usually well to establish the order of participants before you begin any round.

Two precautions may be helpful. Try to keep the starting

phrase from sounding too much like part of a song familiar to the children. It does not matter if the starting phrase sounds familiar to you. Usually our first creative efforts are similar to music we know. However, if the starting phrase is too much like a song he knows, the child will very likely continue with the familiar song rather than with a new phrase which he spontaneously sings. The other precaution has to do with advice on handling a situation after it occurs; there is not too much you can do to keep it from happening. Sometimes in the development of one of these spontaneous songs, one child will sing as his contribution a phrase which brings the melodic line to an end. Melodies do go that way, and a particular succession of tones may have a very strong sense of finality, or conclusion. When that happens, your best reaction is to accept that contribution as a natural ending for that particular spontaneous song. Then get another one started.

Try to vary the starting melodic bits in mood, rhythm, and feeling. You will find that in these continuous spontaneous songs, the initial melodic fragment establishes the mood of the song. If that initial bit offers a slow, smooth melody, the rest of the spontaneous song will very likely be consistent. Similarly, if you start off with a jerky, rhythmic melody, the spontaneous song will carry that type of jerky, rhythmic melody on. A very interesting phenomenon takes place. The melodic development seems to take control. If you discuss what happens during the growth of a spontaneous continuous melody, you will find that the portion of the melody which comes before any particular participant has his turn has a compulsion that will not be denied. The participants, adult and children, can just relax and let the momentum of the previous melody take hold. Their own individual contribution seems to come out of them almost of its own volition.

If a tape recorder is available, you and your children will be interested in recording a spontaneous song for different purposes. At first, no special preparation is necessary or desirable. Do not practice and repractice a particular continuous song you have already developed merely in order to record it. After some experience with this kind of spontaneous continuous singing, when the children have developed a good sense of timing in picking up the melody, record a fresh start with its development. Listening to such a recording can provide an exciting experience. Your children and you may sometimes want to work on a particular spontaneous song, modifying here, changing there, so as to develop a really fixed song of your own. Or you may want to continue developing more new continuous spontaneous songs.

Needless to say, for this activity to attain its maximum value, you must try for maximum participation of the children in your class. All of them should participate. Special efforts should be made, as unobtrusively as possible, to ensure the participation of those children who have not reached control of the singing voice to the extent that they might be able to reproduce a given melody. Since the spontaneous continuous song has no given melody to reproduce, these children should be able to participate in the song development without difficulty. As they gain confidence in this use of their singing voices, their attitudes toward singing remain positive, and the reproductive control can develop that much more readily. Keep in mind that the primary factors in helping children achieve control over their singing voices to the extent that they can reproduce given melodies are their attitudes about singing and about their own voices, and their desire to sing.

Other Aids to Spontaneous Singing

Many teachers have found that singing directions to young children provides a good technique for use during the important transition periods from one activity to another. For example, the teacher may sing, to a melody she spontaneously makes up, the directions, "Take your chairs very quietly and go back to your places." Or, "Put away your pencils, put away your books, and form a big circle over here." This melodic extemporizing by the teacher is quite a bit easier than it may at first sound. The initial plunge may be the hardest. Once in, the going is smooth. Again, if you are at all doubtful about your ability to do this spontaneously before the children, try it out in private ahead of time. The technique serves many purposes. It not only provides a quieting, very effective device for success in moving children from one activity to another, but also sets the scene for reciprocal and corresponding spontaneous creation of musical responses and questions from the children. It also helps to set the scene of the classroom, to build an atmosphere in which music is alive, vibrant, and part of the ongoing classroom living.

Another device has particular value early in the term. Teacher sings, again making up the melody as he goes along, or using one he made up privately the night before, "My name is Mr. Brown. What is your name?"

He points to a child, who is supposed to sing his name. "My name is Jonathan Wildere. What is your name?" He then points to another child. And on and on it goes, until each child has had an opportunity to make up spontaneously a little melody to his name.

The first child pointed to may speak his name instead of singing it. The teacher might continue his directions, singing, "Sing your name; then ask another child what his name is."

Or the first child, mistaking the teacher's intent, might sing back exactly what the teacher sang, including both the melodic fragment and the same words. He might sing, "My name is Mr. Brown," using the same tones Mr. Brown did. Children who have been exposed to the traditional "matching pitches" of the too prevalent "nonsinger" approach of some music specialists are particularly prone to this error. Teacher might then point out, singing not speaking, that that is his name, encouraging the child to sing his own name.

TEACHING A SONG

The best way to introduce a new song is to sing it for the children several times. You will feel more comfortable and make a better presentation if you know the song quite well yourself. A colorful, dramatic presentation is both unnecessary and undesirable. Sing the song simply, with as good tone quality as you can muster, and sing it clearly so that the words may be easily heard and understood. No elaborate preparation of the children for the song should be made; do not tell the story of it, or concoct a dramatic setting for it. Let the song speak for itself. The song should carry its own motivation. Too often motivation has been interpreted in the sense of, "How can I get the children to want to do what I want them to do?" A song which requires selling on your part or coercing probably should not be used. If the song is not of the caliber which your children respond to because they like it, drop that song and choose another.

Rather than an elaborate introduction consisting of the story of the song or a story about the song, you may merely want to say something like: "I know a song I think you will like." Remember to keep the song comfortably pitched for you and your children. You may want to experiment with the pitch. If you find the children straining to reach high tones in the song, try starting it a bit lower.

Sing the song a couple of times, and then have the children join you where they can. Indeed some eager youngsters may be

An informal atmosphere is conducive to relaxed enjoyment of a song session.

Crow Island School addition, Winnetka, Illinois. Photo by Gordon Coster. Courtesy of Perkins & Will, Architects.

so anxious to sing with you that they will want to join right away, even though they never heard the song before. If some children know the song, have them join you in the presentation.

Do you remember how you learn a song at a party? After you hear it a few times, you tentatively join in where you can. You do not learn the new song all at once, nor do you learn it line by line. You learn it gradually, a bit here and a bit there, and probably do not learn it from the beginning straight through. You probably first get on to a few snatches here and there, and only gradually fill in the gaps between the snatches. Try the same procedure with your class. Use the whole method first. Sing the song through several times and encourage the children to join you in the parts they remember. Do not try to teach the song in one day; it may well be from several days to over a week before you feel that all the children know the song. After a number of days in which you have done the entire song, you will want to focus attention on the trouble spots. Be sure to return to the whole song after that focus on a part, so that the children may constantly keep the whole song in mind. Keep your primary goal constantly before you: to provide a joyous experience with singing. Do not stick with the song on any one day beyond the point of interest of the children. Do not resort to mere repetition in order to fix the song in their minds. If you do use repetition, always offer a purpose for that particular trial. Encourage all children to sing; do not leave any child out merely because he does not seem to be singing "in tune." Do not apply false standards of tone quality or tone production. Do not hush the children or demand a light head tone. Your objective is to get the children to sing that particular song enthusiastically, with gusto if appropriate, and to have pleasure doing so. If you achieve this objective, others become possible. If you do not achieve this objective, any others offer almost insuperable obstacles.

Using Phonograph Records

Suppose you do not feel comfortable with your singing voice. Perhaps you are a vocal cripple due to no fault of your own. There are a vast number of good phonograph records of songs you can turn to for help. The criteria you may want to use in selecting a record are simple:

1. The song itself should meet the same standards previously discussed about good songs for children.
2. The record should be of good quality, with clear tone and accurate reproduction.
3. The voice of the singer should be simple and direct. You would be well advised to avoid the highly colored voice of the operatic star or dramatic vocalist. Children do not accept such voices readily.
4. The words of the song should be clear and distinct and easily heard and understood.
5. The accompaniment should be appropriate. Many folk songs are recorded with simple guitar accompaniments which serve our purposes splendidly. Nevertheless, do not rule out other accompaniments just because they are different. You will have to judge whether or not the voice comes through clearly and evaluate the effect of the total presentation.

In using phonograph records, play them on the best phonograph you can find so as to achieve good reproduction. It seems ironic to purchase a good record and then play it on a poor phonograph. Often the tinny sound you hear on many phonographs is the fault of the instrument itself and not of the record. It is poor economy for a school system to purchase cheap and inadequate phonographs merely because they can thereby purchase more of them. Fewer instruments of high quality will get more use from teachers because of the quality of sound.

Let us assume now that you have selected your song and record. Play it a number of times yourself so that you know it well. Try singing the song with the record yourself. After you have done this a number of times, you will want to try to see if you can sing the song alone without the record, at least in the privacy of your own room. With the same kind of introduction you might use if you were going to sing the song yourself to the class, play the record for the group. After a couple of hearings, encourage the children to sing along with the record where they can. Join in yourself.

As the children learn the song, you may want to turn down the volume of the phonograph so that the children's voices dominate. When you feel that they know the song fairly well, have them try the song without the record. Together focus on the weak spots and listen to the record again without singing. Then try the song again without the record. Gradually, over a period of time, the children learn the song. It is likely, too, that if you try this with your children a number of times, another year you might know that particular song well enough to try to present it without the record.

Do not feel that you are cheating your children if you use phonograph records to teach them songs. Other things being equal, the teacher presenting the song himself probably offers the best medium for children to learn songs. Nothing can really substitute for that firsthand contact of a teacher singing the song. However, with the many fine records now available in increasing quantities, this method runs a close second. With some songs, it may even be possible that the record approach is superior, and many teachers confident of their singing voices may still want to use records to present certain songs to their children.

STANDARDS

In order to help children develop good standards for their singing, start by keeping these three factors well in mind:

DO	DO NOT
1. Pitch the song comfortably for your class.	1. Pitch the song too high.
2. Encourage enthusiastic response.	2. Shush the children into a light head tone.
3. Pick songs your children will like.	3. Pick songs to teach technical problems.

Developing Children's Standards

In the beginning accept any enthusiastic response in song that you get from children as legitimate. Once children begin to sing enthusiastically, the development of good standards becomes possible. The application of critical standards before children sing enthusiastically very likely will kill the possibility of engendering any enthusiasm at all. At first you may consider the children's singing ragged and extremely unmusical. However, if the children respond well and enjoy the process, you should be satisfied with this ragged, unmusical singing at the start.

Let us assume now that your children have learned a song and know it well. This means, for now, that they are familiar with the words and sing both the words and the melody with gusto and an easy familiarity. Furthermore, you can tell by the enthusiasm of their response that they like the song. They ask for it; they sing it out of class. When these things happen, you will begin to help the children listen more carefully to their singing and ask them to suggest ways of singing the song better. Exactly when to do this cannot be determined specifically. The "when" becomes a timing decision, part of the art of teaching, the kind of decision that good teachers must feel. The best clues have been indicated above. Watch for:

1. Enthusiastic response, indicating that the children like the song
2. Easy familiarity, indicating that the children know both the words and the music
3. Requests for the song, indicating that they know and like it and, therefore, want to sing it often

When you feel that the time is right, begin to help the children focus their listening critically on their singing.

You might put it this way to your children: "Let's listen to our singing this time and see if anyone can think of a way to make it sound better." Then have the children sing the song through again. You should not be too surprised to hear the children express some of the criticisms you have felt yourself, but which you suppressed.

Someone may say, "We're singing too loud," or even, "We're shouting, not singing."

To this comment, you might well respond, "What would you suggest?"

The child might answer, "Let's try to sing this song a little softer."

The class would then try the song a little softer and see how they like it that way. If the song musically requires softer singing, the class will in all probability prefer it that way. If, however, they do not, you should not make an issue of it. The group may need the feeling they get from the enthusiastic, loud response more than the immediate sensitizing to the desirability for singing a particular song softly.

In developing children's own standards, your objective is to generalize the specific criticisms of individual children, and subject them to the test of trial. Some suggestions may be rejected by the group as a whole, and you must be willing to accept such rejection. If you disagree with the rejection, keep it in mind for later use, perhaps on another song. The factor of readiness must also be kept in mind as we help children develop their own critical standards.

Your first approach, then, to the problem of helping children develop critical standards is to help them focus on their singing so that they hear what the whole group sounds like when it sings a particular song. It is an interesting phenomenon that children just approaching the enjoyment of singing frequently do not hear the sound of the whole class; sometimes they do not hear themselves. They cannot possibly understand critical elements addressed to the group product until they begin to focus on and specifically hear that group product.

Your second problem is to help the children express their own critical feelings about the group singing. Keep in mind and stress with your children that criticism does not mean "what is bad," but rather "what is good and bad." A music critic attempts to evaluate a performance or a new work or an interpretation, attending to both good and bad elements, and indeed to points between these two extremes. In the process of helping children criticize, help them to learn how to express their opinions of both strengths and weaknesses. Furthermore, when they suggest a weakness, try to help them suggest a way to correct that weakness. Help them, too, to learn how to make a criticism without hurting anyone's feelings.

Another problem we must often face is that children will tend to tell adults not what they really feel, but what the children think the adults want to be told. As good teachers, our objective must be to get the children to have enough confidence in us so that they respond as they actually feel. This is not always easy to accomplish. Honest reactions from children are usually a function of the level of the interpersonal relations which exist between teacher and children. Children must have confidence and trust in their teacher before they reveal their true feelings. They must know that teacher respects their right to feel different from others and different from teacher about important matters. They must know that they will not be ridiculed for expressing an honest feeling, even if it is different. They must know that they will not be rejected by the teacher for revealing some honest differences in opinion from what they think he wants or would like them to have. The ease with which any teacher can accomplish this high level of mutual confidence will vary with individual situations, and will be affected by such things as the child's general feeling about adults, his previous experience with teachers, and the teacher's success in building trust and confidence.

Further Development of Standards

You may be surprised at first at the variety and level of critical responses that children perceive. In some cases you will be able to develop all the standards you think desirable from the children's suggestions. These are the most desirable critical elements to apply to any class singing. You may want to call the attention of your group to other aspects of their singing which they have not criticized. Be careful how you approach that, however. Ordinarily, unless a particular standard is felt by at least some of the children in the class, it should not be applied. We run the risk of needless application of adult standards imposed on children's creative work, a process which can easily stultify and restrict their creative development.

In singing, the imposition of adult standards can easily cause your children to reject the activity. Consequently, the items in the following sections are ones to which children usually respond critically. In some cases you will want to focus their attention on the disability which you see or hear. If they agree and suggest ways to improve, then their horizons have been broadened to include that critical aspect. Or they may have sensed that particular point, but may have been unable to articulate it. In any case if the children in your class do not readily accept a critical point which you suggest, drop it. A child may bring up the same point in criticism of another song. At that time you may be able to apply it. If, however, the class rejects a critical point and no one brings it up again, it merely means that that group is not ready for it. Drop it completely for a long time.

Tone Quality

When we sing, we use the human body as a musical instrument. Just as in any musical instrument, we find a vibrating object, a means to modify those vibrations in order to change pitch, resonance chambers which amplify and modify the tones produced, and a way for the vibrating air to escape to the surrounding air. However, the human body does not use metal tubes, wooden pieces, reeds, or nylon strings for these purposes; it uses a very complex combination of flesh, bone, sinew, and muscles—the entire body.

The trained singer learns how to control many muscles so that he may be able to produce the loveliest tone his body is capable of producing. This kind of control cannot be an objective in school music. The trained singer also learns, however, that in singing, his feelings or emotional tone reflect on his muscle tone, that his intellect affects his physical control both consciously and unconsciously, that good tone quality as reflected in truly musical singing is greater than the sum of the individual parts of muscle control. He learns that the great enemy to good singing is tension, and that tension is an emotional reaction which affects his ability to control his muscles and express his feelings in music. He spends much time and practice developing his ability to relax any unwanted tensions in any circumstances.

The most important single contribution the teacher can make to the development of good tone quality is the creation of an atmosphere free of tension, one of relaxed enjoyment of the song. In such an atmosphere the muscular structure of the children's bodies will be in optimum condition for the best production of tones. Consequently, tone quality will be good.

The voice is a function of human personality, not only of physical structure. Our voices, barring physical defect, reflect us as people. The more closely a song "reaches" us as individuals, the better we are able to sing that song. A song which children understand and which affects them deeply will be better sung in terms of tone quality than the song which they do not understand or to which they may be indifferent.

The teacher's problem basically is the selection of songs which really have meaning to children, songs which they can feel deeply.

Confidence in one's ability to sing is an extremely important aspect of good tone quality. The person convinced that he cannot sing, truly cannot sing. You will recall the discussion of vocal cripples in Chapter 2. Vocal cripples are made, not born; most of them are made by teachers who, in their honest zeal to help children, use unfortunate devices which serve more to create feelings of inadequacy than to develop control.

As a teacher, be realistic about tone quality. Never sacrifice any children on the altar of good tone quality. Encourage all children to sing along with the group. Even those children whose control of their singing voices has not developed fully should be encouraged to sing with the class. Create a feeling that they are a part of the group singing. Better that a few voices carry along "out of tune" than that any children develop the feeling that they cannot sing. Their desire to sing and their attitudes about their own voices will do more to help these children develop control over their singing voices than any combination of so-called training devices.

Enunciation

Words are important aspects of songs. In a good song, words and music become part of a single whole. One of our objectives with children in developing good standards of singing should be to make words clear and easy to understand when a song is sung. Following the suggestions made before, teachers should wait until the song is well known to the children before attempting any approach toward improving enunciation. When the teacher asks for suggestions about making the song sound better, one of the children may direct attention to the words. If no child does so, the teacher may want to focus the children's attention on the clarity of the words.

One way of doing this might be to suggest that the class share a few favorite songs with another class. In preparing for this, one or two children could be posted at the front of the room with their backs to the class. As the group sings, these two children listen especially to the words to see if they can understand them and hear them easily and clearly. Their report to the group leads to discussion of how any difficulties in understanding words may be cleared up. Keep in mind in this aspect as well as in others that we try to help children develop their own standards of good singing; we do not impose adult standards on them.

Breathing

As teacher, you may want to focus children's attention on the problem of where to take a breath during a song. Ordinarily, the entire class should probably take new breaths at the same points in the song, although for some purposes uniform breathing would be avoided. The breathing places should be as natural as possible in terms of both the flow of the melody and the flow of the words. Ordinarily, any place which feels as if the melody seems to stop flowing momentarily could be a good place to catch a new breath. After the children know the song well, you might want to ask for suggestions about good breathing places. Have the class try out the various suggestions and come to a mutual decision.

You will find, probably, that most of the suggestions will coincide with the ends of musical phrases. A musical phrase is a rather complete musical idea. At the end of a phrase we feel a kind of break in the onflowingness of the melody. The end of the phrase is a place where we feel that the melody seems to pause for a second or so before going on to another phrase or musical idea. It sometimes feels as if the musical line seems to catch a breath before continuing. Consequently, phrase endings are logical places for singers to take a new breath.

There can well be disagreement about the proper places in a song for a new breath. A group decision leading to everyone catching a new breath at the same place would be the standard to help children achieve.

Attacks and Endings

A standard comparatively easy to achieve which adds considerably to the effectiveness and quality of group singing, but which children will usually not be aware of until you call it to their attention, is the matter of starting and ending precisely together. Once again this standard should not be attempted until the criteria for developing standards have ripened. At that time you may want to call the attention of the children to the fact that they do not all begin the song at precisely the same instant. The objective to achieve is a precise start, everyone singing at exactly the same moment, rather than a ragged start with different children starting at slightly different times.

These two ways of beginning might be diagramed as shown in Figure 4.

Figure 4. ATTACKS

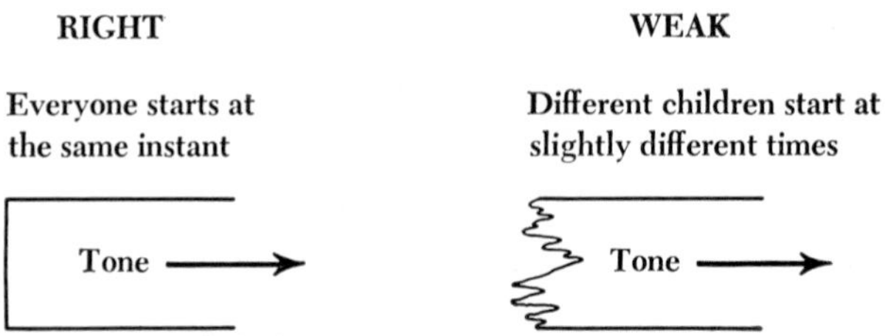

RIGHT   WEAK

Everyone starts at   Different children start at
the same instant   slightly different times

Tone ⟶   Tone ⟶

Similarly, the endings can be precise or ragged and might be diagramed as shown in Figure 5.

Figure 5. ENDINGS

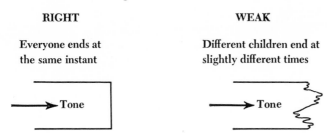

You will want to agree with your children on cues for starting and for ending. The conductor, teacher or child, should present the agreed-on cue. This standard of precise attacks and endings is easy to achieve and usually readily accepted by children.

Expressive Quality of a Song

The expressive quality of a song as a standard will probably emerge from your children. Are we singing the song so that we express its meaning? How could we make the meaning clearer? Does our singing make people who hear us feel about this song the way we want them to feel, or the way the composer seems to have wanted people to feel about his song? These are representative of the kinds of questions that your children may ask, or that you may want to ask when the time is right for helping the children develop good standards.

In the development of this particular standard, intellect plays its role. The meaning of the song must be comprehended before it can be expressed; it must be comprehended fully before it can be expressed fully. Furthermore, we see in this an early application of a quite advanced aesthetic principle, that emotional feeling may be enhanced through the intellect. The total emotional impact of a song on both the singer and the listener may be increased when the feeling content of the song becomes more sensitized through the intelligent control of the singer.

CONDUCTING

In any group effort in which many people attempt to do the same thing at the same time, a leader who provides the cues for changes and who coordinates efforts can make the group effort easier. Singing in groups offers such a problem; we have a group of people, each person offering his own contribution to the effect produced by the whole. A leader who provides the cues for changes and coordinates the different efforts of different people aimed at achieving a common purpose can help considerably in improving the group effort. A conductor is merely such a group leader.

In the elementary school the role of the conductor must be interpreted generally and broadly. Since it offers such splendid developmental potential for children, all of whom need to learn to be both leaders and followers, the leadership role ideally rotates through the group of children. No more should be expected of the child leader than that he stand in front of the group, cue them on when to start, "keep time" by waving his arm or the baton rhythmically, and cue them when to end.

KEEP IN MIND

The following items summarize the major content of this chapter. Individual items may be used for debate, discussion, report, or research topics.

1. Singing, one of the most rewarding of all musical experiences, should be an important part of every music program.
2. To sing well, children must *like* to sing and *want* to sing.
3. A good classroom atmosphere contributes to the development of healthy attitudes, including attitudes toward singing.
4. The primary criterion in the choice of a song is the appeal that song has to the children in the particular class.
5. Folk songs offer many splendid choices of good songs that children enjoy singing.

6. Songs of the great composers, songs of the Great Tradition, and many other types of songs offer many potential sources of good song material.

7. A good balance among various types of songs, while a desirable objective, has no abstract existence. It must be sought in terms of the feelings of the individual teacher and the reactions of the specific class of children.

8. Interpret any grade-placement labels of songs with great latitude. The most valid limitation on flexibility of grade placement is the relationship between the meaning of the words and the experience level of the children.

9. The development of skill in spontaneous singing precedes the development of skill in reproducing a given melody.

10. The development of good spontaneous singing depends on the presence of a good classroom atmosphere.

11. The musical continuous story, singing directions, and singing names are some techniques to use in developing spontaneous singing.

12. The best way to teach a song is to sing it for the children several times as well as you can.

13. The process by which children best learn a song may be described as a vague idea of the whole, to a gradually increasing remembrance of parts, to a better idea of the whole.

14. In teaching a song, constantly remember that the primary goal is to provide a joyous experience with singing.

15. Phonograph records offer a fine method for the teaching of some songs, especially valuable to the teacher who does not have adequate confidence in his own voice.

16. The development of good standards of singing in children is possible only after enthusiastic singing has been achieved.

17. The first step in helping children develop their own standards of good singing is to help them focus their listening on their own singing.

18. In developing standards, generalize the specific criticisms offered by individual children and subject them to the test of trial and the response of the class.

19. Tone quality, enunciation, breathing, attacks and endings, the expressive quality of a song are some of the important aspects that you will want to help your children focus their attention on as they develop standards.

20. The conductor provides cues for changes and coordinates the efforts of the group.

CHAPTER FOUR

Movement and Music

THE WORD *moving* has two specialized meanings. We use moving to connote some body action or reaction. We move our legs. We move our arms. We move our bodies. We move from place to place. We move our eyes, ears, lips, tongue, toes, fingers, hands, etc. In this sense moving refers to an overt body action or reaction involving spatial relocation.

In another sense we speak of moving in a feeling way. We speak of being moved by a great piece of music. We speak of a work of art as being moving. In this sense we refer to our emotional reaction when we are touched deeply by a great work of art, when our feelings are aroused. The word *move*, then, has these two connotations: one, a physical reaction and the other, an emotional reaction. The dual use of the word *move* is very suggestive. Our emotional reactions are related to physiological reactions. Our bodies are involved when we react emotionally. The word *emotion* contains within it the root *motion.*

The expression of emotion through motion—that is the purpose of a program of bodily movement.

Life almost always involves movement. One of the tests for

the presence of life is the search for movement in the organism. Movement in life almost always takes place in its natural form on a rhythmic basis. Our very lives in terms of the physiology of our beings depend on rhythmic motion. Our heartbeats, our breathing, the operation of various organs within our bodies, our stomachs, our digestive processes, all of them function rhythmically. Our daily life cycle of sleep and wakefulness occurs in rhythmic patterns. Man's labor through the years has been eased by his ability to do his work in rhythm. Countless songs of folk origin probably were initiated by the necessity for performing work in a rhythmic fashion to make it easier and to do it better. Songs of the chain gangs, of spinning and weaving, of the smithy, and many, many others point clearly to the utilization of the rhythms of our bodies harmonized with a rhythm of work involving movement, tending to lighten the work load and make it easier to perform.

Who has not seen and admired the natural grace and rhythm of the movement of a cat, the bounding of a deer, the playing of children when they are on their own, free to do the things they want to do? The joy of many children's games comes from the physical activity performed in a rhythmic manner: jumping rope, swinging on swings, the up and down of the seesaw, bouncing balls—all rhythmic motions involving bodily activity.

It seems likely that the emotional reaction one has to music is related to a kind of submuscular reaction of our bodies. That music has the power to modify natural body rhythms, while not tested in its entirety, has been satisfactorily demonstrated. We have clear indication that certain kinds of music increase the pulse rate. We know that other types of music can slow down the respiration rate. While the causes of the physiological reactions to music are not well understood in specific terms, we find clear evidence of their existence. This offers one clue to the values of building programs of creative bodily motion as related to expressing reactions to music. Instead of these reactions being limited to submuscular ones, they become overt reactions, using the large muscles and the entire body.

We speak later of listening to music as being an active and

not a passive process. We will point out that the listener creates toward the intention of the composer. What better, then, than to have that creation toward the intention of the composer through the whole body?

With children, the body response to music is a very natural one. Our adult world in its inhibition and social conventions places barriers between physical reactions to any emotions and the natural desire to express emotion physically. It is not considered manly for one to cry when one is hurt. A little boy is constantly being reminded not to be a baby, but to be a man and restrain his physiological reaction to hurt. Our society tends to control body reactions. In terms of the tremendous emotional response to music, which is the primary response, we

Circle games and dances offer additional opportunities for rhythmic body response to music.

Pocantico Hills Central School, Pocantico Hills, New York. Photo by Bill Hedrich, Hedrich-Blessing. Courtesy of Perkins & Will, Architects.

need to look more to the expression of emotion through overt bodily motion.

The child who finds difficulty verbalizing his reaction to music may have no difficulty demonstrating his feelings about it through movements of his entire body. The total physical response of children to any situation is very normal and natural to them. They do it constantly when they are out of school. We need to tap this tremendous resource through our schools and encourage the development of physical response to all kinds of stimuli. The shy child, the retiring one who in many verbal activities finds himself on the periphery of the group, may be able to express himself and begin the process of socialization through bodily reaction in response to an emotional stimulus of music. The aggressive child may find outlet for his excess energies or vent his hostilities in constructive rather than destructive ways.

The socialization process, the manner in which all children come to know and understand themselves in relation to other children, is eased through the expression of emotion through motion.

In harnessing this expression of emotion through motion, three types of rhythmic activities will be described as possibilities within the scope of a music program, and within the competence of the classroom teacher with little or no special facility or technical training in music. These are formal, informal, and creative rhythms.

FORMAL RHYTHMS

In formal rhythms the actual movements of the children fall into commonly expected patterns, predetermined by the teacher. The music played is usually labeled by the teacher as calling for a particular type of reaction on the part of the children. He may play a record for them announcing, "This is skipping music, children. Let's all skip." He then plays the record, and the children proceed to skip around the room. Or there may be running, hopping, marching, tip-toeing, stretching, galloping, flying, high-stepping-horses music—any one of a number of different types of rhythmic actions. In this type of rhythmic activity the bodily reaction of the children is prescribed by the specific reaction called for by the teacher. Children do not respond to the music itself freely or spontaneously, but only in terms of teacher expectations of what they do.

Miss A's first-grade class was seated in chairs placed around the periphery of the room. The tables had been pushed back against the wall to clear the center of the floor. Miss A said, "I'm going to play some skipping music for you, children. You are to skip in time to the music. Class—stand. Face—right." The children thus stood in a large circle. As Miss A played the skipping record, the children skipped around the room in the large circle.

As the record ended, Miss A immediately spoke to the class. "Stand where you are. Form the circle again." When the formation had been retrieved, Miss A continued, "Some children aren't listening very well. You are supposed to skip in time to the music. Let's play it again, and this time, everyone, listen carefully while you skip." The record was played again; the children skipped around their circle again. Miss A carefully noted the children who successfully had skipped in time to the music, the ones who had skipped but not in time, and those who had difficulty skipping. She planned to give special attention and help to both of the latter two groups. All six-year-old children have not mastered the physical skill of skipping, and she wanted to help them learn this skill. Not all children who skip are able to do so in time to the music, and she wanted to help them learn, too.

The next day, instead of playing the record, Miss A used a drum. Tapping out the characteristic long, short, long, short skipping rhythm, she had small groups of children skip around the room, starting with those who skipped in time to the music the day before. Next she had those who could skip but had not done so in time to the music try. When their skipping again did not conform metrically to the drumbeats, she had the group of children clap hands to each of the long drumbeats. She then had them try the skipping again, praising those who had made some progress.

Miss A was not quite sure what she should do with those children who could not skip at all. Nevertheless, she had decided to try to help them, and try she did. She tapped the drum slowly and then quickly to see if the varying speed might help. She had the children hop on one foot for a while and then try skipping again. She decided that that was enough for the session and resolved to work with the children on skipping consistently.

On another day the floor had been cleared, and Miss A's children were again seated around the periphery of the room. "We have something special for rhythms today," Miss A said. "I have some special lion music for you, and you can all be lions. This music was written by a composer whose name was Saint-Saëns and is part of a long composition called *The Carnival of the Animals*. The lion is a rather large animal, but he walks quite softly since he is part of the cat family. Of course, a lion walks on four feet. Try to make believe you are a large animal, walking quietly, just as a lion would. Class—stand. Face—right."

As the record played, the children stalked around the room on all fours, imitating as well as they could the description of the lion that Miss A had given them.

At the close of the record Miss A said, "That was very well done. Remember that the lion has a large mane of hair. Try to imagine yourself as a lion with a big mane, and shake your head from side to side the way a lion would."

"Miss A." Johnny's hand was waving as he called. "The lion roared in the music. Can we roar?"

"Perhaps we can roar later, Johnny," Miss A replied. "If you are all good lions this time, you may roar the next time we play the music."

The children did quite well on the following playing and were permitted to roar quietly on the playing after that.

The most important advantage of this type of rhythmic activity is that the children have a clear sense of direction. They know what is expected, and react to the music in those terms. The overt physical reaction is limited, however, to the one called for. True, some children when beginning this activity may not know how to skip, and they may possibly learn in the process as the music helps them move rhythmically.

The major value is the provision for a physical response to music by children using their large muscles. If our major objective were to have children do things "in time," then formal rhythms of the type described might be included as a desirable activity. Because of large limitations, however, and the stereotyped nature of the responses, this kind of rhythm must be considered comparatively limited in actual value. Children do not respond to the music itself in formal rhythms; they respond to the label of the music as given by the teacher. The only relation with the music is a kind of metrical one: their skipping or running or hopping or high-stepping horses will ultimately be "in time," with the major pulsations of the music reflected in the major body actions of the children.

Another possible value of the formal rhythms occurs in those situations where children have not had very much freedom of action. Where their actions have been quite inhibited because of their previous experiences, formal rhythms may serve to loosen them up. If you have inherited a group of children in a new situation, you may find that one of the ways in which you can get them moving is to have some formal rhythms. If in the past they have always been expected to sit quietly in their seats, the children may not be quite so disturbed by the apparent conflict when you tell them how to move to the music. Since the stereotypes usually used for formal rhythms are ordinary, everyday ones, this approach may provide some relief for children's anxieties and at the same time serve to introduce a movement program for you.

The values inherent in the formal-rhythms program are, however, very limited. Consequently, it would be wise to move on to other types of rhythmic activities just as soon as you can. In most situations the formal rhythms can be eliminated without any sacrifice at all. Their values are of such a limited nature that the sooner you leave them for more expressive types of rhythmic activities, the better off your children will be.

If you feel the need for starting with formal rhythms, you will have no difficulty getting started. You may want to begin by playing a phonograph record. Records labeled for various types of common movement experiences of children are available. You may play one of them and simply say to your children, "This is skipping music, children. Let's listen to it first and then we will skip." Play the record for them, and then have the children respond to the music. They will, of course, then skip around the room.

Avoid structuring the movements, though. It is unnecessary to keep the children in a circle. Also, avoid the formal commands depicted in the illustration above; it is better not to assume the role of a drill chief. Keep the approach relaxed, with the major emphasis on the fun and pleasurable aspects of the activity.

If you have the skill, you may want to play some appropriate music at the piano. You may also want to provide a characteristic rhythm on a drum for formal rhythms. A skipping rhythm would consist merely of tapping the drum in a long, short, long, short series. If you have previously labeled this as skipping rhythm, most children will have little difficulty "keeping time" to the drum taps. You will have no difficulty characterizing various other basic types of children's movement with a drum. A series of heavy, evenly spaced beats on the drum might be walking music or giant steps. In order to establish a rhythm you might want to try some of the actual movements yourself in privacy to get the basic flow of various types of rhythms.

The great disadvantage of the formal rhythms is in the stereotyped nature of the responses expected and the limitation of the children's reactions to those particular responses. The long, short, long, short rhythm could just as well be played without labeling it as skipping rhythm; then different children might respond in different ways to it. No one of these ways would be correct or incorrect—they would merely be different.

INFORMAL RHYTHMS

In informal rhythms the type of physical response is not labeled. Most often, however, the expectations are quite clear to the children. The kinds of physical movements expected of the children are conveyed either by the context of the rhythm or by the words which may accompany the music that is used.

If children have previously been involved in a formal-rhythm program with the long, short, long, short alternation of drumbeats associated with skipping music, their later reactions to such long, short, long, short rhythms will too frequently be skipping movements. Children quickly learn to associate certain types of responses with certain types of music. If you have been involved with a formal-rhythm program, you will find it necessary to try a different approach in order to move to the informal rhythms. Running music, hopping music, high-stepping-horses music, if used as part of the formal-rhythm program and labeled as to the type of physical response expected for the particular type of music, will be difficult to break away from as long as the same types of music are used.

There are ways of starting informal rhythms, however, and you will want to try some of them if you have previously been engaged in the formal-rhythms approach.

An illustration may serve to demonstrate one possible approach. A record entitled "Building a City" tells what is involved in building a city in quite simplified terms and with simple, rhythmic music. Included in the record are a steam shovel, painters, carpenters with their hammering and sawing, wheelbarrows, steam rollers, and the like. The procedure is a very simple one. Play the record for the children, and discuss the general content. Do not discuss various bodily motions; you want the actions to come from the children, not from you. Then ask the children which of them would like to be painters or carpenters or steam shovels or any of the other things included in the record. Do not discuss the type of movement that would be appropriate for each. The responses of the children in terms of the physical activity they select for particular types of music will, of course, be determined by their experiences in living. With this particular record, "Building a City," if your children have never seen a power shovel, then obviously they may be unable to demonstrate it in rhythmic body activity. However, even if their direct living experiences have not brought them into personal contact with the sight of power shovels in operation, they have perhaps heard of them, read about them, seen pictures of them, or been told about them. Their interpretation through rhythmic body motion will reflect their understanding based on their experiences. Such operations as painting or hammering are usually well within the experiences of most children. Indeed, with the building program of the last decade, most children will have encountered power shovels and steam rollers as well.

You may, of course, want to relate this record to some of your activity in social studies and may be able to arrange a trip to a construction site so that children will see many of the operations portrayed in the record actually going on.

After you have played the record and discussed it with your children, and have indicated various children who want to represent various parts of the record, play it again, and encourage the children to respond with rhythmic body movements as they choose. Do not stereotype the movements. It is not necessary for all painters, for instance, to paint the same way. Do not tell the children what to do or how to do it. When they have completed the first session of rhythmic body motion to this record, have a discussion with the children about the actions they used. At all times keep the discussion, actions, and reactions on a fun-pleasure basis. Do not make a formal exercise out of it; the object is not to develop skill in specific movements, but to encourage children's bodily reaction in basic terms to the music.

You might start the discussion after the first series of body motions by asking each group—the painters, for example—to tell what they thought of their own painting. If this is an early experience of the children in terms of rhythmic bodily movement, the chances are that they will have remained in one spot and painted the same board over and over. Some of the painters themselves may have noticed that they remained in one place. Some children may say, "We never dipped our brushes back in the paint can." Someone may point out that the painters painted only a "little, tiny spot." Encourage free and open discussion, indicating at no time a right or wrong way to react to the music. Always, however, encourage free bodily motion, which most often, in the beginning at least, will mean encouraging larger body motions, even to the extent of exaggerating them. Some children may have been painting with just a small finger or wrist movement. Encourage them to use their whole arms, their shoulders, indeed their whole bodies in the painting, hammering, sawing, or other operations.

An approach to formal rhythms was previously described in which the *Carnival of the Animals* was used. This composition might also be utilized for informal rhythms. The approach would be somewhat different.

In this composition various animals are depicted in music. No verbal context accompanies the performance of the music. Each of the sections, however, was labeled by Saint-Saëns, the composer. The double satiric implication in the music can be ignored at the elementary school level. Saint-Saëns depicts musically such things as lions, elephants, donkeys, cuckoos, fossils, the swan, an aquarium, and others. The entire composition takes about one-half hour to play, but each of the segments extends only from two to five minutes.

We have already described Miss A's use of this composition in a formal-rhythms approach. In the informal-rhythms program, the teacher might tell the children the name of the section of the music which she was to play. After playing it, she could prompt some discussion about the music. Following the discussion the next step would be to have a group of children depict in bodily motion their interpretations or feelings about what the music meant. Since the segment had previously been entitled "Lions," the likelihood is that the children in their interpretation would picture a number of lions roaming through the jungle. Since no specific lion movements have been predetermined by the teacher, this becomes informal rhythms rather than formal rhythms. Had the lion movements been decided on in advance and related to the children in any form as Miss A did, the activity would have characterized the formal-rhythm approach. Even though all the children were lions in informal rhythms, it is reasonable that they would have enacted many different kinds of lions in the activity. The children's movements would not be controlled, as in a circle, but would be comparatively free in use of the space available. The children's actual movements would also be freer than in formal rhythms, limited by the context established by the name of the composition.

These illustrations may help to clarify the idea of informal rhythms. We have a free reaction to the music on the part of the children within the limits established by the verbal context of the music. That context describes in some way or other, thereby limiting the type of reaction of the children. However, the teacher does not limit children's reactions by prescribing the type of movement.

This type of bodily reaction in rhythms is of greater value to the children than the completely stereotyped formal rhythms.

CREATIVE RHYTHMS

Since the basic purpose of the rhythms program is to further children's development through the free expression of emotion through motion, the most important types of rhythmic activities are the creative ones.

Two kinds of creative rhythmic activities may be discerned, depending on the relationship between music and movement. In one kind of creative rhythmic activity children's rhythmic motions are based on music played to them. They interpret their feelings about the music through bodily motion. In the other kind of creative rhythmic activity, children express their feelings through bodily motion and the music follows, accompanies, and enhances the children's motions. In the first, movement follows the music; in the second, music follows the movement.

In all creative rhythmic activities no verbal directions impose controls on the activities of the children in their interpretations and expression of bodily movement. Creative bodily movement offers a means of encouraging children's participation in expressing their own feelings through overt muscular reaction.

In a comparatively recent reaction against limiting the rhythms program to physical interpretations of music, there has been an emphasis on movement itself as the primary operation. "Movement is not the handmaiden of music," has been emphasized. Rhythmic movement in recent years has achieved increasing recognition through the medium of modern dance as an authentic art form in its own right, an art form of particularly expressive quality, which, while related, is not subsidiary

Creative rhythmic activities lead to highly individualized responses and opportunities for the expression of personal feeling.

Richmond Public Schools, Richmond, Virginia. Photo by Arthur Clarke.

to music. A truly creative rhythms program would, of course, place emphasis on the physical expression of feelings by children without inevitably basing that expression on the interpretation of music; but it would also recognize that the communication of emotions is very powerfully done by music and that the overt muscular interpretation of those emotions by children should also receive equally important emphasis in the over-all program.

Both of these types of experiences are extremely significant for children. Both of them are creative. Both of them are expressive. Both of them have very important values in the development of young people.

Motion Follows Music

Approaches to body movement based on the *Carnival of the Animals* have previously been described. In one instance this composition was a basis for formal rhythms; in the other it was used for informal rhythms. This same composition may also be used as a basis for creative bodily movement.

In order to place this interpretation in the creative category the music would be played for the children without prior labeling, merely as another composition. Following the playing we have two alternative procedures in utilizing this music for creative rhythms: one is based on discussion, and the other eliminates words as an intermediate step between the music and the motion.

For the first alternative, following the playing of the music, a discussion with the children might bring out various possibilities of what the music meant to various individual children in much the same manner that any new composition would be discussed with your children. After the children discuss the music, they proceed to depict in physical motion various interpretations they may have discussed. The other possibility, which seems to be somewhat superior, is for the children to depict in movement the feelings that they got about the music without any intervening discussion at all. The focus then would be on emphasizing and encouraging a very wide diversity of bodily responses to the music.

While the music seems to indicate lions to those who know the title, it does not necessarily indicate them to all who hear the music. In any group of children who do not know the title there will, in all likelihood, be some who hear lions in the music, but there will be many who hear different kinds of animals. There will also be a number of children who will move to the music without attempting to depict any one thing specifically; their movements will reflect the music itself, but without any pictorial or representational relationship.

Any musical composition may be used to spark children's dynamic body reactions. The basic approach in creative rhythms is to encourage children to react to the music as they feel it. These feelings may be literal, pictorially interpretive ones, or they may be abstract motions depicting their own emotional feeling or reaction to the mood of the music itself. Be careful not to convey to the children in any way any feeling that one mode of reacting to the music is superior to other modes. There is no superior mode of reaction, nor is there a single correct interpretation. There are merely different ones. Just as in listening to music each individual hears in his own way, in terms of his own experiences, so in reacting to music through physical response, the individual depicts his feelings in his own way.

No two people hear music in exactly the same way; no two people, therefore, would necessarily interpret it physically in exactly the same way. Some children feel freer in expressing their feelings through bodily motion. Other children may take their cue from these leaders. Guard against continuation of such imitation, even to the extent, if necessary, of selecting carefully the make-up of small groups of children who would respond to different music at different times. Eliminate coercion of all kinds from the activity. Ordinarily, children enjoy this type of activity so much that you should have no difficulty getting everyone involved.

Not only may phonograph recordings of all types of music be used for creative body motion, but also improvisations at the piano or at the drums or other rhythm instruments. In this type of creative rhythms the children's bodily reaction is based on the music played and the interaction between that music and the children themselves. They respond as they feel the music, as the music "moves" them. The children's motions will reflect their emotional responses to the music.

Music Follows Motion

In the historical development of man it is likely that music reflected the physiological make-up of the human organism. Rhythm and movement existed prior to the expression of rhythm and movement in music. Consequently, rhythmic movement on the part of children should not always be based on music heard. At times the music should follow the movements of the children. Movement in such cases then becomes an expression of children's feelings, and the musical accompaniment serves to highlight the movement itself. In these circumstances music serves as a supporting medium rather than a sparking medium. Movement becomes primary and music secondary. The focus is not on the interpretation of music, but on the interpretation of feelings. In the creative type of movement described above, the interpretation stemmed from the music itself. The bodily reaction reflected the feelings of the children about the particular music. In this type of creative rhythms the feelings of the children are primary; the expression of those feelings through physical response results from the feeling itself. The music then follows the feeling.

A problem which may immediately occur to you is how do we get this kind of creative bodily movement started? Is it not curious that children whose lives are full of boundless energy and boundless motion provide problems for us when we want to control the release of that motion in our schoolrooms? No one needs to suggest how a child should move on the playground in order to express his exuberance or his sorrow or his fears. Some of the most natural and delightful movements of children can be observed in their natural habitat, the playground. These natural movements are ordinarily unconscious, spontaneous, and unplanned as movement. The body performs in response to stimuli, and the child is rarely aware of what his body does as movement itself. Our major task seems to be to bring into the classroom an element of conscious approach to moving, maintaining the spontaneous, free outburst of motion which characterizes movement in play.

Children revel in movement for its own sake. A very creative kindergarten teacher heard that one of her families was discarding a crib mattress. She asked for it, and it was brought to her classroom. The mattress was placed in the middle of a clear area of the floor, and the children took turns running up to it and jumping on it. To an observer, it immediately became apparent that the activity had a very real fascination for the children. In attempting to analyze this fascination no easy answer was found. The children stood back about twenty feet, raced up to the mattress, leaped, and landed on it in various positions. The mattress took quite a beating and probably did not last long, but since it had originally been destined for a junk pile anyway, that did not matter. Some of the children threw themselves forward as they jumped, landing on their stomachs as one might belly-flop on a sled in the snow. Other children jumped and landed on their feet on the mattress. Still others jumped and landed in a sitting position. Perhaps part of the fascination came just from jumping on a mattress, an action probably frowned upon at home. Part of the fascination, however, must be attributed to the joy of a different quality of movement.

It became apparent quickly that each child in his run up to the mattress, his leap, and his landing created a rhythmic pattern, each one distinctive and different from the others. Although it is difficult to present any rhythm specifically in words, we shall try to represent the spacing of the pattern made by their feet as they touched the floor in their run across the room by spaces across the page of this book.

One child started with slow but evenly spaced steps, grad-

ually sped up until he came near the mattress, then made one
additional slower step, a leap, and a landing. It might be something like:

ta . ta . ta . ta . ta . ta . ta . ta.ta.tata . ta .. boom!

Another child sidled up to the mattress with a kind of gallop
consisting of a series of alternating long and short steps like:

ta . ti – ta . ti–ta . ti–ta . ti-ta . ti-ta . . . boom!

Another youngster used almost a stride up to the edge of the
mattress, and then he flopped, like:

ta . ta . ta . ta . ta . ta . ta . ta . boom!

Still another raced up to the mattress as fast as he could run
and then flopped, like:

ta . ta . ta . ta . ta . ta . ta . ta . ta . ta . ta . ta . ta . . . . boom!

Under some circumstances this activity could have provided
an opportunity for the teacher to pick up a drum or just a
couple of sticks and tap out the rhythm each child used as his
own characteristic rhythm in running and jumping on to the
mattress. The children might have imitated the others' runs.
Each child's characteristic rhythm differed from every other
child's. The values of the activity, basically the expression of
exuberance, might have been enhanced by bringing the characteristic rhythm of each child from the unconscious level to
an aware and conscious one. Certainly, there would have been
no justification for letting the conscious-rhythmic aspect of the
activity spoil or in any way hinder the natural, spontaneous
expression of the children. It could be handled in a manner
which would help the unconscious rhythm of the activity become more conscious without hindering its spontaneity.

Many of children's spontaneous movements that occur in
the ordinary course of the day could be the basis for developing splendid rhythmic motion. When you discover them, try
to tap them out, or encourage children to tap them out, and
help bring them from the unconscious to the conscious level
while maintaining their spontaneity.

Dramatic Play

This book does not need to detail all of the many varied aspects of dramatic play in the lives of children. Suffice it to say that through dramatic play children explore and examine the environment in which they live. Through dramatic play they also explore and examine their own feelings about this environment and about themselves. They enact and reenact their own experiences and in the process clarify meanings for themselves. They express their feelings about the meaning of feelings. They enact roles that they wish were prevalent in their own lives. They enact their own wishes, their hopes, their expectations, their dislikes, their thinking, their plans, their disappointments, their worries, their fulfillments, their understandings. The lives of children are full of dramatic play, and it is to this primary life-fulfillment activity of children that we can turn for another important aspect of creative bodily movement of the type in which movement is primary and music follows movement.

Any incident, any story, any happening can serve as the springboard for the dramatic impetus to creative rhythmic movement. This approach, valid for children of all ages, is particularly appropriate for older children. One may very readily have six-year-olds act as butterflies or interpret the first crocus peeping through the snow, but eleven-year-olds are likely to scoff at such "babylike" activity. More robust interpretations are suitable at older levels, just as simpler dramatizations are more suitable for younger children. As the classroom teacher you will be in the best position to determine the suitability of any dramatic content for your particular group of children. Suitability is a function not only of the age of the children involved, but also a function of the kind of experiences they have had and of their developmental level. No one is in a position to know the children in your class better than you. Consequently, no one else can really determine just what dramatic incidents will appeal to your children.

The key difference between dramatization utilized for rhythmic movement purposes and that dramatization ordinarily used as part of the language arts program is the use of words: in creative rhythms we eliminate the use of words in favor of pantomime.

Emotions, feelings, and stories can be communicated in many different ways. Words are one of the means man has evolved to help him communicate with others. Indeed, words are one of the most important attributes of the thinking process. Nevertheless, communication takes place in many different ways and through many different mediums. We can express feelings, ideas, and emotions through pantomime as well as through words. The elimination of the verbal aspects of communication provides an important stimulus to increasing children's ability to express their ideas and communicate by using bodily motions.

A third grade, doing an area of work on Indians, planned a dramatization of the lives of an Indian tribe. Part of this dramatization included a period of drought. A long time in which no rain fell caused the Indians' crops to dry up. What better way, then, to convey the feelings of the Indians than to provide an opportunity for the children to create an Indian Rain Dance in which they plead with the Great Spirit to give them rain. The importance of the crops to the Indians and the essential nature of the life-giving rain were discussed by the children, who as city children had never experienced personally the vital nature of rain to an agrarian group.

This third-grade class planned a series of group movements depicting the planting of crops, the growth of these crops, their gradual drying up, and the meaning of the drought to the Indians. Then the children formed a circle and provided opportunities for each person in the group to come to the center and show his own personal prayer for rain through movement. All of this, of course, was in pantomime. The movements were accompanied by a variety of drumbeats.

That we must always be careful not to attribute adult motives to children, or to hold out for adult standards in the activities of children, is clearly exemplified by one youngster's interpretation of this rain dance when she was in the center of the circle. Actually she seemed to be standing still, in a kind of hunched-over, head-down, dejected position, and it appeared that she could think of no movement at all that was appropriate. Her dejection was at first misinterpreted as representing her own shyness and lack of ideas. Then we noticed that as she stood there, the fingers of her hands were moving up and down, up and down in various patterns. We realized then that she was trying to represent the rainfall with her fingers and that her dejected bodily stance represented her interpretation of the Indians' feelings about not having any rain. Since she was a very withdrawn youngster who had not previously participated very actively in the doings of the class, this representation of hers seemed just as appropriate for her as were other representations in which some children leaped high in the air as if to the sky in an apparent effort to pull down the rain.

At a sixth-grade level this creative bodily movement has just as many values. The product that would be suitable for the sixth grade would be determined by the maturity level of the children. It is in order to caution at this point that the word *dance* should not be used with the older grade levels. The word *dance* to many of the boys connotes a kind of sissy activity in which they will have no part. Of course, this attitude changes later in adolescence. But at the prepubescent stage the boys tend to reject any activity so labeled. Consequently, you may find it advisable to refer to this activity solely as rhythmic pantomime.

The following account tells how the activity developed in a sixth-grade classroom.[1]

A sixth-grade class started a variant of charades with rhythmic accompaniment. A small group of children, formed on the spot, would concoct a brief dramatic incident which they enacted to a rhythmic accompaniment. One of these was "Custer's Last Stand," pantomimed by two soldiers and two Indians. "Cus-

[1] An account of this experience appears in Adele Franklin, Constance Coveney, Alfred Ellison, and Mabel Hawkins, "Good Education for Older Children," New York State Council for Early Childhood Education, New York, 1953.

ter's Last Stand" captured the imagination of several of the boys, who wanted to participate in it. Off the group went to the gymnasium to see what they could develop. Another day the rest of the class went with this group to watch. More children wanted to join the activity. After some discussion to see what all the children could do, the whole class became involved. At this time there was no intention of developing a performance for anyone or any occasion, merely enjoyment in expanding an interesting activity.

Because of its origin as a charade, the children permitted no speech or sound other than the accompaniment. For this particular activity the accompaniment consisted of improvised music at the piano; it could just as well have been a rhythmic accompaniment provided by drums.

The action grew from simple beginnings by group discussion, evaluation, and suggestions by the children. At first one merely saw the soldiers coming into the gym, setting up their camp, and being attacked by the Indians, who entered through another door in the gym. No props of any kind were used. The activity grew, and the group finally decided that they would like to share it with other classes in a sharing assembly. Originally when this decision was made, there was no intention of using costumes or any special lighting effects. The day before the performance, however, the children decided to add costumes: cub-scout shirts inside out or other blue shirts plus dungarees for the boy-soldiers, and dungarees plus bright plaid shirts or blouses for the girl-Indians, who also wore a distinctive headdress of a ribbon plus one feather. That same day, lighting effects were added, and two children painted two large paper panels depicting a barren tree to set the scene in the West. A vulture waited patiently on the branch of one of the trees.

At last performance time arrived. Off went the lights in the gymnasium-auditorium. Two boys walked up the center aisle to the middle of the large floor and turned to face the audience seated on the floor in the rear half of the large room. As the boys reached the middle, they stepped into the circle of the spotlight beamed from the railing of the balcony. Behind them half the gym floor was lit by two floodlights, and at the end of the gym was the stage with its curtain closed.

"Our class presents 'Custer's Last Stand.'" The boys continued with a brief outline of the story, ending with, "You won't hear us say anything. It's all in pantomime. Some of you may think we're just playing cowboys and Indians, but this is all true American history."

They left through the aisle to the rear of the gym. The music started, and two of Custer's scouts came loping in, up the center aisle, out into the clear half of the gym floor. They circled one of the two folding screens on which the trees and a vulture had been painted (the only props on the floor) and saw two Indians who had come in from the front door to the left of the stage. One of the scouts very slowly crept toward the two Indians, who did not see him. The scout took careful aim, made the motion of a gun recoil, turned, and quickly rode off to join the other scout. One Indian was wounded and quickly helped off by his friend. Meanwhile the scouts rode around the gym floor, located a camping place, and rode off to report.

Custer's troops galloped in, found the camping place, and set up camp. They watered their horses, cut wood, cleared some ground, set up tents, made supper, played cards, wrote letters, talked together, dreamed of home—all in rhythmic pantomime. Night fell; the spotlights turned to blue. The men gradually turned in for the night, rolled up in their blankets, until the only movement was the quiet walk of the sentries.

The curtain parted slowly as the music took on an Indian flavor, and the audience saw the camp of the Indians on the stage, "miles" away. The Indians who saw Custer's troops reported at the campfire meeting about their encounter. One after another, braves solemnly arose to describe the coming of the white man and what it had meant to them. They told how they had been robbed of their land. The killing of their buffalo deprived them of food, and they faced starvation. Without buffalo hides they had no homes and no clothing. In some barren places, without buffalo dung they had no fuel for their fires. Raids on their villages and the tragedy of their squaws and papooses and brave warriors who had died in battle were dramatized briefly in pantomime. Tension mounted. Each brave recounted his harrowing tale with more vigor. Frenzy grew. The anger of the Indians and their determination to strike at the cause of their trouble became obvious. The camp-fire meeting, begun so solemnly, ended in a war dance.

The curtain closed, and the scene shifted to Custer's camp on the floor of the gym. The sentries still picketed the camp, poking now and then at the imaginary bushes on the fringes. The Indians crept out at the sides of the stage, one by one, slipping from the ends of the curtains. Down the stage steps, gradually onto the gym floor, around the sides of the camp, along the gym walls they came. Across the middle of the gym, between the camp and the audience, they crept, until Custer's men were surrounded. One brave, "knife" in upraised hand, approached a sentry from behind and signaled the onslaught on the camp by killing the sentry.

The battle scene was short but gory. Indians wildly circled the camp, shooting their arrows at Custer's men who, roused from their sleep, set themselves into the traditional formation. The uneven battle ended with Custer and his men sprawled awkwardly all over the floor, joined there by a number of Indians. The other Indians finally left, and Custer's camp was a wild, desolate, and dreary sight.

Wait! One soldier still lived! He crawled forward painfully, dragging himself haltingly. He reached out with one arm, as if toward home. Alas, he suddenly slumped forward and then, all was completely still.

The curtain parted slowly, and again, "miles" away, one saw the Indian campfire. The Indian braves, fewer in number, once again sat around the campfire, cross-legged and solemn. The chief arose and in brief emphatic motions indicated the fate of all who would drive the Indian from his land. He raised his arms high to the Great Spirit and was joined then by the others in a victory dance. The curtain closed.

It must be clear that an elaborate final production is not an important part of this activity. The process, again, takes precedence over the product. It is the doing that is most important, not the performing. Performing has values of its own, but they are secondary to the process of developing the activity. This group which did "Custer's Last Stand" spent more time on the individual rhythmic charades, which probably took no more than two or three minutes each, than they spent on the entire production. This group happened to get very much excited about "Custer's Last Stand" and apparently saw tremendous potentialities in it. This captured their interest, and the teacher capitalized on it. Eventually the program was recognized as possible. The children did not start out to put on a performance; the performance came as a result of their activities. After they had worked it out, the children decided that they would like to share it with other groups in the school. It was not developed, however, in order to prepare an assembly program.

There is no single correct way of proceeding in order to develop a program of creative bodily motion. You do not have to be a devotee of the modern dance in order to help your children develop this activity. No technical dance movements are involved. Indeed, they should be discouraged. The freedom of motion, the integrity of gesture, and the expression of emotion through motion are the roots of the program. You do not have to tell the children what movements to make—that would be quite the wrong approach and would tend to stifle rather than stimulate creativity.

Most important is your attitude. The classroom climate must be one of mutual confidence and regard. The children must feel that you really want them to express their own feelings and wishes and not merely reflect the stereotypes of what is traditionally expected of them. Once there has been agreement by the group on the particular dramatization or pantomime, your role as teacher is primarily that of stimulator and guide to help the children determine what they want to do, how they want to do it, and how they will organize.

Expressions such as, "How do you think we should start it?" or "Who has an idea about what we can do next?" "Which way do you think would be best?" will be most useful to you. Children are naturally creative unless somewhere along the line they have been blocked. Our job is to make sure of two things: one, that we do not block their natural creativity; and two, that we free those who have been blocked.

Figure 6. MOVEMENT AND MUSIC

TYPE	MUSIC USED	CHILDREN'S RESPONSE
Formal rhythms	"Type" music, labeled by teacher, title or verbal content.	Specific movements as indicated by teacher: skipping, running, hopping, etc.
Informal rhythms	"Type" music, not labeled, expectations clear, often stereotypes.	Not specified externally, movements limited by type, stereotype, or verbal context.
Creative rhythms based on music played (movement follows music)	Any music, nontyped, untitled at first, without verbal context.	Free, creative bodily movement stimulated by the music alone. The expression of emotion through motion.
Creative rhythms based on children's feelings (music follows movement)	Improvised—piano or drum accompaniment.	1. Generalized creative and expressive bodily motion as felt by child; no external stimulus. 2. Creative and expressive bodily motion as felt by child in relation to dramatic pantomime.

KEEP IN MIND

The following items summarize the major content of this chapter. Individual items may be used for debate, discussion, report, or research topics.

1. The word *moving* refers both to overt body action or reaction and to an individual's emotional reaction.
2. Life almost always involves movement.
3. Patterns of living are characterized in function by rhythm.

4. Music has the power to modify natural body rhythms.
5. The primary purpose of a program involving bodily movement is the expression of emotion through motion.
6. Formal rhythms are those in which the actual movements of the children fall into expected patterns which are predetermined by the teacher. The bodily reaction of the children is prescribed by the specific reaction called for by the teacher.
7. Formal rhythms are limited in value because of the stereotyped nature of children's responses.
8. The main use of formal rhythms is in those situations where children previously have not had freedom of action; formal rhythms may serve as a good introduction to bodily movement for such groups.
9. In informal rhythms the type of physical response is neither labeled nor predetermined precisely by the teacher. However, the context of the rhythm or the verbal accompaniment of the music usually conveys expectations of the types of movement.
10. Informal rhythms are superior to formal rhythms as an activity for children in that the reaction of the children is freer and within broader limitations. Those limitations are established by the context of the music rather than the prescription of the teacher.
11. Creative rhythms involve those physical activities of children which freely express their feelings.
12. In one type of creative rhythms the children react through bodily motion to the music which they hear, unhampered and unprescribed by any force external to the music and to themselves. Their interpretation is of their feelings about the music which they hear.
13. In another type of creative rhythms children's rhythmic bodily movement is based on their feelings, and the music follows the children rather than the children following the music.
14. Rhythmic dramatic pantomime is an important aspect of creative rhythms.

15. Any musical composition may be used to spark children's dynamic bodily reactions.

16. Since no two people hear music in exactly the same way, no two people, therefore, would necessarily interpret it physically in exactly the same way.

17. In creative rhythms our major task is to bring an element of conscious approach to movement, while maintaining the spontaneous free outburst of motion which characterizes movement in play.

18. Through dramatic play children explore, examine, and come to understand their environment, as well as their feelings about both this environment and themselves.

ℑ CHAPTER FIVE

Playing Music

WHEN WE PLAY music, we produce an ordered progression of
sounds on some suitable medium. Singing is such an important activity in the elementary school because every child can
sing and, therefore, can participate in making music. Also,
every child can participate in playing music. In playing music,
however, the child does not use the human body as the instrument for producing the sound as in singing; he uses another
medium which he controls.

Composers have many reasons for creating music, for planning the orderly progression of sounds. They may have a need
to express some feeling, using sound as a medium, just as a
painter expresses feeling using color, mass, line, and texture
as mediums. When a person plays music composed by someone else, he re-creates, toward the intent of the composer, an
expression of feeling. The music which the player reproduces
creates within him some feeling. This feeling may or may not
be the same as the feeling which the composer expressed
through his composition. It need not be the same. Nevertheless,
good music creates some feeling in the player. What he feels
comes out in his playing. In this sense the player of music

creates as he plays, even when he plays the progression of sounds composed by someone else. The musical score, the notes on paper, is not music. It is merely a way by which we communicate what the music could be. The score must be translated by a human being before it becomes music.

A person who has never produced music through singing or playing never fully feels music to the extent felt by those who have engaged thus in producing music.

Those who play music, however, need not, indeed, should not, restrict their playing to the music composed by others. They may also determine the progression of sounds which they will play. Playing music, both as a creative and a re-creative activity, can be engaged in by all children. Teachers without technical training in music can help their children participate in this very important musical activity.

PLAYING RHYTHMS

Music is an organized, produced, and perceived progression of sounds. Playing rhythms can be an important part of playing music, even though rhythm is but part of music. In a symphony orchestra no one instrumental player plays the entire composition; he plays but a part of it. One instrumentalist or group of instrumentalists may play the main melodic line. Another instrumentalist may play a counter melody. Other instrumentalists may play parts that fill in the harmonic structure or that fulfill the rhythmic pattern. Each player contributes toward the realization and fulfillment of the composer's intent, but no one of them plays the symphony or can play the symphony alone.

We need not feel that each child, when he plays, must produce an entire composition. Indeed, there are few instruments on which that can be done. While the piano can fulfill the melodic, harmonic, and rhythmic intent of compositions written for the piano, transcriptions of orchestral music when played on the piano cannot fulfill the tonal color, the dynamic range, or the full feeling of the composer who wrote with the orchestra in mind as the medium of expression.

Over the course of years, children might learn to play instruments which serve melodic, harmonic, and rhythmic functions. At any one time, however, they usually need to play together with others, in ensembles, in order to fulfill the intent of the composer.

What Instruments First?

As we examine the possibilities of various instruments and consider the appropriate ones for children, there is an additional component. What muscular dexterity would be required for specific instruments? What reasonable expectations of mastery can we hold for success with a particular instrument with children of various ages? Do specific instruments require special competencies and complex muscular coordination? How can our knowledge of children's growth and development be utilized to help make determinations?

As young children grow, their large muscles come under control before the small muscles do. The young child's arm movements are ordinarily easier to coordinate than his finger and hand movements. Fine muscle coordination will usually not develop until after large muscle coordination has developed, although in some children smaller muscle coordinations do develop before some of the large muscle coordinations. In nursery schools and kindergartens children are given large paint brushes with which to paint, brushes which may be 12 inches long with bristles a half inch to an inch wide. Very few younger children have developed the finer muscle coordination necessary to handle small, fine brushes. The tiny pans of water-color paints that ordinarily were the limited and limiting painting experience many of us had when we were in elementary school are not really suitable for young children. With large brushes the child makes strokes utilizing arm motion and sometimes even some shoulder motion.

Similarly, when it comes to musical instruments, we discard for most young children those instruments which require coordination of the small muscles in favor of those with which they can utilize the large muscles of the arm.

Further, our consideration must include provision for satisfying experiences quickly, particularly for young children. Success encourages and failure kills interest. In choosing instruments we need to select those which children can utilize quickly and master sufficiently to meet their own needs for success in playing.

These factors suggest that rhythm instruments provide an excellent medium for introducing playing experiences with children. At all ages children can have satisfying, musically valuable experiences with rhythm instruments. For those just beginning to explore the world of instruments, rhythm instruments provide an opportunity to order progressions of sounds without any accompanying necessity for great skill and control. The ease with which young children can produce sounds on rhythm instruments and organize them in a satisfying way argues strongly in their favor.

For our purposes an instrument must be broadly defined. We have said before that music in its broadest sense is an orderly progression of sounds. The child who produces sound in some way that makes sense to him makes music. The child often produces sounds by experimentation. He may knock objects together, tap a pencil on the table, kick a wastebasket, drum rhythmically with his knuckles on a table, clap two spoons together, strike a metallic object with a nail, stretch a rubber band over a box and strum it. These experiments with sound are similar in effect to experiments in playing musical instruments, the making of music through the ordering of sounds.

With very young children you may want to use objects found in the immediate environment or readily procurable on loan or gift from the home. Any objects producing sounds pleasing to the child can serve for the initial attempt at playing rhythm instruments. Sticks clicking together, nails hung by a string and struck by another nail, pot lids, a wastebasket turned upside down, wooden blocks, or pieces of dowel sticks of various sizes can be used at first to produce sounds from the immediate environment.

Encourage children to be attentive to the sounds produced by varying objects. Encourage their experimentation. The only cautions that need to be applied are those common-sense ones to protect furniture from needless scratching and scraping and hard knocks. Damage to furniture certainly does not contribute toward the ultimate objective anyway and teaches children undesirable lessons.

Young children of nursery school age would probably be satisfied with quite simple sound-producing instruments, defining instruments in the broad terms which we have previously used. If professional rhythm instruments cannot be purchased, you can still provide in any classroom situation for the contributions which playing rhythm instruments can make to children. These improvised instruments lead to highly satisfying musical experiences.

Naturally with young children you would not attempt much in the way of organizing or helping children organize the

Rhythm instruments introduce a variety of musical possibilities for experimentation with organizing sounds.

Richmond Public Schools, Richmond, Virginia. Photo by Arthur Clarke.

sounds of the various instruments. It might be possible for gross groupings of instruments according to the type of sound produced to take place, and even three- and four-year-old children may make decisions about which instrument or group plays next. Keep any organization at this level simple, brief, and uncomplicated.

Too often rhythm bands have been considered suitable only for very young children. In actuality it is only as children grow and develop to a certain point that they are able to achieve the higher values stemming from the organization of orchestrations on a quite complex level. Orchestrations on such levels are of great advantage and make many contributions to the furthering of children's sensitivity to all music. Consequently, it is highly recommended that rhythm-orchestra activities continue throughout the elementary school years and even into the junior high school level.

The Rhythm Orchestra

The rhythm orchestra, when properly developed, holds the interest of children of all ages and offers high potential value for the development of musical feeling. Rhythm is part of living; indeed, rhythm accompanies all life. Rhythm must be felt through the body. We find it difficult to intellectualize about rhythm, which almost invariably includes either actual bodily motion or submuscular reactions.

Too often the potential assets of the so-called rhythm band, while dimly perceived, have not been adequately realized. Rhythm bands in most schools have been limited to the kindergarten and at times extended to the lower grades. The activity has too often been overformalized and teacher dominated in presentation. The organization of the orchestration, which determines which instruments are to play and when they play, has ordinarily been made from a cumulative, atomistic point of view. Children, assigned specific instruments, were taught to respond on certain beats in the measure. Instruments maintained their individual identities. Orchestrations were built up on the basis of accumulating the sounds of specific instruments to be reproduced on various beats of each measure. With the large variety of rhythm instruments possible, several difficulties were encountered. A complete orchestration became a very complex affair, which almost necessitated that each instrument have a score of its own. This meant that the composition would be difficult to play unless the children were able to read a rhythm score with skill. Consequently, the problems of score reading interposed between the satisfaction of the children's desire to play and the music. They had to read music notation before they could play.

Since very young children were unable to develop this facility in reading the rhythmic notation, the activity was simplified in two ways. One simplification merely amounted to using fewer instruments so as to reduce the complexity of the orchestration. The other simplification was the creation of song materials about individual instruments. Then the children who had those instruments could play while the rest of the class sang the song. Too often, of course, the song material developed for this purpose was inferior musically, and the same objections can be raised to it that were treated previously in Chapter 2.

To differentiate from this former method of proceeding, we shall call our collection of rhythm instruments a rhythm orchestra instead of a rhythm band. Our recommended procedure will be analytical and organismic rather than cumulative and atomistic. As we start our rhythm orchestra, the children begin with vague ideas of the total sound, first of the music alone, then with the rhythm instruments added. Through a process of gradual differentiation, sounds of groups of instruments are made more specific. Also through differentiation from the vague ideas of the whole, we shall develop ideas, feelings about and understandings of foundational musical elements present in all music: the basic rhythm, the melodic rhythm, and the phrase rhythm. After each step of differentiation, the new element developed is reintegrated into a new understanding of the whole composition. Learnings grow from whole to parts to new whole to new parts to still newer whole in an almost unending cycle.

A Rhythm Orchestra in a Third Grade

The following description tells a composite story of how a rhythm orchestra might develop in a third-grade class. Probably in no one specific classroom would the rhythm orchestra develop in precisely this fashion. Further, the development of the rhythm orchestra might take place in somewhat similar form in a second-grade or a fifth-grade classroom. The crucial differences among the grade levels may be found in the maturity level of the children and in their previous experiences with rhythm instruments. For our third grade we have assumed that while the children had had some experience in the kindergarten, there had been little previous development of a rhythm orchestra.

The class had a few manufactured instruments: two drums, two triangles, and a tambourine. They had made a number of other instruments, simple ones to be sure, but nevertheless effective in producing different kinds of sounds. (For instructions on how to make rhythm instruments, see Chapter 6.)

You may want to read the following material twice. The first time read through the account of what this third grade did so that you will get an over-all picture of the development of the activity. Then go back and read it again, this time referring to the explanatory material for additional understanding of what was done.

Miss Wilson glanced around the room. She saw that her eager eight-year-olds were quietly waiting for the music, their instruments on the floor below their seats.

The temptation to play an instrument one holds is almost unsuppressible no matter who holds the instrument, teachers or children. If you need quiet with no miscellaneous clicks, clangs, or booms as various children submit to the overpowering urge to hear what the instrument sounds like, have the children place their instruments on the floor under their seats. Removing the instruments from physical reach this way serves better than constant admonitions for quiet, admonitions which may be very difficult to obey.

"The first time, we'll just listen to the music," the teacher suggested. "After that we can play."

The focus constantly begins with the music itself, not with the playing of an instrument. Playing music involves listening. Listening includes the phonograph record in this case. Later it also includes listening to the sound of one's own instrument and listening to other instruments.

She put the needle in the groove of the record and adjusted the volume knob of the phonograph until the music sounded just about right. The stirring sounds of the main part of Sousa's "Stars and Stripes Forever" filled the room.

The standard admonition for playing a record would be "not too loud, not too soft." More teachers, however, tend to err on the side of not playing the record loud enough. Try to approximate the level of sound of the original combination of instruments, modified by the exigencies of the size of the room you are in. If your building is not modern and you must also be concerned about disturbing your neighbors, you might try to pick a time when they are at recess or on a special-purpose mission.

Miss Wilson watched the children's faces with satisfaction as she saw that they were quite obviously interested in the music. "How many of you liked it?" she asked as she lifted the needle from the record at the end of the part she was playing. She grinned with satisfaction, intermixed with relief, at the immediate response of the children, all of whom enthusiastically raised their hands.

Since our basic objective still holds—to provide pleasurable experiences with music—the music selected for rhythm-orchestra work must appeal to the children in itself. If the children had not liked the composition, Miss Wilson would have put it aside and selected another. We must take children as they really are, not as we would like them to be. Our job is to help them develop as far as their potential will permit from the point at which we find them.

"Get your instruments ready quietly now. This time we'll play with the record." There was a clashing, clanging, clicking noise as the children lifted their instruments from the floor and fiddled with them.

Miss Wilson knew that some noise was bound to accompany this getting-ready process. She remembered very well her own experience with an in-service teachers' group. She could hardly resist sounding her instrument when she got her hands on it. She decided to ignore this noisiness.

She held up her arm in the signal for "silence," and was pleased at how quickly the children responded. "This time play your instruments with the music. Play the way you think it will sound best." Quickly, she started the record again, raised her arms in the typical conductor's position just before the orchestra began to play, and vigorously cued her little musicians when to begin.

As she expected, there was no organizational pattern to their playing. Each youngster was an island unto himself as he sounded his own instrument.

The original response of the children is a generalized one, unorganized, frequently unmusical, sometimes even a bit chaotic. Compounded of parts of curiosity, glee, and exuberance, this initial reaction of the children is quite natural and should be expected. It represents their current level of development. They had been very eager to play their instruments, and it seems quite normal that their first efforts to play them would be to hear how they sound. Miss Wilson was wise to let them react as they did.

Some children had various types of drums. Others had shaking instruments. There were some large spikes that had a pleasant triangle-type sound. She noticed the length of pipe that sounded so bell-like and smiled to herself at the washboard and thimble rhythm. The pot-lid cymbals clanged, and the tambourines jangled.

The jumble of sounds reminded her of the fifth grade she had the year before. "They didn't start out much differently," she thought. "My job now is pretty much what it was with them. I certainly can't expect these eight-year-old children to do what those fifth-graders could do in organizing their orchestra. But third-graders are quite competent. We'll see how far they can go."

The major difference between the third and fifth grades will depend on the individuals in the two classes, their maturity level, and the experiences which they have previously had with a rhythm orchestra. Miss Wilson's fifth grade the previous year had had no background of experience with a rhythm orchestra. Indeed, she had some difficulty pursuading the want-to-be-grown-up fifth-graders that rhythm orchestras were not a "baby" activity. Her major lead that year had been the construction of some rhythm instruments, an activity in which they were far more successful than her present third grade. The dexterity and resourcefulness of those fifth-graders had resulted in some fine instruments, which were well made and had good tone quality. After the instruments were made, she found it possible to help the children satisfy their natural desire to play them. It did not take much experience for them to recognize that playing in a rhythm orchestra was not a baby activity at all. Indeed, it was quite grown up.

The record ended. "What did you think of it?" Miss Wilson asked. Several hands went up.

Wherever possible, help children develop their own critical faculties. By asking them what they thought of the way they played, Miss Wilson worked toward two objectives: she put the children in a position of evaluating, even at this early stage, and she started to build within the children the attitude that they needed to listen to what they did so that they might properly evaluate it.

"I think you should play the record louder. I could hardly hear it," one youngster said.

"Is there any other way we could hear the music better?" Miss Wilson asked.

"We could play our instruments softer," another child answered.

"Is it important for us to hear the music?" Miss Wilson asked.

"Sure. How can we tell how to play if we can't hear the music?" a third child replied.

"Let's play it again," several children pleaded.

"Fine," responded Miss Wilson. "This time let's play a bit more softly so that we can all hear the music."

The children played with the record a second time, more softly than the first. Miss Wilson did not turn up the volume. She watched as the children played and noted that more of them responded to the music instead of playing their instruments haphazardly.

It seems quite likely that during the initial playing of the composition, children would be primarily concerned with producing sounds from their own instruments. Only after they have passed through this stage can they listen well to the music *while* they play. The initial stage of primary interest in producing sounds on their own instruments may last through several playings, not only one. Be patient at this point. With experience the children will be ready to move on.

Miss Wilson realized that the children would have to make many such generalized reactions to music with their instruments before they would be ready to organize their playing. She thought again of the previous year's fifth-graders. "That's one big difference," she mused. "Progress in organization comes much more slowly with the younger children. I must be careful not to push too rapidly."

She decided that they had done enough for that day, and at the end of the record told the children to put their instruments away quietly.

Miss Wilson knew that in her over-all objectives she planned to develop with her children a feeling for the three kinds of rhythms present in all music: the basic rhythm, the melodic rhythm, and the phrase rhythm. She realized that definitions of terms like these would not make much sense to the children; they must feel the three rhythms through their bodies. The rhythm instruments were one way to build toward these goals.

These three rhythms present in all music are developed in more detail later. Let us briefly define them here, however.

The basic rhythm is the underlying pulsation felt in all music. It is the "toe-tapping" rhythm. The melodic rhythm refers to the rhythm in which the specific tones of the melody follow each other. It may be likened to the rhythm of the words in prose. The phrase rhythm labels the succession of more or less complete musical ideas and is the basis of form in music.

Miss Wilson had other major objectives in her work with rhythm instruments, besides. She wanted to help her children begin to hear the sounds of instruments quite consciously, to be able to differentiate among them. Further, she wanted to help them learn to organize sounds reasonably and with consideration of the over-all effect of those sounds. Since she knew, however, that the learning process includes the gradual differentiation of separable parts from vague feelings of the whole, she was quite content for the initial experience to be on the level of generalized reactions to the music.

For a number of music sessions with the instruments, Miss Wilson continued to play different phonograph records, and the children responded on their instruments as the music impelled them. She varied the type of records she played. The children also played accompaniments to their songs. After about two weeks, she felt that the children were responding well. Their playing seemed to be in keeping with the music. She felt that they were ready for the next developmental step.

This kind of decision is one of the key problems in teaching. The right time to introduce a new activity or to change from one aspect to another or to drop an activity altogether is an aspect of the art of teaching rather than the science of teaching. The proper timing is more often felt than determined objectively. Developing a sense of good timing is often a function of experience. We find it comparatively easy to tell afterwards that we should have changed an activity just before we lost the interest of the class. Good teachers, through critical self-evaluation, gradually develop this sense of timing. They can tell by the beginnings of restlessness of a small group of the children, or by a kind of glazed look in the eyes of some other children, just when the time is ripe for changing an activity to avoid losing the group. Similarly, teachers become sensitive to the cues that tell them when the group is ready to move on. Good teachers are constantly aware not only of what they intend and what they do, but also of how children receive and perceive what is done and intended.

Miss Wilson now selected one of the children's favorite records. She played it for them as usual. After the playing this time, however, she led into a different kind of discussion.

"I noticed while you were playing that some of you were playing one kind of rhythm and others were playing a different kind of rhythm. Both of these rhythms are in the music we heard." Miss Wilson knew from past experience that some children discover the difference between the basic rhythm and the melodic rhythm by themselves. Others recognize the difference only after it has been pointed out. "Did anyone notice these two kinds of rhythms?"

A logical, cumulative, atomistic approach would have us teach the basic rhythm first and then the melodic rhythm. After the children know each of these rhythms separately, those who adhere to this kind of approach would permit us to have the children combine the two rhythms. Certainly, this seems logical enough. However, the analytic, organismic approach recommended here insists that learning depends on differentiation of separable elements from vague ideas of the whole: we start with the whole and then separate it into its parts. Miss Wilson started with a total response to the whole music. She now began the process of differentiating the basic rhythm and the melodic rhythm from the hitherto undifferentiated whole.

"Some of us were playing softly, and some playing loudly," Steve responded.

"Yes, that's true," Miss Wilson agreed. "But loudness or softness isn't rhythm, Steve. Any rhythm could be played either loud or soft. The rhythm is part of what we play. The loudness or softness is a way of playing it."

"Marie was playing something different from what I was playing, Miss Wilson," Barbara said. "I tried what she was doing, and it fit the music, too."

"Let's hear what you were playing, Barbara," Miss Wilson suggested. "Then we'll hear how Marie played."

Barbara played a succession of evenly spaced beats on her drum, "tumm TUMM tumm tumm tumm TUMM tumm tumm . . ."

Then Marie played a different kind of rhythm: "tumm TUMM tada tumm tada TUMM — — tada TUMM tada tumm tada TUMM — tumm — . . ."

"That sounds like the 'Stars and Stripes Forever' that we were playing," irrepressible Jimmy called out.

"How could it?" practical Janey wanted to know. "I didn't hear any melody."

"Play it again, Marie," Miss Wilson asked.

Marie played again.

"That's the rhythm of the melody," Miss Wilson said. "Barbara was playing what we call the basic rhythm of the music. I wonder if Barbara and Marie could play together, each one playing her own rhythm."

Barbara and Marie played together. After a few false starts, they got it right. Barbara played the basic rhythm, and Marie played the melodic rhythm. We might represent the way they played together this way:

```
{ B:  tumm TUMM tumm tumm tumm TUMM tumm tumm tumm
{ M:  tumm TUMM ta-da tumm ta-da TUMM  —    —   ta-da

{ B:  TUMM tumm tumm tumm TUMM tumm tumm tumm
{ M:  TUMM ta-da tumm ta-da TUMM  —   tumm  —

{ B:  TUMM tumm tumm tumm TUMM tumm tumm tumm
{ M:  TUMM ta-da tumm ta-da TUMM  —    —   ta-da

{ B:  TUMM tumm tumm tumm TUMM tumm tumm
{ M:  TA tumm ta tumm tumm TUMM  —    —
```

For those who read music, the notation of the melody of "The Stars and Stripes Forever" is on the next page. The basic rhythm and the melodic rhythm of this composition are shown on page 139.

You have realized, of course, that the "tumm tumm's" of the basic rhythm are all to be evenly spaced, like soldiers' footsteps as they march, or like our heartbeats. The basic rhythm

consists of steady, rhythmically even pulsations that continue
through the music. In music these basic pulsations seem to
group themselves together in units of twos, threes, fours, or
sixes. Other groupings are possible, but they are found less frequently than these four types.

In the succession of "tumm tumm's" you find that every
fourth one is in capital letters. In our examples the first pulsation of every group is capitalized to make it easier for the eye
to follow. Traditionally, many music theorists have insisted
that the first beat of each group or measure is always accented,
played louder. Actually this is not so. Music played with an
accent on the first beat of each measure is most unmusical, and
no adequate player really plays that way. Indeed, in many
flowing melodies a sensitive instrumentalist may use a kind of
negative accent, playing the first beat of a measure more softly
than the others. At any rate, except in marches and dance
music, accenting the first beat of each measure would create
a choppy, disjointed, and very unmusical effect.

THE STARS AND STRIPES FOREVER

John Philip Sousa
Arr. by A. E.

Using a drum, if one is handy, or your finger on the arm of your chair tap the basic rhythm carefully. Keep the beats evenly spaced. Once you feel this rhythm, tap it with your foot instead of your finger. When you are satisfied that your foot taps evenly, regularly, and almost without your thinking about it, try to tap out the melodic rhythm by clapping your hands. Keep your toe tapping evenly, and fit the melodic rhythm into the basic rhythm. On the first two "tumm's" your clap and

Basic and Melodic Rhythms

THE STARS AND STRIPES FOREVER

John Philip Sousa

your tap will be simultaneous. On the next "tumm," however, you will clap twice for the "tada" in the melodic rhythm while you tap once. Then a clap and a tap come together, followed by two claps to one tap.

One of the problems in any book about music is the reproduction of sounds. Rhythmic sounds presented without notation offer particular difficulties. Try to translate the "tumm, tumm's" and "tada's" into the basic and melodic rhythms of "The Stars and Stripes Forever." The best way to capture these rhythms is through a group experience with rhythm instruments.

"Who can tell us in words how Barbara's basic rhythm sounds?" Miss Wilson asked the group.

"Barbara sounds like soldiers marching along."

"She sounds like jumping rope."

"When I was going to Grandma's one day in the car we heard a sound like that. Daddy said it was the cracks in the road that did it."

"It sounds like a heartbeat. The doctor let me listen to his stethoscope once, and that's what it sounded like."

"It's like a train—the click of the wheels on the cracks in the tracks."

"Good." Miss Wilson broke in. "Now what would you say about Marie's melodic rhythm?"

"Marie's rhythm was sort of jumpy. It had long ones and short ones too, but Barbara's rhythm was even."

"There's a sound for every tone in the melody."

"I could almost hear 'The Stars and Stripes Forever' when Marie played her rhythm. Can you always tell what the melody is from the rhythm?"

"Let's find out." Miss Wilson quickly seized her opportunity. "How many of you recognize this song?" Miss Wilson tapped out this rhythm on a drum:

TUMM tumm tumm tumm TUMM tada tumm — TUMM tumm
tumm tumm TUMM tada tumm — TUMM tumm tumm tumm
TUMM tada tumm — TUMM tada tumm tumm TUMM — tumm —

"Why that's 'Skip To My Lou'!" Several children immediately recognized the rhythm.

SKIP TO MY LOU

Traditional
Arr. by A. E.

Pick your part - ner, Skip to my Lou,
TUMM tumm tumm tumm TUMM ta - da tumm——

Pick your part - ner, Skip to my Lou. Pick your part - ner,
TUMM tumm tumm tumm TUMM ta-da tumm—— TUMM tumm tumm tumm

Skip to my Lou. Skip to my Lou, my dar - ling.
TUMM ta - da tumm—— TUMM ta-da tumm tumm TUMM—tumm——

"One of you play the rhythm of some song we know. We'll try to tell what song it is from the rhythm."

This game of guessing the song from the melodic rhythm is a favorite with children. It can be played in odd moments at any time during the day. As in so many things, all children do not grasp the notion of this melodic rhythm at the same time, nor can all children reproduce the melodic rhythms of various songs with the same degree of adequacy or accuracy. Depending on your group, you may want to vary the procedure Miss Wilson used.

1. A child taps out the rhythm of the melody of a familiar song.
2. Those who recognize it raise their hands.
3. The first child calls on someone.
4. The child called on makes his response.
5. Assuming he is right, the entire class sings the song, then claps the melodic rhythm, while the child who answered correctly conducts.
6. He taps out the rhythm of another song, or calls on another child to do so.

The process continues.

Miss Wilson's suggestion was eagerly received, and Johnny had his turn first.

"Tada tada Tada tada Tada tada Tumm tada Tada tada Tada tada Tada tada Tumm tumm," he played.

A number of hands went up. "Call on someone, Johnny," Miss Wilson said. Johnny called on Ann.

" 'Yankee Doodle,' " responded Ann.

"Good," said Miss Wilson, "now you try one, Ann."

Ann thought. Finally, "I can't think of one," she said, disappointedly.

"We'll come back to you later then, Ann," said Miss Wilson reassuringly.

Be especially understanding of those who "can't think of one." Your attitude as teacher will determine whether or not the Anns ever try again. It is not reasonable to expect all children to have equal facility. Much depends on growth level, maturity, and experiential background. Johnny is not better than Ann because he could do it and she could not. Johnny merely reached the stage when he could do it sooner than Ann did. Ann will reach it, too, unless, somehow, somewhere she gets the idea that she cannot do it. If she thinks she cannot, it will be extremely difficult to help her.

"Who would like to try?" Miss Wilson looked around at the waving arms. "Let's hear yours, Stanley."

"Tumm — t' tumm t' tumm t' Tumm — tumm — Tumm — t' tumm tumm Tumm — — — Tumm — t' tumm t' tumm t' Tumm — tumm ta-da Tumm tumm tumm tumm Tumm — —," Stanley played.

" 'I've Been Workin' on the Railroad,' " Mike guessed when Stanley called him. Then Mike played:

"Tumm tumm Tumm — Tumm tumm Tumm — Tumm tumm t' Tumm — Tumm tumm t' Tumm — t' Tumm t' ta-da-ta Tumm t' tumm t' Ta-da-ta ta-da-ta Tumm t' tumm t' Ta-da-ta ta-da-ta Ta-da-ta tumm t' Tumm tumm Tumm."

Miss Wilson realized that they were taking more time with this activity than she had planned for the day. She also realized, however, that the interest level of the children in the activity was very high. She watched the class carefully, trying to sense the first signs that would tell her it was time to change the activity. When she saw that slight beginning of restlessness, the first loss of interest, she quickly brought the activity to an end for the day, promising to continue again the next day.

Miss Wilson was perfectly willing to adjust her program schedule in order to capitalize on the interest of the children. She recognized that real learning was taking place and that it would have been unfortunate to cut off the activity at this time. The interest level of the children and the quality of the learning experience were more than ample justification for maintaining a flexible schedule.

In the succeeding days Miss Wilson provided a number of opportunities to play this rhythm guessing game based on recognition of melodic rhythm. She also helped the children move on to the next step in playing their instruments. The class was divided into two parts. When they played with the phonograph records, one group played the basic rhythm and the other group played the melodic rhythm. At this point the division of the class into two groups was made rather haphazardly, with large varieties of instruments in each of the groups. The groups changed each day, and all the children had opportunities to play both the basic rhythm and the melodic rhythm.

Notice that Miss Wilson reached a new integration of the whole with her children. The process went something like this: understandings start with vague over-all impressions of a whole thing and proceed by a gradual differentiation of various parts of that whole, which are later reintegrated into a better understanding of the whole. The new integration of the whole, however, is then further differentiated into better understandings of parts of the whole and reintegrated later into still a higher and better level of understanding of the whole. This whole-to-parts-to-whole process can be applied to learning music.

Miss Wilson started with the vague responses of her children to the whole composition. The children's responses were undifferentiated; they initially responded to the music in vague generalized ways. Their responses indicated their then-current understandings and feelings. Her task was to help them gradually differentiate the parts of this vague insight into the whole. Each step of the differentiation she planned, however, would be reintegrated into higher levels of understanding of the whole. She had no intention of making the differentiations ends in themselves.

Two further large steps lay ahead. Miss Wilson knew that the order in which they were to be accomplished did not matter. She wanted to develop a feeling for the phrase rhythm in music, and she also wanted to develop the ability to discriminate among the various instruments according to the sound they made. Both of these objectives were well in mind as she waited for the right time to forge ahead.

Figure 7. WHOLE-TO-PARTS-TO-WHOLE

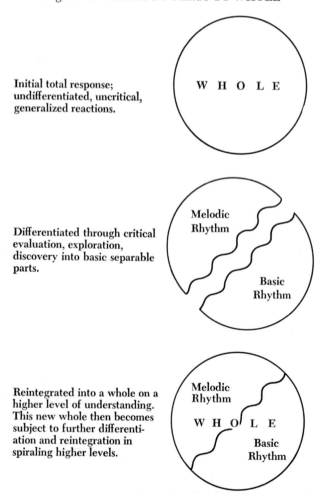

Initial total response; undifferentiated, uncritical, generalized reactions.

WHOLE

Differentiated through critical evaluation, exploration, discovery into basic separable parts.

Melodic Rhythm

Basic Rhythm

Reintegrated into a whole on a higher level of understanding. This new whole then becomes subject to further differentiation and reintegration in spiraling higher levels.

Melodic Rhythm

WHOLE

Basic Rhythm

While the full development of the meaning of phrase rhythm will be treated in the account of Miss Wilson's program with her children, we will describe it briefly now. In music we have ideas just as we have in language. Musical ideas have no specific concrete meaning content of their own. The flow of music, however, does proceed with a kind of idea progression in a similar way. These musical ideas are called phrases. Each phrase contains a more or less complete musical idea. We feel the ends of phrases in music. The entire development of musical form depends largely on the progression of musical ideas or phrases.

The development of the ability to discriminate among various instruments according to the sound they produce can be carried on successfully at the rhythm-instrument level just as well as it can be carried on at the symphony-orchestra level. The difference between the sound made by an oboe and a clarinet, for example, is a difference requiring discrimination of tonal color. The difference between drums and shakers varies from the difference between clarinets and oboes only in degree, not in kind. If we can start children at young ages developing their ability to discriminate among the sounds of different instruments, starting with rhythm instruments, we will lay the groundwork for later discrimination among the various symphonic instruments.

Miss Wilson saw her opportunity when one of the children suggested, "Why don't we have all the drums play the basic rhythm and the rest of us play the melodic rhythm."

"Good idea." Miss Wilson seized the opportunity. "Let's try it and see how it sounds."

The drummers were grouped together in one section of the room. When the music played again, these drummers played the basic rhythm, and the other instruments played the melodic rhythm.

The children were pleased with this development. One suggested that they reverse the procedure and have the drummers play the melodic rhythm and the others play the basic rhythm. They tried it that way, too. As they discussed the way they sounded, they came to the conclusion that for parts of the music it sounded better when the drums played the basic rhythm, but for other parts it sounded better when they did not. With Miss Wilson's help, the children made decisions about which parts of the composition the drums would play basic rhythm and in which parts the others would play basic rhythm. They tried out various suggestions and made their group decisions.

Miss Wilson very wisely did not decide which instruments would play the various parts of the composition. The children made suggestions. The group tried the various suggestions, and the class made the final decisions. Miss Wilson made suggestions just as any other member of the group did, but she invariably encouraged the children to make their decisions in terms of their best judgment of the suitability of the effects wanted and the effects achieved. Miss Wilson did not, however, abrogate her responsibility. She recognized her objectives and seized all possible opportunities to further them.

The next opportunity came for Miss Wilson when one of the children suggested that, "We don't all have to play all the time. I think it would sound nice if just the triangles would play in the part that goes...."

They tried that, too, and were delighted with the results. Miss Wilson saw that she should now take a hand. "There are some other instruments that sound quite like the triangle," she suggested. "How would it sound if we put them together to make a group?" The children looked somewhat skeptical, but were willing to try.

Miss Wilson had now made a suggestion that would help develop the objective she had in mind: the grouping of instruments and the development of the ability of the children to discriminate among the sounds of the different instruments. It would probably be very economical in terms of time spent for Miss Wilson to tell the children which instruments to play together. Too often this is the procedure followed. However, such a procedure would reflect Miss Wilson's decision on grouping instruments, not the children's. It would give them no opportunity to test the sounds of the different instruments in comparison with each other. While they have heard their own instruments and have heard the effects of all the instruments, they have not compared the various instruments with each other to see which sounded most nearly like each other. This is the next step that Miss Wilson was developing with her children.

"Which instruments do you think sound at all like a triangle?" Miss Wilson asked. The class responded with loud sounds as they tried their own instruments again to see if they sounded like the triangle. Finally, they decided that they would make a group consisting of triangles, the small bells, and the long nails or spikes.

"Maybe we could put some other instruments that sound like each other together and make some other groups," was the next suggestion, this time coming from one of the children.

The process of differentiating instruments according to their sound was now under way. Some of the instruments were easy to classify; others were more difficult. Miss Wilson did not predetermine the number of groups, realizing that the number of groups and the classification of instruments into specific groups were not nearly so important as the process of listening to the sound of individual instruments and of making decisions about which ones should play together.

After several sessions spent listening to the individual instruments and discussing their grouping, the class finally decided to have four groups of instruments: drum-type, shaker-type, clicker-type, and tingle-type. Miss Wilson accepted the decision of the group in all cases. She noted that the shakers included all rattle-like instruments, both those with metallic cases and those with cardboard or papier-mâché cases, despite the difference in tone. The shakers also included the sandblocks and other scraping-tone instruments. The tinglers included everything with a bell-like tone.

It would have been possible to divide the class into four groups quite different from those decided on by the children. These were the groups that emerged in this particular situation, and Miss Wilson was willing to accept the decision of the group. Which groups came together did not matter nearly as much as the fact that the children were listening carefully in order to discriminate among the sounds of the various instruments.

The class now experimented with different combinations of groups. They started a musical composition with the drums playing the basic rhythm and the clickers playing the melodic rhythm. On signal from their child conductor, they shifted to the shakers playing the basic rhythm while the tinglers played the melodic rhythm. They decided ahead of time which two groups would play in combination and agreed on the cue they would watch the conductor for in order to make changes together.

Notice the importance of the child conductor. He has specific responsibilities. At times, offer the conductor opportunities to determine the specific orchestration or instrumentation that he would like the class to try at the particular time. It is his responsibility to cue accurately, a responsibility it would be well for all children to experience. Take turns with your child conductors, and try to make sure that all children have opportunities to explore this leadership role.

Miss Wilson noted that the conductor's cues for changes naturally came most frequently at phrase endings in the music. Phrase endings are natural breathing places in the onflowingness of a melody, places where the melody seems to pause for a moment before continuing. This was as good a time as any to develop the feeling for the rhythm of the phrases.

"Let's try something new today." Miss Wilson started another session. "I wonder if you can play in your groups as you have been, but change from one group to another as the music plays."

"We've been doing that," Johnny pointed out. "The conductor tells us when to change from one group of instruments to another."

"Do you think you could change from one group to another without a conductor, though?" Miss Wilson asked.

"How would we know who is supposed to play?" Sandy wanted to know.

"That will take good listening," Miss Wilson pointed out. "We'll decide first which group of instruments will start and which group will come next and the one after that. The first group will start with the beginning of the music. They will play until the music seems to come to the end of its first idea. There you will hear a place where the music seems to pause for a second, as if it were catching a new breath. When the players in the first group come to that place, they stop playing. The players in the second group start then and play with the music until it comes to another little breathing place at the end of another musical idea. There we change again. The second group stops, and the third group starts. At the end of the next musical idea, the third group stops, and the fourth group starts."

"Will you give us a signal?" Sondra asked.

"You won't need a special signal from me," Miss Wilson replied. "The music itself will give you the signal. Most of the conductors have been giving their cues to change at these places anyway. I think you will hear them without the conductor very well."

"We'll all play the melodic rhythm this time. Let's have the drums be the first group to play. Then, shakers, you be group two; tinglers, come next as group three; and clickers will be group four."

Miss Wilson thus simplified the playing of the instruments and the orchestration. All the children played the melodic rhythm this time. With the introduction of any new activity or problem, permit only one complicating factor at a time. The children were now to develop a feeling for phrase rhythm. Therefore, the children should not simultaneously concentrate on developing orchestration. Miss Wilson suggested that all children play the same type of rhythm—the melodic rhythm in this case. She could just as well have had everyone play the basic rhythm. Which rhythm they played would not have been as important as the fact that they were playing only one rhythm and that the new problem was introduced in a context of old, familiar, uncomplicated skills.

Miss Wilson started the record, and off started the drums. She watched closely as the music came to the end of the first phrase and carefully guarded against giving any kind of cue to the children, even as much as the blinking of an eye. She listened as the drums played:

"Tumm TUMM tada tumm tada TUMM — —." Two of the drummers stopped at this point, but the other four continued, "tada TUMM tada tumm tada TUMM — tumm." At this point all the drummers stopped. Without hesitation, the shakers continued with the music.

"TUMM tada tumm tada TUMM — — tada TA tumm ta tumm tumm TUMM — —." The shakers stopped, and the tinglers continued:

"Tumm TUMM tada tumm tada TUMM — — tada TUMM tada tada tada TUMM — tumm —." Here the tinglers stopped, and the clickers continued:

"TUMM tada tumm tada TUMM — -da tada TAda tada tada tada TUMM — tumm." The clickers finished, and the whole class burst out in spontaneous applause for themselves. They were excited that they had been able to do it. It sounded so difficult when Miss Wilson explained it, but it was easy to do after all.

It is true that it is much more difficult to explain this material in writing or even orally than it is to do it. Do not be discouraged if the explanation seems complicated. Try it. You will find that the doing comes much more readily than you imagine.

"That was fine, boys and girls." Miss Wilson praised them. "Now we can talk about musical phrases, because that was what you were playing. The drums played the first phrase, the shakers played the second, the tinglers the third, and the clickers played the fourth. A phrase is just a word that means a musical idea. We can tell the end of a phrase, because the music feels like the end of a phrase."

"Now we can decide who will play what on each phrase and play without a conductor." Sandy experimented.

Now we find the beginnings of the development of a much more complex orchestration. Such orchestrations actually depend on understandings of the phrase rhythm and the phrase development within a composition. The orchestration development relates also to the process of whole-to-parts-to-whole spoken of previously. By and large, until this point, orchestrations have been conceived in terms of the whole. The differentiation at this point will come in terms of the parts of the whole, the musical phrases. Nevertheless, the whole will constantly be kept in mind.

"Yes, that's possible," Miss Wilson agreed. "How many phrases were there in the 'Stars and Stripes Forever'?"

"Four."

"Do you think we can play these phrases with different groups playing in a different order?"

"Of course."

The class experimented with different possible arrangements. They varied the order of the instrumental groups. To make sure that everyone would know in what order to play, they worked out a form which they wrote on the board.

RHYTHM ‖	PHRASE			
	1	2	3	4
Melodic	Clickers	Drums	Shakers	Jinglers

Depending on the age of the children with whom you engage in this activity, you may want to develop the symbolic representation of the score described in the next section before you develop the form of the orchestration using the word names of the instruments.

The children then wanted to try both the basic and melodic rhythms by phrases. They planned this orchestration and used the blackboard to make it easier to follow.

RHYTHM ‖	PHRASE			
	1	2	3	4
Melodic	Clickers	Jinglers	Clickers	Jinglers
Basic	Drums	Shakers	Drums	Shakers

Their next step was to vary the instruments playing the melodic and basic rhythms: those who played melodic rhythm on phrases 1 and 2 now played basic rhythm on phrases 3 and 4. Similarly, those who played basic rhythm on phrases 1 and 2 now played melodic rhythm on phrases 3 and 4. Their orchestration looked like this:

RHYTHM ‖	PHRASE			
	1	2	3	4
Melodic	Clickers	Jinglers	Drums	Shakers
Basic	Drums	Shakers	Clickers	Jinglers

At this point the class decided that they could use symbols instead of words to indicate the various groups of instruments. They decided that they would use as symbols the drawing of one of the main instruments of each group.

The symbols for the four groups were decided on:

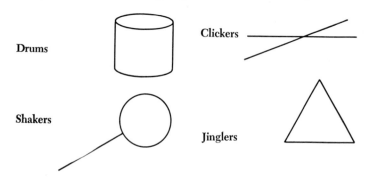

Using the symbols, their last orchestration looked like this:

RHYTHM	PHRASE			
	1	2	3	4
Melodic	(clickers)	(jinglers)	(drums)	(shakers)
Basic	(drums)	(shakers)	(clickers)	(jinglers)

Several days later, Sandy brought up another point. "Miss Wilson," he insisted, "I think there's a place in the middle of the phrase where we could change instruments, too."

"Yes, that's right," Miss Wilson responded. "When we first tried to see if we could hear the phrases, I remember that some of the drummers thought that would be a good place to change."

Musical phrases have subparts just as sentences in prose literature. In the particular composition played each of the long phrases consisted of two subphrases. It was these subphrases that Sandy referred to.

Miss Wilson continued, "Would you suggest how we might try it, Sandy?"

"Sure. Have the drums play the basic rhythm of the whole first phrase. The shakers could play the melodic rhythm of the first part, and the clickers could play the second part."

They tried it, liked it, and wanted to see if it could be done through the rest of the composition. They thought there was too much drum and settled on the following orchestration:

RHYTHM	PHRASE			
	1	**2**	**3**	**4**
Melodic	⌐O △	⌐O △	⌐O △	⌐O △
Basic	⊔	✕	⊔	✕⊔

This orchestration was quite satisfying to the group, and they played it for quite a while. They developed similar orchestrations for other compositions they liked. Inevitably, they tired of playing it the same way and experimented with other orchestrations, which grew more complex as the children became more adept at translating the combinations of sounds into organized patterns.

Further differentiation of the sounds of the instruments came also. The children came to recognize, with Miss Wilson's help, that the shaker group really had two types of sounds. One of these sounds was a rattlelike tone, and the other was a scraping kind of sound. So the scrapers were separated from the shakers and formed a different group. After some experimentation the children decided that some of the rattlelike instruments had a sound that was closer to the scraper sound than to the other shakers. This was the difference between the metallic-toned shakers and others with cardboard cases which had a softer quality. They also came to a greater realization of the possibilities of the tambourines with their tingling, rattling, and banging potential.

However, as Miss Wilson attempted to develop these new groups and help the children work through orchestrations involving them all, she quickly realized that she was losing the children. For some reason they no longer responded as they had. She tried to pinpoint in her mind the time at which the children first seemed to lose interest. As she thought back, she realized that the loss of interest had come with efforts to orchestrate for six groups. At that time the orchestrating became mechanical. Realization of the idea of organizing patterns of sound gave way subtly and almost imperceptibly to a kind of mechanical way of listing the groups of instruments just to have a way to play rather than find a way to organize the sounds.

When things go wrong in the classroom, the good teacher invariably asks herself two questions: "What did I do that I should not have done?" and "What did I not do that I could have done to make the situation right?" Miss Wilson recognized the failure of this immediate step. She wisely reviewed her whole process and tried to come to some understanding of why it was that this process did not succeed. Her decision as to why the activity had not succeeded, however, was incorrect. She came to a wrong conclusion and needed to look in other directions for the solution to the problem.

Miss Wilson pondered the phenomenon and tried to work out in her own mind the reasons for it. She reached back into her own experience as a teacher and her knowledge of children. She thought of her experience the previous year with fifth-graders and remembered how the challenge of organizing six groups had stimulated them.

"Perhaps," she thought, "I'm doing too much work with the rhythm orchestra. The children could be tired of it as an activity." She decided to use the rhythm-orchestra time for other activities. After about a week, however, during a planning session, one of the children asked, "Let's have our rhythm orchestra today. We haven't played our instruments for a long time." The favorable reaction of the children led Miss Wilson to reconsider her decision.

"So they are still interested in the rhythm orchestra." Miss Wilson pondered the problem. "If the problem is not disinterest in the activity itself, the root of the difficulty must be in the way I'm handling it."

She decided to backtrack a bit, and during the next planned rhythm-orchestra session, she suggested that the children play some of their old orchestrations, the ones with four groups. Their response told her what had been wrong with her planning. "These children are just not ready to organize more than four groups of instruments at a time," she decided. "Instead of trying to work with six groups, we could develop the four groups we had and do some more orchestrations. The children still can grow in their understanding and feeling for the music we play with the four groups."

Miss Wilson had been misled by her fifth-grade experience into expecting too much of her third-graders. When she had accurately appraised the situation and determined where the difficulty lay, she found that the interest of the children revived. There were many more learnings in developing orchestrations with four groups, and it was along these lines that the group proceeded.

They played old favorites in orchestrations they had already developed and composed new orchestrations both to music they already knew and to music new to them. They invited other classes in to listen to them play and offered a concert in a sharing assembly for the rest of the school.

These children did not prepare an assembly for the rest of the school in the sense of being assigned a date and told that they must have a program ready at that time. When in the normal development of their classroom program they were ready to share with the other children some part of what they had been doing, they indicated that they wanted to participate in a sharing assembly on a chart in a central place in the school. They picked their own date for this from the possible dates which teachers had agreed on and accepted then an obligation for producing their program at the sharing assembly.

The Continuous Rhythm Story

In Chapter 3 we suggested the continuous melodic story as a device for encouraging the spontaneous development of a melodic line. A similar procedure can be used with rhythm instruments. Someone starts a rhythmic pattern. When the starter comes to the end of his statement, a second person continues the feeling and flow of the initial rhythmic suggestion. He does not reproduce the same rhythm; he modifies or changes it in any way that feels appropriate at the spur of the moment. The mood established by the initial rhythmic pattern continues without specific planning. When the second person stops, a third person picks up the rhythmic progression and continues its feeling and flow. On and on the development of the initial rhythmic statement goes through as many people as have decided to participate.

In the initial stages of the activity it may be better for you as the teacher to start the first rhythmic statement. However, it would be possible for a child to do so. Also in the initial stages it is not essential to pay much attention to the progression by which various sounding instruments follow each other. The idea is to develop a rhythm story regardless of the tone of the instruments themselves. After some practice, however, if in developing the rhythm story you disregarded the sound of specific instruments, you may want to develop with your children a specific planned progression of instruments. In such cases ask the children to suggest an instrument to start. Then, through discussion, determine the specific pattern in which various sounding instruments succeed each other.

Rhythm instruments provide small-group as well as large-group activity.

Montclair School, Oakland, California.

A rather interesting phenomenon takes place in this continuous rhythm story. The rhythm itself seems to take over, and the individual frequently can respond by continuing the rhythmic pattern without specifically thinking through what he will play. His body senses the previous rhythm and continues that rhythm without an actual interposition of specific intellectual planning; it becomes a feeling thing.

Rhythmic Improvisation

Instead of this rather forbidding label "rhythmic improvisation," you may want to use the more familiar term "jam session" with your children.

In the rhythmic improvisation we start in the same way that we do with the continuous rhythm story, with one person playing a very distinctive rhythmic pattern. However, instead of the first person stopping when the second one begins to play, he continues. The others in the group begin to play when they feel that the time is ripe. They come in at different times, together or separately. There is no preplanning of who plays what or when. The rightness of the timing depends on the feeling of the individuals in the group. We have a group improvisation. Various players start and stop as they interact with each other with various rhythmic patterns. There is, of course, no rightness or wrongness about the playing. There are no notes to follow and the sole determination of what happens is the kind of feeling which the individuals in the group develop about the overall effect produced.

This description may suggest chaos to you, but it rarely is chaotic in result. The activity fascinates children of all ages. Indeed, adults, too, are fascinated by it. Small groups of children often gather together on a playground with collections of various tone-producing gadgets to have a jam session. It is the spontaneity of effect tied together by the underlying rhythm with which the pattern started that seems to be its major attraction. The values for children are many. Hold on to the spontaneous attractiveness of the activity which brings children to it of their own volition.

A rhythmic improvisation is one of the simplest of all activities to get started with your children. It may present difficulties only if the children are inhibited or fearful of letting themselves go with sound-producing instruments. In this activity, even more than most others, the feeling of the actual rhythm itself can permeate the entire group. The total group efforts, though spontaneous, are controlled; they are all influenced by the rhythm with which the improvisation started. What individuals do to enhance, modify, change, add to this original rhythm really controls its development. Individuals come in, play louder or softer, drop out according to their own feeling of the rightness of what they do, their feeling about the total effect produced.

The first time you try this you may be somewhat amazed at the results. It is possible though that the first effort might not be successful, particularly if you face the problem of freeing your children to play as they feel. Try doing this several times, however, and see how the results improve over a period of time.

You may also want to record some of these spontaneous improvisations, so that the children can hear the sound of the total group effort. Utilize the recording to develop critical evaluation with your children. "How could we make it sound better?" is a good question to ask. You will not want to impose adult standards on this activity either. You do want to help children develop their skills in critical listening and their own standards through the playing of instruments as well as through singing.

HARMONIC AND MELODIC INSTRUMENTS

Although they present somewhat more difficulty in playing than rhythm instruments, some harmonic and melodic instruments are simple to play and well within the scope of the classroom teacher with little or no technical facility in music.

The Autoharp

A harmonic instrument such as the autoharp is played with simple movements. Various tone bars stop certain strings of the instrument from vibrating; when one of the bars is depressed, a simple sweeping motion of the hand across the strings produces a harmonious chord. The instrument may be purchased with five, twelve, or fifteen bars; each bar produces one chord. Since a considerable amount of song material is available marked with autoharp chords, this instrument provides a comparatively simple means of providing accompaniments to songs. Children learn to play the autoharp with little difficulty and should be encouraged to experiment with various chord progressions as well as in playing accompaniments. If an autoharp is available to you, by all means keep it in your classroom easily accessible to your children. Encourage them to experiment with it, and experiment with it yourself.

Xylophones

The most suitable instruments for young children are those which require only simple muscular reactions to produce tones, preferably one large action per tone. Instruments such as the xylophone or orchestral bells are suitable for the lower grades. Orchestral bells are now being made with individual tone bars mounted on a resonating block, with each tone individual and separate. These can be either placed next to each other and played in the same way as a xylophone or they can be distributed among children in small groups for various types of melodic playing.

With all instruments it is best to start the playing with a song the children know and love. Pick a comparatively simple one in both range and variety of tones. Approach the playing of these melodic instruments from the experimental point of view. See how the children discover the melodies on the instruments. Encourage the creation of little three- or four-tone successions of tones, called motifs. Develop a game approach in which one child makes up a motif, and other children try to play it after they hear it but once or twice.

Instruments for the Intermediate Grades

For the fourth grade and up there is a very wide choice from among a large number of suitable instruments. Teaching children to play orchestral and band instruments themselves is beyond the scope of the classroom teacher who has no background of training in music. The utilization of band and orchestral instruments at the elementary school level may have been overdone anyway. A considerable amount of time, energy, and effort as well as a high proportionate budgetary allotment have frequently gone into teaching a comparatively small number of children to play band and orchestral instruments. For a lesser investment of time, energy, and money, all children in the elementary school could learn to play some of the recreational instruments, which would provide all of them with a basis for more advanced band and instrumental work at the junior high school level. The elementary school must not become merely a recruiting ground for the junior and senior high school band and orchestra at the cost of the full development of all of the children.

If the school budget is large enough to provide for a specialist who can teach instrumental music to small groups of children and at the same time also provide opportunities for *all* children to play the various simpler instruments, the recreational type, the school is justified in doing so. However, if the total group approach is sacrificed for the intensive training of a small proportion of children, such false emphasis on regular instrumental playing at the elementary school level cannot be adequately justified. The elementary school is the place for experimentation and widespread involvement in music. All children should have opportunities for playing some types of instruments. We would not see the total group sacrificed for the technical excellence of a comparatively few children.

While the development of children's skill in playing band and orchestral instruments is ordinarily considered beyond the scope of the classroom teacher, he may very readily attempt one of the many kinds of simple, easy-to-play instruments. Most musicians no longer scoff at the values of this type of instrument. Many of them in the past were considered inferior because of poor tone quality and improper tuning as the result

Intent on their recorder playing, these children are oblivious to everything but their music making.

City and Country School, New York City.

of poor manufacturing standards. When we see, however, the higher standards of many instruments presently available and the values the children gain from playing them, we no longer take them lightly.

One of the very popular groups of such instruments is the recorder and those derived from the recorder. The recorder itself is an old instrument with a very simple method of producing the tone. The mouthpiece is called the fipple-flute type; all we need to do is blow into it lightly in order to produce a tone. The principle of tone production is exactly the same as in an ordinary whistle. The recorder, now having a renaissance, at one time held a highly respected place as a regular musical instrument, and many noted composers wrote music specifically for the recorder.

The tone of the recorder is comparatively pure, somewhat thin and light. The recorders made vary in price according to the quality of the instrument. They are, however, comparatively costlier than instruments discussed later. Because of the expense of recorders, different kinds of plastic instruments have been developed, such as the tonette, flutophone, symphonette, song flute, melody flute. The tonette and the song flute are variants of the old favorite, the ocarina, popularly known as "sweet potato," which in itself is another possibility in this group. The ocarina type differs from the recorder type in that the air column is enclosed. The tonette, for example, is similar in principle to an ocarina, although it has a different shape. The tone is very similar to that of the ocarina.

The flutophone and symphonette are plastic modifications based on the recorder. The melody flute is more like a fife or simple flute.

The ukelele and harmonica are other possibilities which should not be ignored. Comparatively easy to master, they, too, can provide genuine musical experiences. The guitar, although somewhat more difficult for youngsters to play, may be used at the sixth-grade level and is a very rewarding instrument.

Tonettes, flutophones, symphonettes, song flutes, melody flutes, and harmonicas can be purchased for as little as a dollar.

Fairly well tuned, they are fairly accurate in pitch. You may want to purchase one of these and experiment with it yourself to see how easy it is for you to learn to play. In the beginning do not be concerned about reading music with it. Try to master the principle by which the instrument is played, and play little melodies on it "by ear." Indeed, learning to read notes should never be confused with learning to play an instrument in its initial stages. Beginning efforts both by you and afterwards with your children should be from the song approach. Only after a certain familiarity with the tonal possibilities of the instrument has been achieved and after a number of simple melodies can be played on it should any approach be made to note reading.

We previously stated in Chapter 2 that if notation was to be taught at all in the elementary school, it should not begin before the fourth grade, and then only if a rich experience in music preceded it in the primary grades. We also urged that any approach to note reading be through an instrument. It is through these various easy-to-play instruments that the best approach to notation can be made.

As you help your children develop skills in playing any instrument, remember that mastery of any instrument is a tool and not an end in itself. Your primary purpose is to provide a pleasurable experience in making music. Keep the activity on an enjoyable level for the children, and do not let it deteriorate into drudgery. Would that more instrumental teachers, both public and private, considered themselves primarily as music teachers, not as instrumental teachers. The elementary school level is not the place for the exploitation of the talented few who will later make a profession of their instrumental skill.

The "Law of Practice"

We have suggested that at all times you should keep the activity of learning to play an instrument on a joyful, pleasurable level. Do not let it deteriorate into meaningless, repetitive drill. Children constantly practice themselves when the skill is one which they want to accomplish. There seems to be a

kind of "law of practice" which children follow naturally and
normally of their own volition. Some children learn new skills
very, very easily. They take to new accomplishments readily
and seem to master them with little difficulty. Other children
do not learn physical skills quite so readily. However, they
will practice a skill that they themselves want to learn over
and over and over again without any outside stimulus.

Have you ever noticed a youngster first learning to bounce
a ball? To us this seems to be quite a simple task. Many children learn to do it without any difficulty. The one-two-three-
a-larey type of activity offers no challenge or difficulty to some
children. Many children, however, need to learn to coordinate
their muscular responses in order to control how hard they
must hit the ball and control their hand position so that when
they hit it, it will bounce back straight. The coordination of the

*Tonettes with autoharp accompaniment provide valuable ensemble op-
portunities.*

Richmond Public Schools, Richmond, Virginia. Photo by Arthur Clarke.

bouncing and passing the ball under the leg also presents some difficulties to some children. These children practice over and over again without any outer stimulus. No one needs to tell them to practice. A child learning to jump rope can take a rope off to one side, alone, and practice incessantly, day after day, until he masters the skill. Boys will throw a ball against a wall or practice a tennis stroke for enormous lengths of time. It is similar with any activity in which any dexterity is required. If it is an activity in which the child is genuinely interested, if it is one which he himself feels that he wants to accomplish, no one needs to tell him to practice. He will stick with it until he accomplishes his goal or frustrates himself.

Self-imposed Discipline

If a child is really interested in and wants to master an instrument, no one will need to insist that he practice. Consequently, learning to play any instrument can be kept on a joyful, pleasurable basis rather than on a drudgery basis. Do not let it degenerate into a tug of will. If you start the activity at all, be very responsive to the children's feelings about what they do.

Encourage experimentation and creation. Make up little melodies on the instruments. Try the continuous melodic story with the instruments as well as with the voice. See how many of the songs the children know they can discover and reproduce on the instrument.

This kind of informal approach to playing simple instruments could be enlarged to include all kinds of instruments. If more piano, string, and other instrumental teachers would ensure that the primary function of mastering an instrument is the ability to produce music satisfying to the player from the instrument, the development of skill on the instrument would come more readily, and the mortality rate would be lower. How many adults in our population today remember that they took piano lessons for a number of years and then rebelled against the drudgery of practice. Today, most of them wish they could play the instrument they gave up. The conclusion to be drawn is not that people be forced to practice, but that the approach to learning to play any instrument be changed from mastery of the skill to the production of music satisfying to the player. Skill develops after the desire to produce music is recognized. Children begin instrumental lessons eagerly. They want to make music and play the instrument. We negate their desire when we sacrifice the production of music for a temporary achievement of skill. The major discipline of playing music must be self-imposed, not imposed by a teacher or parent, if the playing of music is to be a lasting, rewarding, and enriching activity that continues throughout life.

KEEP IN MIND

The following items summarize the major content of this chapter. Individual items may be used for debate, discussion, report, or research topics.

1. Playing music is producing an ordered progression of sounds on a suitable medium.
2. When a person plays music composed by someone else, he re-creates, toward the intention of the composer, the expression of feeling.
3. A person who has never produced music through singing or playing never fully feels music to the extent felt by those who have engaged thus in producing music.
4. Playing rhythms can be an important aspect of playing music, even though rhythm is but part of music.
5. In considering the appropriateness of various instruments for children, the required muscular dexterity must receive important consideration.
6. Rhythm instruments provide an excellent medium for introducing playing experiences to children.
7. Rhythm bands as traditionally presented have usually been overformalized, teacher-dominated in presentation, and based on a cumulative, atomistic point of view.
8. The rhythm orchestra is developed from an analytical and

organismic approach, starting with vague ideas of the total sound, followed by a process of gradual differentiation of the sounds of various groups and types of instruments. Also through differentiation from vague ideas of the whole, basic rhythm, melodic rhythm, and phrase rhythm are developed.

9. The music selected for rhythm-orchestra development must appeal to the children in itself.

10. In developing the rhythm orchestra we help children utilize their own critical faculties rather than apply adult standards. Children's critical faculties develop through a process of evaluation, listening, and discussion.

11. The *basic rhythm* is the underlying pulsation felt through all music. The *melodic rhythm* is the rhythm in which specific tones of the melody follow each other. The *phrase rhythm* is the succession of more or less complete musical ideas.

12. It is possible to identify a particular song by the rhythm of the melody alone, without any tonal elements.

13. Understandings start with vague over-all impressions of the whole and proceed by a gradual differentiation of the various parts of that whole; these are later reintegrated into a better understanding of the whole. This new integration is then further differentiated into better understandings of new parts and reintegrated again later into still higher and better understandings of the whole.

14. The development of the ability to discriminate among various instruments according to the sound they produce can be carried on successfully at the rhythm-instrument level just as it later may be carried on at the symphony-orchestra level.

15. When any new activity or problem is introduced, simplify the surrounding context; introduce only one complicating factor at a time.

16. The procedure in developing a spontaneous continuous rhythm story is similar to the development of the continuous melodic story.

17. The rhythmic improvisation is a spontaneous creation of a succession of rhythmic patterns by children playing various types of rhythm instruments.

18. The improvement of both the rhythmic continuous story and the rhythmic improvisation is based on children's self-evaluation and the development of critical judgment on the part of the children.

19. Some harmonic and melodic instruments are well within the competency of classroom teachers with little or no technical facility in music.

20. Children learn to play the autoharp with little difficulty and should be encouraged to experiment with various chord sequences as well as accompaniments to songs.

21. In the elementary school all children should have opportunities to play some type of instrument; it is better for all children to play recreation-type instruments than to sacrifice the large majority for intensive training of a small proportion of the children on regular band or orchestral instruments.

22. Recorder, tonette, ocarina, flutophone, symphonette, song flute, melody flute, harmonica, ukelele, and guitar are some of the possibilities for instrumental work with all children.

23. Learning to play an instrument in its initial stages should never be confused with learning to read notation.

24. The initial stages of instrumental playing should be approached from familiar songs, with experimentation encouraged in the tonal possibilities of the instrument.

25. The activity of learning to play an instrument should be kept on a joyful, pleasurable basis.

26. Children who want to learn a skill will practice that skill over and over without outside pressure if it is genuinely a skill that they themselves want to accomplish for their own purposes. This may be termed a "law of practice."

ᕓ CHAPTER SIX

Making Instruments

ALTHOUGH MANY SCHOOLS purchase a complement of rhythm instruments, children may make effective instruments of their own to supplement the purchased ones. The instruments made by children will most likely not look just like the professional ones. In many cases the tone quality will not be as desirable as in the purchased manufactured instruments. Nevertheless, the assets accruing when children make their own instruments are very considerable and outweigh the liabilities.

The construction of instruments, while frequently related to musical activities, is *in itself* most frequently not a musical activity. The making of instruments as an activity is very desirable, since constructive-manipulative activities of all kinds have many contributions to make to the development of children. Do not confuse these values. Making the instruments does not become a musical activity until children begin to play them. Let us recognize that the benefits to children from the construction of the instruments basically stem from the nature of the activity as a potentially creative constructive-manipulative one and from the stimulus to playing the instrument that comes from making it. The musical aspect of the activity enters only

169

when children begin to listen to the sounds of the instrument and play them.

There is nothing very difficult about constructing simple but satisfactory rhythm-orchestra instruments. If in your school you find a cooperative-minded industrial arts or arts and crafts specialist, you may want to undertake the construction of these instruments as a joint venture. Do not, however, permit the development of manual skills to become an objective of this construction except incidentally. Let such skills come as a pleasant extra value. Also try to keep the focus on the process of constructing rather than the product. Making instruments satisfying to individual children in your class should determine how the activity is handled. Do not let adult standards of craftsmanship determine your children's feelings about this activity.

Even though you have no specialist assistance, you, as the classroom teacher, need not hesitate to undertake the activity alone. The satisfactions which will greet the children's efforts more than outweigh the minor difficulties that might be en-

Children can make a wide variety of instruments.

Brown School, Denver, Colorado.

countered. Do not strive for professional appearance; the instruments do not need to be highly finished. No effort should be made to push the children toward standards of artistic endeavor and satisfactions more suitable for adults than for children. Suggestions can always be made to children, but pressures should not be placed on them to modify their work to meet standards of adult satisfactions.

MAKING RHYTHM INSTRUMENTS

For a rhythm orchestra we need a large variety of different kinds of sounds. The development of critical listening over a period of time can result in improving the quality of sound and the quality of the instruments that children make and use. Initial efforts may be quite crude in terms of both the instruments used and the sounds produced. Improvement should be a function of growth and comes from the development of self-evaluation and critical judgment.

Almost any kind of sound may serve a purpose in our rhythm orchestra. Sounds which children enjoy and which satisfy them should be the sounds used initially in the building of an orchestra.

As children grow older, they will tend to be less satisfied with the use of instruments selected solely from the clicking, banging, and knocking of objects from their immediate environment. As this stage of development appears, help children see possibilities in making various types of instruments. The nature and complexity of the instruments which older children want to use and which they can make increases considerably. The activity of making and playing their own instruments should actually continue through all the school years of a child. Indeed, we can hope that the activity will continue on into adulthood.

Drums

Drums are among children's favorite instruments. A drum consists of a large hollow body and a taut head fastened to the body in various ways, depending on the material used.

The simplest types of drumlike instruments are hollow-body objects struck in the condition in which they are found. A tin can struck by a pencil will produce a crude, metallic kind of drum sound. Oatmeal boxes, coffee cans, and other types of hollow objects such as hat boxes can be used in their raw state, especially with very young children and at early stages of development. Later, however, the children will be interested in producing better kinds of drums. In order to make one, some of the same implements may be used. The dull thudlike tone that usually attends cans or cereal boxes used as drums is the result of inadequate vibration of the head. To make better drums, we can use the same type of body we used before but improve the drumhead itself.

DRUMHEADS. The best drumheads are skin or parchment. For an inexpensive drumhead, purchase a used drumhead from an instrument store. When the head on a professional drum tears or rips, it ordinarily does so in a comparatively small place. Professional drums are usually much larger than the drums which we would help children make. Consequently, the part of the drumhead which remains after the torn part is eliminated can still serve a long and useful life. These heads can be purchased rather inexpensively at most stores that sell or repair musical instruments.

Sheet rubber makes good drumheads also, although it tears easily if the sheeting is too thin. Inner tubes from automobile tires have often been used. Today's tubes, however, are thicker and heavier than the ones formerly used, and it is difficult for children to stretch the rubber inner tubing taut enough to get good tone.

Linen and unbleached muslin may also be used for satisfactory drumheads. These should be shellacked after being fastened to the body of the drum.

DRUM BODIES. One of the favorite bodies to use for the drum is a wooden nail keg. With the current packaging of nails in small plastic containers or cardboard boxes, nail kegs are not as easy to find as they once were. Nevertheless building supply houses and large hardware stores still sell nails in sufficient quantities so that they may have nail kegs around. Small barrels also serve well and make a superior drum. Wooden mixing bowls or salad bowls and metal wastebaskets can also be used for the body of drums. The large number 10 size vegetable, fruit, or soup cans make quite good drums.

A drum may be open or closed at the bottom. A few holes in the bottom of a closed drum improves the tone. A tom-tom has a drumhead at both ends of the body.

DRUMS WITH WOODEN BODIES. Before attempting to fasten the drumhead to any drum body, soak the parchment in water for about a half hour until it is soft and pliable. Soap will not hurt the parchment, and if the drumhead you have purchased is soiled, during the soaking process use some soap to wash off the dirt. If the body of the drum is wood, fastening the parchment head to it is quite simple. The parchment should overlap about an inch and a half all around the body of the drum; cut it about three inches larger in diameter. After the parchment has been soaked to make it soft and pliable, it will tear more easily than dry parchment. Be careful not to rip holes in it. Fasten the skin about three-quarters of an inch below the edge where the skin turns over the body. This will leave you about three-quarters of an inch to the edge of the parchment. Upholstery tacks, with their large heads, serve very well for tacking. After you have put one tack in, stretch the parchment across the top of the body as tight as you can, being careful not to pull so hard that the parchment tears where the first tack was fastened. Tack the head securely on the opposite side. Halfway around the rim, between the two tacks you now have in place, stretch the skin tightly and secure that side with another tack. Directly opposite the third tack, stretch the skin again and secure with a fourth tack.

You now have four tacks inserted which divide the drumhead roughly into quarters. From this point on, put two or three tacks, depending on the size of the drum, between the tacks you have now placed. Pull the parchment taut each time before you tack it down. Space the tacks evenly around the top of the drum. Do not be concerned if you find that even after you stretch the drumhead and tack it securely it is not as tight as you think it should be. Refrain from playing the drum while the drumhead is still wet. As it dries, the skin shrinks, and it will be much tighter after drying than it was when you finished tacking it.

Some nail kegs have a metal band around the top. Remove this hoop, stretch the head over the keg, and then replace the hoop. Tack the hoop back in place through the original nail holes.

If you decide to use a wooden mixing or salad bowl, do not be concerned if there is a crack in it. This crack will not affect

Figure 9. SALAD BOWL DRUM. Stretch drumhead, soaked until pliable, across top of salad bowl and tack.

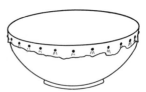

Figure 8. NAIL KEG OR BARREL DRUM. Remove iron hoop around top. Stretch drumhead, soaked in water until pliable, across top of keg. Replace iron hoop and tack down, stretching head before placing each tack.

Figure 10. SUGGESTED ORDER FOR TACKING DRUMHEADS. Work to opposite sides as much as possible. Stretch head before placing each tack.

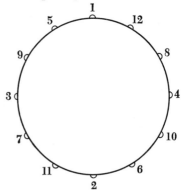

the tone of the drum at all. You may find that a neighboring storekeeper has put away some wooden salad or mixing bowls he has been unable to sell because they cracked. You may find the price marked down considerably because of this flaw which will not affect the tone of the drum at all. The procedure with the wooden bowls is the same as with the nail kegs. Since the bowls are made of hardwood, they will be harder to nail than the kegs.

DRUMS WITH METAL BODIES. If you use a metal wastebasket or a large metal can as the body, you will have a different problem fastening the head of the drum to the body. You will not be able to tack the head down and will devise some other method of fastening it. If there is a metal bead or lip or rim around the edge of the container, stretch the wet skin over the top and then tie six or seven turns of good strong twine around the body of the drum below the lip to hold the skin down. Put one or two turns of the twine tightly around the body over the skin. Then, holding the twine tight, pull the skin under the twine as taut as you can, stretching it over the end of the body of the drum. The more turns of twine you tie around the body, the more securely the head will hold. Tie the knot quite tightly so that it will not loosen up. Again, put the drum away without playing it; then the skin can have a chance to shrink as it dries. Instead of twine, you may use heavy wire around the body to hold the skin tight.

In both instances, when you have tacked the head down on the wooden body or tied it down on the metal body, you may want to hold the edges of the parchment tight against the body with some tape so the edges will not stick out after the skin dries. After the parchment does dry, you may take the tape off and trim the edges with a sharp scissors or a single-edge razor blade.

Tom-toms

To make a tom-tom, you will need a body open at both ends. With the regular drum, the body must be open at one end where you fasten the head; it may be open at both ends. For the tom-tom, however, the body must be open at both ends and a drumhead fastened at each end. All you need do is secure the drumhead to the top and bottom of the body in a manner similar to that described for the drum itself.

In making a tom-tom, the two heads may be laced together over the body. Use parchment strips or shoelaces or any other strong lacing material. Parchment or leather strips about one-eighth inch thick serve very well for the lacing, since they may be soaked and will shrink on drying, thus serving to tighten the drumhead. In order to lace the drumheads punch holes around the edges of the parchment after you have cut it to size. The heads should be cut to allow about an inch and a half overlap over the top and bottom of the body. Punch the holes about three-quarters of an inch in from the outer edge, and try to space the holes evenly around the head approximately an inch and a half apart. Match the holes of the top and bottom drumheads.

Figure 11. A TOM-TOM. Use large can or wastebasket open at both ends for the body. Two drumheads, placed top and bottom after soaking to make them pliable, are laced together.

When the heads have been prepared, place one on the working surface, topside down. Put the body over it, centering the body on the head. Your circle of punched holes will appear about half way between the edge of the body and the edge of the head. Place the other parchment head on top of the body, centering it. Start with two different pieces of the lacing on opposite sides of the parchment heads. Lace the two heads together, lacing through the holes from inside to out. Lace up and down, trying to keep the skin as taut as you can. Be careful, however, not to pull too tight because of the weakness of the wet parchment. Pull until you feel the parchment beginning to give. Try to judge the strength of your pulls so that you do not pull the hole through and yet get the head as taut as possible. If you should accidently pull one hole through the edge of the skin, make another hole near the one that ripped and continue to lace.

Go around the tom-tom, lacing up and down, lacing the two heads together until the laces meet. Tie knots as securely as you can at that point, but before you make the knot permanent, go back around the lacing to see if you can pull it any tighter without tearing through the holes.

Drumsticks

Drums are frequently, and for children most often, played with the fingers. However, if a drumstick is desired, it can be made very simply with a quarter-inch dowel stick. Fasten a clump of absorbent cotton at the end of a 12-inch length of dowel, and cover it with a piece of unbleached muslin or other available thin material. Tie tightly, enclosing the cotton around the end of the dowel. Or a baby's or doll's sock may be stuffed with cotton and pulled over the end of a piece of dowel stick. Fasten securely. These serve as padded drumsticks and produce a pleasing, not-too-loud sound.

If you want sticks more nearly like regular drumsticks, round off the ends of two lengths of dowels. Sand them so that they are smooth and have no sharp edges. They produce a much more brilliant tone than the padded sticks.

Playing the Drum and Tom-tom

Drums are best played in the rhythm orchestra with the fingers. Since the vibrating drumhead produces the sound, the fingers must be drawn off the head very quickly after it is tapped to avoid stopping the vibrations. You will find it easier to do if you think of "pulling" the tone out of the drum with your fingers. Tap the head with your finger, lifting your hand away from the drum instantly. The "pulling" notion will help you get your fingers off the head so that it can vibrate freely.

Notice that you can produce different tones with your drum depending on where you strike the head, near the rim, part way in, or near the center. Encourage your children to experiment with and listen to the different tones produced so they can use them in the rhythm orchestra.

Tambourines

Tambourines have a vibrating surface similar to a drumhead and also have affixed to the rims objects which jingle when shaken. The instrument can be played either by shaking it for a jingling sound or by striking it sharply on the heel of the palm to produce the combination of drum sound plus the jingle.

You can make crude tambourines with two paper plates. Lace the plates together with cotton or string. Place small metal bells around the edge periodically as you lace the plates together. While the paper plates themselves may not last very long, the effect they produce will be tambourinelike.

More elaborate tambourines may be made using metal pie plates with bells fastened around the edge. In order to make holes in the pie plates use a sharp nail and hammer. Be sure to place the part you nail through over a piece of scrap wood. A center punch, which can be purchased very inexpensively at a hardware store, is probably the best implement to use for making the holes. The plates may be wired together or tied together. Place the little bells around the rim as you lace. Metal bottle caps may be used instead of the metal bells. Remove the cork disks from the bottle caps, put holes through the center, and fasten them in pairs to the rims of the pie plates.

More elaborate and realistic tambourines with better tone quality can be made using embroidery hoops and parchment drumheads. Professional tambourines always use parchment heads. The drumhead should be about one inch larger all around than the larger embroidery hoop—about two inches greater in diameter. Soak the drumhead for about a half hour as you did when making drums. Stretch the parchment as tightly as you can over the inner embroidery hoop, and place the outer hoop over it to hold the parchment tightly. Lace some bells or bottle caps around the outside hoop for the jingle effect.

Jingle or Bell Sticks

Bottle caps can be used quite effectively to make jingles. You need a piece of wood approximately six inches by two inches, or a six-inch length of broom handle will do nicely. Also any piece of shaped wood, such as the "fly-back" paddles that look like ping-pong paddles, can be used. Make a hole in the middle of each of two bottle caps, after removing the cork insert. The hole should be large enough to permit the caps to slide easily over a one-inch flathead nail. Put the nail through these holes,

Figure 12. **BELL STICK.** Fasten bells to end of stick. Shake or slap stick on palm.

Figure 13. **JINGLE STICK.** Flattened bottle caps fastened loosely to stick. Shake or slap stick on palm.

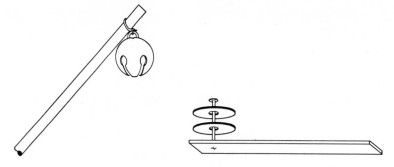

and hammer it into the wooden handle. Drive the nail in firmly, but not so far in as to stop the bottle caps from jingling against each other.

These can be played either by shaking them or by striking the backs of the handles against the heel of the palm.

Small metal bells, procured in the five-and-ten, may be fastened to a handle to serve as bell sticks. They are played in a similar way.

Shakers

Shaking instruments may be made from almost any kind of container. Inside the container we place small objects of almost any hard type. Handles may be fastened or not, according to the desires of the person making the instrument. The tone quality will depend on the material used for the container and the materials used inside the container. The easiest type of shaking instrument to make is the kind that uses any common container that might ordinarily be scrapped, such as metal cans or boxes, cardboard boxes or wooden boxes. Inside we insert such things as pebbles, buttons, rice, small plastic beads or disks, wooden beads, gravel, or other small objects.

These instruments may be simple or complex, depending on the age of the children and the time you want to spend on the activity. The simplest type of shaking instruments would be those fashioned from metal containers which already have a top, such as Band-aid cans or typewriter-ribbon cans. Two aluminum tumblers or metal screw-on jar tops can easily be taped together. Insert the small hard objects, close the lid or tape the two containers together, and you have a shaker whose tone will vary depending on the materials used.

Food cans of various types may also be used, but ordinarily the tops of these are removed when we take the food out. Frozen food cans, such as frozen orange juice cans, tomato juice cans, small vegetable cans, may all be used for shakers. Another closing will have to be made for these cans, however. The easiest way to do this is to cut a cardboard disk exactly the same size as the open end of the can. Through this disk insert a clothespin, or a length of half-inch dowel stick or broom handle, so that it goes completely through the cardboard and extends through to the opposite end of the can. Nail this handle securely through the bottom of the can so that it is affixed permanently. Insert the rattling objects inside the can, push the cardboard down over the handle, and tape it firmly over the end of the can. The shaking instrument is now complete except for any decorations you may want to add.

One of the simplest shaking instruments you can find is a large metal salt-and-pepper shaker usually used for cooking purposes. These ordinarily are available for about five or ten cents. They have a screw-on top and a convenient handle just about the right size for children. Unscrew the top, insert the rattling objects—anything from the size of dried rice on up through such things as marbles—and when the lid is replaced, the shaking instrument is ready to produce rhythmic tones.

Cardboard containers of various sizes and shapes may also

Figure 14. SHAKER. Use tin can as base, cardboard disk to close open end and dowel-stick handle. After inserting rattling objects, slide disk over open end and tape. Decorate to suit.

Figure 15. A CANISTER SHAKER. Metal kitchen salt-and-pepper shakers. Various types of rattling objects placed inside vary the tone.

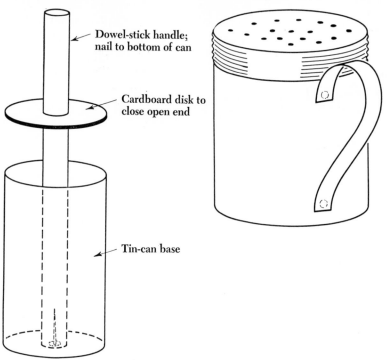

Dowel-stick handle; nail to bottom of can

Cardboard disk to close open end

Tin-can base

be utilized: small cereal boxes, small milk containers, or cardboard tubes such as the ones found inside rolls of toilet tissue or inside kitchen toweling. With the tubing you will need to devise a means of containing the inserted objects. Wrapping the entire tube with aluminum foil or taping cardboard cutouts to the ends will do.

Tea strainers taped together with some rattling objects inside make very effective shakers, and with handles already there, too. Even a burlap bag filled with marbles can be used. Clam shells with some small beads inserted and the shells taped together can also be effective. In making these instruments let your imagination go, and see what you and your children can concoct together in the way of ingenious ideas. More and more packaging is being produced using plastic containers, many of which form fine bases for shaking instruments.

Figure 16. **COOKIE-CUTTER SHAKER.** Two cookie cutters taped together after some small hard objects are placed inside. Tone varies depending on material used.

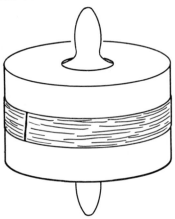

Avoid the use of glass bottles as containers; they crack or break too easily and may then be dangerous.

Somewhat more elaborate shaking instruments may be made of papier-mâché. These seem somewhat more desirable and offer more creative potential. In making a papier-mâché shaking instrument almost any object can be used as the molding form. Children particularly seem to like to use a fruit or vegetable. For example, a green pepper may be the form in which the shaking instrument will be made. You may apply the following directions for a green-pepper shaker to any fruit or vegetable desired.

Coat the pepper with petroleum jelly or some other greasy substance so that the papier-mâché will not stick directly to the vegetable. Use your favorite recipe to make the papier-mâché. Actually, paper hanger's paste, sometimes known as fox-paste, water, and strips of newspaper will do. After you have coated the pepper, put about six layers of papier-mâché around it, and put it aside to dry. After it has dried completely, slice it carefully through the middle, remove the pepper, and insert the rattling objects. In making papier-mâché instruments it would be better not to use dried vegetables, since they pick up moisture from the papier-mâché and may prove difficult to shake loose later. Insert the rattling objects, perhaps beads or pebbles or nails or buttons, fit the two halves of the papier-mâché pepper together again, and put several more layers of papier-mâché around the outside binding the halves together. After it has dried, paint the instrument any color you choose.

Another rather interesting instrument may be made with papier-mâché using a burnt-out electric bulb as the base. Again, coat the glass surface of the bulb with some greasy substance, and cover with about six layers of papier-mâché. Do not slice this open, however. When it dries, strike it sharply against a hard surface to shatter the bulb inside. The glass will, of course, remain inside the papier-mâché. You may want to put a few more layers on after you shatter the glass to make sure that none of the glass pieces come through. A painted design then will enhance the appearance of the instrument.

Newspaper, of course, makes fine papier-mâché. If you plan to paint the instrument, the last few layers should be unprinted newsprint or paper toweling, because it will be easier to cover with the poster paint usually used in schools, without having the print show through.

Scrapers

A scraping, scratching sound at first thought may seem to be rather forbidding. It is possible, however, to make scraping instruments which have a very pleasant tone, quite useful in our rhythm orchestra. One of the simplest and most frequently used of the scraping instruments is the sandpaper blocks. To make these, all you need is two pieces of wood sized to fit a small hand. Cut sandpaper so that it is large enough to overlap the sides of the blocks. Thumbtack the sandpaper, grit side out, to the blocks, placing the thumbtacks along the sides, not the surfaces, of the blocks. When the blocks are scraped together, a rhythmic swishing sound can be produced. They may be clapped together as rhythm blocks for a clicking sound.

Other rhythmic sounds are sometimes used which offer additional potential for development of the orchestra. A common door spring of fairly large size is held at one end. A metal object, such as a spoon, may be rubbed up and down the length of the spring so that a rasping kind of rhythmic sound results. The small washboards that are sometimes used in the kitchen sink or bathroom sink are easily portable. Metal thimbles on the fingers run across the ridges of the washboard produce an interesting rhythmic sound. With older children a common grater can be used as well. The kind used to grate potatoes or onions produces an interesting sound when a metal spoon is scraped across the rough edges. Be careful of scraped knuckles, though.

Figure 17. **WASHBOARD SCRAPER. Thimbles on fingers, scrape across ridges. Also tap on wood frame.**

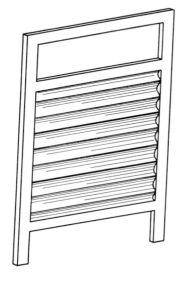

Bell Tones

Although there are many possibilities in producing bell tones for our rhythm orchestra, keep in mind that for now we want to produce tones that may be varied rhythmically, not melodically.

A fine trianglelike tone can be produced by using large building nails or spikes. The larger ones produce better tones than the small ones. Try to get some spikes at least 8 inches in length. Tie a thin piece of cord loosely at the head of the nail so that you can dangle the nail from the cord. Strike it with another nail. It will produce a very pleasant ringing tone.

The small metal bells that we spoke of before in making tambourines can also be used in various bell-tone instruments. A number of them can be tied, tacked, or nailed to the end of a piece of broomstick for a bell stick.

A vegetable brush can be used for a handle and the framework and bells tied around the metal edge for an effective bell instrument. Or a metal vegetable spoon, the large kitchen kind with perforations, can also be used. Here the bells can be tied through the holes and rattle and clang against the metal spoon.

Metal bells can also be sewn to an elastic band and slipped over the hand to form wrist bells. A bell may be fastened to the eraser on a pencil and played rhythmically.

Louder bells can be made by using a length of common iron or aluminum pipe. The longer the pipe, the lower the pitch of the bell. A plumber friend may have a length or two of scrap pipe around. Get him to drill a hole completely through the pipe about one-quarter of the way along the length of the pipe, so that a small wire can be inserted through it. This wire serves as a handle, and the length of pipe is struck with a nail or other metallic object. The metal pipe really rings out and should probably be reserved in the rhythm orchestra for special effects.

Figure 18. **NAIL TRIANGLE. Large building spike tied loosely at head. Hold by string handle and strike with another nail.**

Miscellaneous Types of Instruments

As you and your children begin to make instruments, you will be alert for many other possibilities that are not mentioned here. Some possibilities not yet included within the various categories are briefly indicated below.

Some wooden spools from sewing thread may be strung over a wire clothes hanger or on heavy cord. When shaken, these spools, usually made of hardwood, produce a pleasant clicking sound.

Canister covers take handles very easily. For these handles

you may want to use small lengths of broomsticks or some drawer pulls from the hardware store. These serve as clicking instruments or as cymbals depending on their tone.

Some natural growths, such as gourds found in various parts of the country, can be used as shaking instruments. All you need do is let them dry out. The seeds inside the gourd serve as the rattling objects. To speed the drying, cut open one end and remove the pulp and seeds. After the gourd is dry, put some pebbles inside and cork the hole closed. Gourds of all kinds may be painted gaily.

A length of bamboo can be used either as a shaking instrument or as a scraping or striking one. To use it as a shaking instrument, cut off a length of bamboo so that you have a completely hollow length. Insert the rattling objects, pebbles do nicely, and cork up both ends. To make a scraping instrument, use a triangular file to make gouges crosswise along the side of the bamboo. Scrape a pencil or other thin object along the length of the bamboo. A rhythmic scraping sound can be produced. Good clicking instruments result from striking together two lengths of bamboo.

Wooden cooking spoons can serve a dual purpose. Cut off the spoon end of two of these, drill small holes through the part closest to where the handle was, and tie them together with a loop to slip over a finger. They are well hollowed out for use as castanets. The handles, just as any length of hardwood dowel, may be used as clicking instruments.

Put metal thimbles on the thumb and fingers to produce finger castanets. Bottle caps, after the cork is removed, may be tied to the finger ends for metal finger castanets as well.

Scraping instruments may be made out of rhythm sticks, which in their simplest form are merely two lengths of hardwood. Dowel sticks serve admirably. Merely use a triangular file to make gouges or ridges across the stick.

MAKING MELODIC INSTRUMENTS

Melodic instruments are somewhat more difficult to make than rhythm instruments. They do not appear as plentiful in the environment of the child as do the potential rhythm instruments. More accuracy is required in their construction. Consequently, except for experimentation with tuned water glasses and bottles in the lower grades, we do not recommend the actual construction of melodic instruments for very young children.

With precut wooden blocks that are tuned by others, first- and second-grade children can arrange a certain number of tones in sequential order from lower to higher. Making melodic instruments should ordinarily be deferred until the child is about nine years of age. Even then, the approach to making melodic instruments should be slow and careful, without undue pressures. String instruments offer special problems in making them strong enough to withstand normal use and still stay in tune.

Although the details of construction cannot be included here, it is possible for middle-grade children to make melodic instruments such as xylophones, shepherd's pipes, and simple flutes or fifes.

Tuned Water Glasses

Playing and experimenting with tuned water glasses and bottles offer a very rewarding experience for children. Different-size glasses produce different natural pitches. We tune the glasses by adding water or pouring some water off. As we add water to the glass, the pitch achieved when the glass is struck lightly at the rim will be lower. The glass itself vibrates. As we add more water to the glass, it vibrates at a slower rate, therefore producing a lower pitch. If you plan to tune water glasses, take three of the same size and shape to start. Find the natural pitch of the glass by striking it lightly on the rim. Add water to the other two, about twice as much to one of them as to the other. Adjust the water level until you can produce the tones of a simple melody such as "Hot Cross Buns." This melody contains tones that correspond to *E, D, C,* or for those of you who know syllables or numbers, *mi, re, do,* or *3, 2, 1.* Experiment with your children, or have them experiment, adding different quantities of water to the glasses to see what happens to the tone or pitch of the glass when water is added or taken away.

Perhaps, though, you do not know "Hot Cross Buns," cannot tell *E* from *C*, *mi* from *do*, or *3* from *1*. Do not count yourself out of this activity. Use any simple song you and your children do know well. By experimenting with different-size glasses and different amounts of water in them, your children will still be able to make a set of tuned glasses or bottles on which they can play a familiar song. Do not expect them to complete the job in a single session; it may take a number of tries. Allow ample opportunity for the kind of experimentation that leads to familiarity. At each session be satisfied if they can locate a couple of tones that sound right to the group. If you do not have confidence in your own ability to hear when a correct tuning is reached, let the children decide. It is a better activity for them when their decisions are followed anyway. They learn from their mistakes; do not be concerned if they make some. The main bit of equipment you need is not the glasses; your attitude of experimentation and encouragement is most important.

Tuned Bottles

The tuning of bottles is slightly different, depending on whether we strike the bottle or produce the tone by blowing across the top of it. If the bottles are to be struck with a mallet, the instructions for tuning are the same as those given for tuning glasses. When we blow across the top of the bottle, the basic pitch is determined by the size of the bottle, but the bottle itself does not vibrate—the air inside the bottle vibrates. Consequently, you raise the pitch when you add water to the bottle, since a smaller quantity of air vibrates. This process is quite the opposite from tuning water glasses. The basic pitch of three equal-size glasses might be considered the *E* (*3*, or *mi*) for "Hot Cross Buns." We add water to the other glasses to get pitches lower than *E*. In water bottles, however, the basic pitch is the pitch of the empty bottle which in "Hot Cross Buns" would be *C* (*1*, or *do*). We add water to two other like-size bottles in order to get the other two higher pitches for "Hot Cross Buns."

Once, through a process of experimentation and trial and error, your children have tuned three glasses or bottles accurately, have them make up little three-tone melodies. If you plan to use the same bottles or glasses another day, mark the water level on the glasses or bottles by pasting a strip of paper there or by noting the level with a grease marking pencil. You will then be able to add water if some evaporates and find the same pitches again without going through the whole experimental process that you originally used.

You may want to continue the activity, especially with children eight years of age and older, by tuning an entire octave of a scale properly. You will need eight glasses or bottles for this purpose. You will find it easier if you start with four of one size and four of another size. For the bottles, four Pepsi-Cola bottles and four Coca-Cola bottles are just about the right size to continue through a full octave of a scale.

The music corner in this third-grade classroom contains a homemade bottlephone as well as a complement of rhythm instruments.

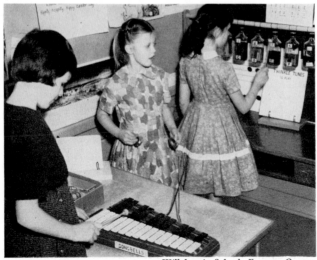

Willakenzie School, Eugene, Oregon.

♫ CHAPTER SEVEN

Listening

LISTENING TO MUSIC holds many exciting possibilities for the growth and development of children. To fulfill this potential, we will have to replace the traditional notion of listening as a passive process. Listening can be quite an active process, and only as an activity does it provide an important contribution to individual growth and development. Our role as teachers becomes one of stimulating the active listening to music.

FREEING THE LISTENER

Listening is influenced by attitudes, and attitudes result from many different factors. We first examine some of the factors that influence the way we listen.

Control by an Elite

Musicians and music critics ordinarily tend to operate within the framework of a kind of hierarchy of musical values. Certain music is "good" music; other music is "not good." People not trained musically are inclined, of course, to follow the lead of the critics who play such an important role in establishing this hierarchy of musical values. This seems natural enough. After all, the musician trained in his field seems to be in a proper position to determine "good" and "not good" in music. While this process seems natural, it is only apparently so. Acceptance of this process as proper serves to maintain an unfortunate reservation of the enjoyment of music for a fortunate elite who, having received specialized musical training, maintain a special privilege of determining "good" and "not good" music—a privilege they are reluctant to grant to others not so specially trained.

We can properly have no quarrel with the right of the musician to make up his own mind about what music he considers good and not good. We can and should, however, quarrel with the critic and the musician when they attempt to determine, directly or indirectly, what can be considered good and not good music by others.

The musical layman who may disagree with the critics in judging a particular composition frequently feels himself inadequate to judge music on the same basis as the critics. He reacts, in deference to the musically trained elite, too often by concluding that his own feelings about music are deficient. Such feelings of inadequacy can lead an individual to withdraw from listening to music and to reject it.

The great attribute of music, however, is that it can be all things to all people. What a composition means can be only what it means to human beings. Dewey said, "A work of art . . . is actually, not just potentially, a work of art only when it lives in some individualized experience." [1]

What is good music can be determined for an individual only in terms of what he feels is good. As school people we have no ultimate responsibility for determining great music as different from good music or as different from poor music. Our role, rather, is to help each individual find a place for himself in listening to music for his own personal enjoyment. When we emphasize individual experience in music, we underscore

[1] John Dewey, *Art as Experience,* Minton, Balch & Co., New York, 1934, pp. 108–109.

the importance of helping the individual feel that his own judgment about music is valid for himself as much as the judgment of other individuals is valid for them.

No one should put himself in a position of telling another what he should or should not like in music. The label "good" or "not good" music carries just that connotation. Presumably a good composition is one which should be liked, and a bad or not good composition is one which should not be liked. The connotation of good music carries with it the corresponding connotation that here is music that people generally should approve of. It is good music; the critics have approved of it; it has stood the test of time. Therefore, we should like it. Similarly, music which has not stood the test of time or which is disliked by the critics is presumably music which the ordinary person should not like.

But, you ask, if those who know music think a composition is not good, why should those untrained musically like it? The basic fact is, however, that what is good can be good only as people as individuals enjoy it. That enjoyment comes from something internal to the individual. One likes it or not. Whether or not one likes a particular composition can be determined only by the person listening to the composition for himself. If one individual in listening to any composition feels within himself that he does not like that composition, no judgment of any musical expert helps him truly to like it. Expert opinion may exert subtle pressure on the individual so that he may verbalize that he likes the composition. Often, however, the individual who dislikes a composition that he is told he should like tends to feel that music is just not for him; he "doesn't get it!" The *expertise* cannot change a person's internal feelings or reactions. It can lead the individual to the conclusion that his own feelings or reactions are bad or wrong.

Does one like Wagner, or dislike Wagner? Disliking Wagner is just as legitimate for any given individual as is liking Wagner. One listener may like Wagner and dislike Stravinsky. Another listener may react just as strongly liking Stravinsky and disliking Wagner. Each of these positions is entirely reasonable and proper for the individuals holding them. What is good musically is merely that which individuals like, and what is not good is no more than that which individuals dislike. Both favorable and unfavorable opinions can apply to the same composition at the same time, as different individuals hear it simultaneously.

We need to encourage children in the independence of their judgments, and we should start the pattern of helping children express their judgments freely and frankly from very early ages. Some techniques for doing this will be presented later in this chapter. For now let us emphasize and reemphasize the primary importance of the individual person's reactions to music and the encouragement of the feeling on his part that the way he feels about the composition is right for him at whatever stage of listening development he may be. We encourage him to express his feelings openly, freely, and frankly, and at the same time encourage him to respect the opinion and judgment of others about the composition whether or not they agree with him.

Music as a Temporal Art

Music as an art form takes place in time rather than in space. We look at a painting and can see it all at once. Time passes as our eyes wander over the painting. We may pick out a thread of color, follow that, look at the content, look at various parts of the painting. And as we do so, time passes. At any one given instant, however, we can step back and look at the painting as a whole. We speak of painting as taking place or existing in space.

In music, however, we cannot do this. At any one given instant we can hear only a single tone of a melody or a group of tones struck simultaneously to produce a chord. This is not music; it is but part of music. We have music only when human beings can hear the tone or cluster of tones that occur in any one instant and relate that tone or cluster to what has gone before in the melody and to some extent relate it to what is to come in the music. Hearing tones in the context of the flow of the music requires a certain amount of familiarity with the idiom. This is one of the reasons that Mozartean or Haydnesque music remains so popular. In much of their music we can almost tell what comes next. As a general populace we have heard this kind of music in many different kinds of situations and, indeed, in many different compositions by many different composers. We have a feeling for the rightness of the turn of the melody. We can almost anticipate the following tones. Even when the composer fools us by giving the melody a little unexpected quirk, we get an added fillip from that fooling, but do not lose our sense of orientation to the music as a whole.

However, when the musical idiom, the structure, the form, the flow of the melody depart from the familiar type, we sometimes lose our orientation and our sense of expectation of what comes next. It is, therefore, more difficult for us, sometimes, to listen to music in an unfamiliar idiom without losing our perspective of it. This factor tends to make us generally and too often reject music in a contemporary idiom.

The problem of orienting ourselves to the changes which composers have brought into our music is not a new one. It recurs through the history of music of the last few centuries. Beethoven, Brahms, Wagner, Berlioz, Franck, Debussy, Stravinsky, Copland, Schönberg has each in his turn had unfavorable comments made about his music by some of his contemporary critics.

Some of these composers introduced new kinds of harmonies in their music. These new harmonic structures were in many cases rejected by their contemporaries until the harmonic idiom in its new form became familiar enough so that the music could speak directly to the listener without the difficulty of orientation to new kinds of sounds. Many of these composers were attacked as being tremendously unmelodic in their music. Some critics of his day considered the structure of the Brahms' symphonies thick and turgid, without melodic elements. Our contemporary ears are accustomed to Brahms, and we may have difficulty understanding how he could ever have been considered as unmelodic.

Wagner's harmonic structure was so advanced for his time that one of the favorite cartoons of that era shows Wagner as a small figure standing on the lobe of a human ear, attacking the eardrum with the point of an eighth note.

César Franck was attacked because his *Symphony in D Minor* had but three movements instead of the traditional four movements. He also introduced an instrument that until that time had not been used in the symphony orchestra, the English horn. These new sounds and new formal structures were difficult for some contemporaries to follow. Their orientation, based on the music with which they were familiar, was disturbed. Many reacted with dislike.

With the development of Stravinsky in his early period, we find an even more radical type of attack on the work of a composer. At the first playing of *Le Sacre du printemps, The Rite of Spring*, in Paris, robust fist fights broke out in the audience between those who liked this radically different music and those who disliked it.

We have developed the matter of the familiar or unfamiliar idiom and the matter of the listener's orientation to illustrate more clearly the effect of music as a temporal art and the influences of that factor. The orientation of the listener is at stake. His sense of the fitness of the flow of the melody will in part make him receptive or unreceptive to the music itself. Familiarity with what has gone before in a melody and a kind of sense of what comes next in the melody are among the reasons that we tend to like music that we know. Music that we hear for the first time, even in a comparatively familiar idiom, cannot speak to us as readily as music with which we are quite familiar. A first hearing of a composition cannot carry with it a sense of memory of what has gone before and what comes next. After a number of hearings the sense of familiarity grows, and we can place the things that are going on melodically, harmonically, and rhythmically, as well as formally, in their proper context.

Consequently, while we can certainly encourage children to express their feelings about a composition, even the first time they hear it, we need to help them recognize that they may reserve judgment after hearing a composition for the first time. Initial reactions are valid, legitimate, and need to be respected, although they are initial. However, we would hope to develop an attitude which could say: "This is my reaction for now. After I hear this composition a few more times, I may change my judgment of it. I may like it more; I may like it less."

Program and Abstract Music

Generally speaking, music can be divided into two large types according to whether or not the composer planned the music to tell a story. Some composers have started out to write a composition which depicts as closely as possible some specific story. We call this program music. Richard Strauss in *Till Eulenspiegel* attempts to depict musically the pranks of young Till. In the *Sorcerer's Apprentice,* by Dukas, an old folk tale is told through the medium of music. In these two illustrations a very definite story is related. Other composers have attempted to depict moods and scenes and feelings about things that have happened. Debussy in *La Mer* describes the sea and various aspects of living at sea.

In a symphony, however, or a string quartet, most composers do not attempt to tell a specific story. We call this abstract music.

In listening to music some people make up a story as they listen. In some cases the story that they think of is conditioned by the story that they know accompanies the music. In other cases the story which the listener makes up has nothing to do with the original story. Indeed, it is quite unlikely that anyone not knowing the specific story of a programmatic composition would happen on the original one by himself. Music without accompanying words has no powers of direct description in concrete terms. It has the power of evoking moods, but the precise connotation of meaning which can be conveyed by words has no possibility of transmission in the form of music.

When a group of people unfamiliar with the story of the music listen to a particular composition, it is extremely unlikely that any two of them would agree on precisely what story the music tells. There would probably be as many different stories about the music as there were people who listened to it.

Some people listen to music pictorially; that is, they construct a story to fit the music they hear as they go along. Other people, however, are unable or unwilling to do this. They listen for various elements in the music, but do not particularly hear or think of stories. Indeed, many people in this second large category find themselves unable to hear a story in the music, even when they know the presumed story supposedly accompanying the music. The music, they feel, could so appropriately apply to many different types of stories equally.

Since one of the great values of music is its evocative powers, listening should be free of any coercion in terms of specific stories. By this we mean to reject the traditional approach to listening of telling the title of the composition, the name of the composer, the story of the music if there is one, or even the story which some people have heard in the music when the composer himself did not express any specific story content. At concerts the writer of the program notes often speculates about possible stories that have been associated with the music at various times. The program notes often tell the stories in detail. Such procedures too often limit the reaction of the people hearing the music to the type of story related to them. Free play of their own imaginations in terms of the particular stories which they might make up as the music plays is severely hindered.

Furthermore, many people prefer not to listen storywise. They do not create a story during the process of listening. People like this are severely handicapped if before they hear a composition they hear the official or semiofficial story of a particular composition. Their own listening, despite their best efforts, can be limited by the particular story told to them prior to listening. They may, because they consider it proper to listen to music this way, attempt to follow the story given to them. If they are not able to hear this story in the music and have the typical layman's awe for musical authority, their own reactions are likely to be ones of dismay, with accompanying

feelings of inadequacy. They may distrust their own reactions
to the music and feel that their failure to hear the story they
were presumably supposed to hear was a symptom of some
inadequacy on their part. Such feelings can effectively limit
future listening.

People who create their own stories when they listen to
music may feel that their stories are inferior if they have previously been given a "correct" story which they were supposed to
hear in the music. Trusting the musical authority again, they
would tend to distrust their own responses. This, too, creates
feelings of inadequacy and tends to discourage further listening.

In playing music for children's listening our primary role is
to help build an interaction directly between the music and
the individuals listening. It is far better to say, "Here is a composition. Let's see if you like it," without any prior comments
about title, composer, or story.

We face, too, a general feeling of some people, adults more
than children, that they are supposed to like certain music.
Similarly, they feel it is not so important for them to like
certain other music. We find a kind of status-snob approach to
music: certain composers, presumably great, must be liked;
other composers, not nearly so well known, may be disliked.
Labeling the composer before listening to music in a group
situation can activate this feeling on the part of people whose
background in music is not particularly strong. Surely, Beethoven was a great composer. But that does not mean everyone
will enjoy Beethoven's music or all of Beethoven's music. In
our role as teachers we should not undertake to browbeat or
apply social or status pressures to listeners in order to get
them to verbalize a liking for Beethoven's music. The music
must speak to them or not. It stands on its own feet. Truly
great music will reach people. We do not have to associate a
famous name with a particular composition in order to have
people react favorably to it.

Despite the contentions of some musicians, there is innately
no superior mode of listening in terms of program music or
abstract music. There are individual differences in the way peo-

ple listen, and it is not more or less than a matter of individual differences. People who listen pictorially can also listen to other more strictly musical elements in a composition. People who listen abstractly only do not usually feel the need for programmatic listening. There is no need for us to attempt to pressure any group which tends to listen one way into listening the other way.

Ways of Listening

There can be no abstraction of a right or wrong way to listen to music. The way a person listens is right for him, whatever his current mode of listening. It is not wrong for him, no matter how he listens. As we work with children, we encourage the child, as our first task, to listen whichever way seems right for him.

Our second big task is to help broaden each child's horizons so that he recognizes many different ways to listen. As discussion about reactions to music and ways of listening proceed through a group, each person's recognition of the possible different ways of listening increases. He hears how other people have reacted to the music, and he hears how they have listened in ways different from his own.

There are probably as many ways of listening as there are people who listen. While we cannot say that there is any one right way and that other ways are wrong, it may serve a useful purpose to discuss briefly some of the common ways of listening.

Some people tone bathe when they listen, letting the sounds surround them. They relax and luxuriate in enjoying the sensation of sound. This type of listening tends to be more passive than other types.

Other people tend to listen for the story that is involved in the music. They may like to follow the composer's story if the music is descriptive. At times they may make up a story to fit the music. At still other times they may hear segments of various stories, disconnected from each other. In some cases these segments have no relationship to each other, being merely the spontaneous reactions to particular parts in the music which occur to the listener. In some instances the stories made up by the listener are accompanied by pictures or mental images, and actual scenes seem to form in the listener's mind, which change and shift as the music changes. Sometimes these pictures are part of a single story, and at other times the scenes are disconnected and sparked by various parts of the music.

Some people do not listen pictorially at all. They like to follow the shifting instruments that play in the orchestra. Or they try to identify various instruments and enjoy the identification. Others follow the melodic line. They hear the main melody and then listen for that main melody as it is repeated through the fabric of the various instruments. Others, once they become familiar with the main melody, listen to the countermelodies, the ones which play against the main melody,

Concert-going vitalizes musical experience.

New York Philharmonic's Young People's Concert. Photo by Bakalar-Cosmo.

and follow these shifting countermelodies through the various instruments. Some people follow various melodies as they become familiar with the composition, and they listen for the return of previously heard melodies. Some people, admittedly with more training, will follow harmonic patterns in the music. Others will follow rhythmic patterns. Some combine various elements of these procedures in various ways.

At a concert many people are certainly fascinated by the instrumentalists themselves and by the conductor leading the orchestra. They note the way he cues in various instruments and watch the instrumentalist as he responds to the conductor's cues. Some people hear the harmonic development of a composition or make more detailed formal analysis as the composition proceeds.

No one of these ways is right and all others wrong; all may be right. People listen to music in different ways, and the way in which any one individual listens at whatever stage of development is clearly right for him. We must avoid the artificial development of feelings of inadequacy about one's own response to music. There is, consequently, no one right way to listen.

Above all, we listen to music with our emotions; music is a feeling thing.

LISTENING: AN ACTIVE PROCESS

Activity, in the popular sense, usually involves overt physical movement. Active, as opposed to passive, may refer to more than just physical movement, and listening can be an active process, even though no actual body movement is involved.

The Process of Hearing

The human ear although intimately involved in hearing, of course, can by no means be considered the sole organ involved. Three factors are necessary for sound to exist: one, an object vibrating within a particular frequency range; two, a medium to carry the vibrations; three, a receptor to receive the vibrations. In music the vibrating mediums may be the strings

of the violins or cellos, the reed of the clarinet, the lips of the
trumpet player, the skin of the kettledrum, or the vocal cords
of the singer. These vibrations are carried by the surrounding
air to a human being, the receptor. We do not have music until
the vibrations reach a human being and are translated by that
person into organized sound.

The difference between music and sound is merely one of
organization. Composers plan the organization of sounds, but
listeners organize sounds also. Composers may make music
which is unintelligible to certain listeners. To those listeners
for whom that composer's compositions are unintelligible, there
is no music. Similarly, certain people have listened to the sound
of wind in the trees and discerned organization. These sounds,
frequently termed noises, are transmitted by the organization of
people as receptors into music.

Music, then, connotes organized sounds.

The organization of sound depends upon human experience.
It is not our ears which hear music; it is our whole beings
which hear music. Our ears merely act as part of the receiving
mechanism. The ear transmits the vibrations to the mind, but
we listen with our whole body and our whole experience; our
feelings, our emotions, our intelligence, our previous experiences, our physiological make-up are all involved in the process
of hearing music.

Sometimes when we listen to music, the music is so familiar
to us that the organization of it seems very natural. It seems to
be part of our whole fiber of being. We are aware of no organizing done by us as individuals. In other instances, when we
listen to music of a completely different culture, for example,
the sounds which we receive are so strange and so divorced
from any in our previous experience that we are completely
and totally unable to proceed with any organization. For us,
then, this is not music. To someone raised in that other culture,
for whom those sounds present phenomena within their total
life experience, the same particular sounds have meaning
through their organizational potential. As individuals they are
capable of organizing the sounds. For them, this is music. To

that same person, native to an entirely different culture from ours, our Western music would be completely divorced from his previous experience. What to us is our greatest music for that person would have no significance, would have no organizing potential, and would not exist as music, but merely as sounds.

Remember the traditional philosophical question of the tree falling in the wilderness with no one around? The question is posed: "Is there sound under such circumstances?" This presumably difficult question is not difficult at all. Of course there is no sound; there are merely vibrations. They would not become sound until there was a receptor capable of receiving them. The receptor might be a person present, or it might be a tape recorder set to record those vibrations automatically. In that case the vibrations would be translated to sound when someone listened to the tape recording through a playback machine.

A phonograph record is not music; it is potentially music. It contains on it a recording through mechanical and electronic means of various vibrations. It is not music until it is played back on a device capable of translating those vibrations into ones we are capable of receiving. When we hear the translation and organize the vibrations, there is music.

The process of organizing sounds is an activity. When we organize sounds on any level, we participate in an active process. Actually, listening can be a creative undertaking in which the listener creates toward the intent of the composer. In some instances this creation on the part of the listener may be reacting emotionally to the mood that the composer built into his music. As the listener experiences a mood while listening, he creates toward the intention of the composer. The composer rarely wants a listener to react in precise terms to his music. He does, however, want listeners to react to his music in their own terms. Consequently, when a listener reacts on his own level, no matter what that level may be, in some organizational way to the music he hears, he is involved in an active creative process.

Selective Hearing

All of us are endowed with an attribute which we may call selective hearing. All the sounds which impinge on our ears are not equally transmitted to the brain. Our minds select from the multitude of sounds we hear the specific ones we would like to register. We can focus on those sounds almost to the exclusion of all others. Naturally, there are limits to the possibilities of excluding certain sounds, depending on their intensity. A fire siren may impinge on us, even when we desire to exclude it. However, we have all frequently known the phenomenon of literally not hearing certain sounds.

For a moment try this experiment. Let this book rest on your lap. Close your eyes and listen for half a minute to the sounds that are normally part of this particular time of day. Right now, we can focus on the sounds we hear once we transmit our attention from the task of writing to full listening to the sounds which come to our ears. There is the sound of children playing in a nearby playground. These sounds blend and intermix, and yet we can distinguish screams and shouts of particular children. A counterpoint is played by the rumbling of an automobile and a truck passing by. Then we hear the slam of an automobile door. The rumbling of a bus on a street not too far away presents a swelling and gradually diminishing sound. The clicking and rattling of the Venetian blinds in the room as they wave in the air are also heard. An airplane passes overhead with its noisy motor. We hear a whoosh as another automobile engine starts. The chirping of some birds provides additional sounds impinging on the ear. Unfortunately in this busy metropolis many of the sounds are automobiles and truck motors and tire rumblings. Those of you more fortunately located may find natural sounds predominating. You may even be fortunate enough to hear the babbling of a brook accompanying the grunting of some frogs and the sound of the wind in the trees.

Once we stop to focus on the sounds we actually can hear, we recognize readily that the sounds impinging on the ear are not the ones that always register. We do not hear the constant flow of background sounds that are always present.

Another manner in which this may be readily recognized is to recall the times when, perhaps, you have been engrossed in reading a book or in doing a particular task you enjoy. Your attention was so completely fixed on the task that you did not hear, actually and literally did not hear, someone calling you. Many of us have had that experience.

One of the problems facing deaf people when first fitted with a hearing aid is that of relearning the attributes of selective hearing. The hearing aid amplifies all sounds equally; it has no powers of selection. Powers of selection are functions of human listening. Consequently, not only does the hearing aid amplify the sound of another person's voice, but it also amplifies all of the surrounding sounds and noises. The person learning to use a hearing aid must begin anew to select from the multitude of sounds amplified those most pertinent to what he wants to hear. His selective hearing mechanism must be reoriented and reorganized.

In hearing music we find a similar phenomenon. Those not familiar with a particular composition face the problem of orienting and organizing their selective hearing mechanism. In the chapter on playing instruments we describe the process of separating basic rhythm from melodic rhythm. In this we find an example of the development of selective hearing. Initial experience in listening to a total composition may not include the differentiation among the sounds of the basic rhythm and melodic rhythm. However, as we become more familiar with the composition, we learn to separate out the basic rhythm when we want to hear that and the melodic rhythm when that is what we want to hear. We are able through a process of familiarity and understanding to differentiate between these two rhythmic aspects of a musical composition. This is a process of developing faculties of selective hearing as applied to music.

Similarly, when we listen to the flow of the music in order to determine the phrase endings and get the feeling for the phrase rhythm, we are also involved in refining the process of selective hearing. We learn to listen to the flow of the melody and determine when the musical idea comes to a kind of ending. This process also sensitizes our selective hearing mechanism.

The process of differentiating the sounds of various instruments, too, is another step in the development of selective hearing. As we learn to compare the sounds of various instruments so that we can determine which instruments sound more nearly like each other for the purpose of grouping them together, we sharpen our powers of selective hearing. From masses of undifferentiated sounds, we begin to distinguish the sounds of particular instruments.

As we develop our orchestrations, we learn further to involve our selective hearing mechanism in the application of our own judgment as to which instruments could and should sound together in the various groups, which groups sound best together,

Children's fascination with music includes curiosity about instruments.

New York Philharmonic; Columbia Records.

and which groups should succeed each other in the development of orchestrations for particular compositions.

Later the differentiation of the sounds of symphonic orchestral instruments is merely a further development of these kinds of activities which start on the level of the children's development. These kinds of activities, beginning with rhythm instruments, start the selective hearing mechanism in its process of growth and development. Later on we will be able to help children, basing later activities on these experiences, to differentiate and distinguish among the sounds of the various orchestral instruments. Further, we learn thereby to pick out the sound of any of the familiar instruments from the total warp and woof of an entire symphonic composition. Through this process we gradually learn to focus our hearing, our listening apparatus, our selective hearing mechanism for the furtherance of our total musical enjoyment.

We Learn to Listen

We learn to listen both actively and passively. Normally the child is born with a hearing apparatus. Sounds impinge on this apparatus indiscriminately and register in the young child just as much as in the adult. The organism of the very young child, however, has not learned to interpret these sounds. His experience in living is quite limited; consequently, the sounds which he hears have little meaning or significance. Aside from the startle effect of loud sounds, the very young baby responds more to the quality of warmth that he detects in his mother's cooing to him than to the specific sounds which she makes. She can get the same response of joy and happiness from her baby by talking nonsense syllables as she gets from specific words.

In the beginning the sounds which the baby hears are probably a large undifferentiated mass of sounds. We have previously detailed an account of the probable development of language facility in children. Note how specifically listening ties in with the development of speech and with the progress of skill in communication. Speech and hearing are two different aspects of the individual organism's communication spectrum.

The development of the speaking mechanism closely ties in with the development of aural discrimination. The oral and aural relationship is much more acute than we usually realize. Their interdependence becomes apparent in communication only when there is some recognized impairment of one or the other. In such cases the child's whole communication mechanism is unbalanced, and he needs to be specifically taught to use whichever of the two mechanisms is unimpaired. It is likely, however, that the hearing mechanism is primary and somewhat more important in the development of communication skills than the speaking mechanism. Mute children learn to differentiate sounds they hear more readily than deaf children learn to speak. The growth and development of the hearing apparatus is a process of gradual differentiation and discrimination from among the vast quantities of tones, sounds, and noises which impinge upon the ear. The experience of the individual child determines his ability to organize the sounds which he hears and make them intelligible.

Music as a form of communication is no less dependent upon the experiences of the listener for differentiation and organization of the masses of tones which impinge upon the hearing mechanism. It is quite likely that the development of such listening skills depends on factors of growth, development, and related experience far more than upon specific skill training. Our most important role as teachers in helping children learn to discriminate and organize among the tones that they hear can best be played by helping them focus on sounds, by encouraging them to express their feelings and reactions about the sounds they hear, and by encouraging them constantly to make finer and finer discriminations among these sounds.

The selective hearing mechanism just described may be counted on to provide initial impetus. It is our responsibility to help the selective hearing mechanism develop.

THE LISTENING PROGRAM

Before we make any specific suggestions about the development of a teaching approach to listening, we need to examine what we mean by the listening program and some of the general concomitants of it.

Scope of the Listening Program

In schools the listening program must not be limited to a period or series of periods in which we play records or the piano for children. The listening program encompasses all musical activities which we undertake in the school.

In Chapters 2 and 3 in the discussions of the development of self-standards through self-criticism about singing, we pointed out a process of helping children focus their attention on the sounds they produce when the group sings. Through this process of self-criticism we build within children increased powers of discriminatory listening and help them develop their selective hearing mechanism. They listen to the total effect of their singing. They differentiate from the total mass certain facets on which they concentrate. As these are shared among all the children in the group, each child profits by the stage of the selective hearing growth of the others.

Does one child detect that the class has not all started the song at exactly the same instant? When the child who hears this as a possible defect calls it to the attention of the class and the other children listen to the initial attack the next time they sing, the selective hearing of all the children in the group has been developed further. Does another child call attention to the fact that parts of the song should be louder and parts of it softer? All the children profit by their subsequent focusing on this facet. The singing program is as much a part of the listening program as is the period devoted to phonograph records.

In the chapter on rhythm instruments we discussed the development of orchestrations by the children. We speak of grouping instruments according to their sounds. We are developing the selective hearing mechanism of children. Instruments are grouped according to the way the instruments sound as the children hear them and as the children decide on the groups. Will a particular shaker be grouped with those which sound rasping or with those that sound rattling? This is a problem of aural discrimination. As children differentiate among the sounds of their rhythm instruments, they engage in much the same process they later will be engaged in when they discriminate between the sound of the trumpet and the French horn in the symphony orchestra. Do we pose the problem of determining which group of instruments plays when we orchestrate a particular composition for our rhythm orchestra? Here again is a problem of aural discrimination and the development of selective hearing. From the total mass of sound which we create, how will we order these particular sounds? How will we organize them to create the effect that we want? Involved in this process are not only the beginnings of aesthetic decision, but also the development of aural discrimination while we listen to the music we orchestrate to determine which instruments will be most appropriate at a particular spot.

In creative bodily motion we frequently interpret through our bodies the feelings that we have when we listen to particular kinds of music. Again, the listening apparatus functions as part of the total organism. Hearing is related to the previous experiences of the child and translated by the child into a bodily, physical expression of the feelings involved.

Whether it be in the process of formal or informal rhythms, listening as an active process is involved in determining the appropriate movements to particular music. Leaving both formal and informal rhythms for more creative types of rhythmic activities, listening involves even further discriminations. It also involves total physiological response to music.

All the musical activities that take place in the school are actually part of the listening program and contribute to the growth and development of aural powers of discrimination and to listening as an active process.

Music Suitable for Children

A vast and growing quantity of children's phonograph records are available for use in classrooms. This vast literature is of very mixed quality. A number of records are exceedingly valuable, but, unfortunately, a larger number must be approached with caution.

The listening program in schools, however, must not be limited to so-called children's music, either the recently produced quantity specifically written for children or the works of great composers which have been specifically composed for children. Children can take any music that has been composed,

Young children, too, are absorbed by the combination of sight and sound at a concert.

New York Philharmonic's Young People's Concert.

with but few limitations. Great music appeals to children just as much as to adults. Indeed, young children are less likely to reject music in a contemporary idiom than are their elders. What to an adult may be cacophonic is quite normal to the young child whose ears have not been acclimated solely to music of a classical period or its like. The entire literature of music is available to us to use with children, provided we use it reasonably.

ATTENTION SPAN. The major caution to keep in mind in determining what music is suitable has to do with the length of playing time, since children's attention spans are somewhat more limited than adults'. Nevertheless, even as adults, it is rare that anyone listens with equal intensity to an entire composition. As adults, and this applies to trained musicians as well as to the musical layman, we tend to listen with fluctuating attention. At the beginning of a composition, our attention is ordinarily quite high. As time passes, however, our attention tends to waver as a result of various distractions. At a concert the distraction might be a neighbor waving a program. It might be a latecomer busily settling himself nearby. It might be any one of a dozen things happening in the concert hall which might catch our eye and cause our attention to wander from the music itself. It might, however, be no physical happenstance that causes our attention to wander. It might be some thought that strikes us at a particular moment during the playing of the music.

Our attention ordinarily wanders for a brief time, and then something happening in the music calls our attention back. Our attention to the music continues comparatively high until something or some thought distracts our attention again. Our mind wanders away from the playing for a period of time and then again is brought back. If we were to diagram the attention of an individual at a concert, it might look something like the wavering line pictured below:

High attention

Low attention

We have no reason to assume that the attention levels of children would be any different. Indeed, their attention peaks might be more numerous.

Since children ordinarily do not concentrate on any particular task for as long as adults, it is unreasonable to expect them to listen to a composition at one sitting for as long as adults might. It would be a reasonable limitation to restrict our playing of unfamiliar compositions to approximately five or ten minutes. Within this time span there are no limitations on what compositions to play. Music which is attractive to any adults might attract some children. Consequently, the entire literature of music is available for us to use in schools with the one limitation: the length of time it takes to play.

Even this limitation need not keep us from playing symphonic music for children, since most symphonies are in a number of movements. There is no reason why we should not take a section of a long composition and play that as an entity for a particular session. The limitation that we should observe in this is that the musical segment selected have a kind of unity and wholeness of its own, even though that wholeness is merely part of a larger whole. We could very well read individual chapters in a book to children at a single session. We do not feel it imperative to read an entire book at a single sitting. We select segments which have an entity and wholeness of their own, with breaking points that are reasonable in the story. We would hesitate to stop reading a story until we had reached a kind of natural breathing spot in its flow. Similarly, in music we would hesitate to break off in the playing of a symphony at other than a reasonable breaking point in the flow of the music.

Sometimes we find movements of a symphony whose playing time is within the limitations we have tentatively suggested. Some symphony movements play for about five minutes; others play for no more than ten. Any of these movements might be suitable to play as entities for a single session for children.

TEACHERS' FEELINGS. We have then the entire realm of symphonic music that contains much that is suitable to play for children. There is one limitation other than time that we must place on selections from this vast literature. We previously placed this limitation on the selection of songs. Do not play any music for children that you have negative feelings about yourself. If you do not like the music, your feelings about it will transmit to the children. There exists a real danger that you may limit your children's listening experiences by your own prejudices about certain pieces. The dangers involved in such limitations, however, are much less severe than those involved in prejudicing children against a particular kind of music which you yourself might not like. If you have come this far in this book, the chances are quite good that you have at least an open mind about many different kinds of music. Listen to music of many different types yourself, and pick those compositions which you like and which in your knowledge of your children you think that they will like. Play that music for them.

Do not be afraid that some music might be "too deep" or too difficult for children. Children constantly amaze us by their potential receptivity to all kinds of music. If you play something for them which they do not like, put it away for another time and try something else.

At the end of this book you will find a selected list of music from the great literature which you may want to try with your children. You will also find some suggestions of music either specifically written for children by the great composers or particularly suitable to play for children. You will also find a selection of records from the vast numbers of children's records which have recently been produced. You may want to start with this selected bibliography. Do not limit yourself to it, however. There are other suitable compositions that are not listed here. If there are any compositions which you particularly like, do not hesitate to try them with your children.

Teacher-Child Relationships

Growth and extension of a child's listening horizons depends on two primary factors. First, it depends on the individual youngster's ability to express honestly, frankly, and freely his own reactions to the music he hears. Secondly, it depends on the ability of the child to listen just as openly, frankly, and freely to the feelings others have about the music heard. Neither of these is attainable unless you as the teacher have been able to establish a particular kind of working relationship with your children.

Children tend to tell us what they think we want to hear rather than what they really think, unless they realize that as adults we honestly want them to tell us their true feelings. It is not easy to help children recognize that when we ask for their opinions, we really want to hear their thoughts on a subject and not merely a reflection of what they consider our opinions to be. The development of such an attitude, however, is a goal of all good teachers, encompassing far more than just the music program.

Children inhibited because of an unfortunate previous experience in school or home in which their responses were well controlled by parental or teacher expectations cannot be easily freed. This inhibition can, of course, destroy the growth of the individual child's feelings of personal worth and dignity. In such cases it takes time and real effort on your part to earn the respect of the children so they realize that you actually do want them to express their honest judgments, not merely limit their responses to what they think you want them to say. It may take several months; four to six months would not be an unreasonable time to take to reach this happy goal.

It is extremely difficult for children to respect the judgments and opinions of others unless they feel that their own opinions and judgments are respected. The child's feelings about his own opinions will influence his readiness to give the other person's opinions a hearing. When we use hearing in this sense, however, we do not merely mean a respectful audience. We do not mean to imply that listening to the other fellow's viewpoint merely involves quiet and a fair chance for the other person to express his viewpoint. Certainly, this is involved. More than that, however, what is involved is giving the other fellow's ideas a chance to influence our own judgments.

In adult discussions we frequently use the period of time

while the other fellow expresses his opinion to think up our answers to him. We are polite enough. We listen to him with an open ear, but with a closed mind. We listen only to see the loopholes in his argument. We listen in order to give our own thinking an opportunity to mold what he says into our own frame of reference so that we can control, answer, or modify the other person's judgment.

What we need for true discussion, however, goes far beyond this. An important attribute of respecting the opinions of others is a readiness to accept those opinions for ourselves when we can be convinced of their rightness. The other person's ideas are not always better than our own, nor must the other person's opinions necessarily supplant our own. What we refer to is a readiness to be reasonable in the sense of letting reason dominate; a readiness to listen to other opinions with a readiness to accept and not reject them just because they are not our own. In brief, we hold ourselves convincible.

The various ways of developing this kind of teacher-child relationship in the classroom generally go beyond the scope of this book. However, in terms of the responses to music to which we listen, we will have some specific suggestions later in this chapter. For now, we want to emphasize that the teacher must really want children to respond as they actually feel when he asks for their opinions about a particular musical composition. Unless he feels this way himself, he will not be able to convince children to speak honestly, frankly, and freely of their inner convictions.

A DEVELOPMENTAL APPROACH TO LISTENING

Consistent with the previous discussions in this chapter, we shall suggest a procedure for helping children develop an active way of listening to music. This approach is based simply upon letting the music speak for itself directly to children without any intermediaries, with subsequent open, free, and frank discussion of the children's reactions to that music. It takes advantage of the sharing potential of the variety of ways in which different children in any group will normally react to any given composition.

The Cyclic Procedure

The procedure may be termed a cyclical approach. The steps in each cycle are simple to enumerate: one, an introduction by the teacher; two, playing the record; three, discussion. At later sessions other cycles follow with repetition of these three steps. Each cycle, however, will be on a higher level than the previous ones because of the experience through which the children have lived.

Four questions generally typify the increasing level of the cycles, even though answers to more than one question may be attained within any one cycle. The questions about the music are:

1. Did you like it?
2. Can you tell why?
3. What did you hear while you listened?
4. Can you hear what others heard?

You may disregard the cyclic pattern and apply the four questions in other patterns.

Cycle One

The cycles described present a generalized procedure and are not meant to be followed literally. We cannot determine in advance just what the limits of any individual cycle will be without knowing the particular age of the children involved, the backgrounds of the children, and the whole gamut of factors that go toward making up the group personality of a class. In your situation you may find that the discussion part of any one cycle includes material from the discussion part of succeeding cycles described here. The specific application of the cyclic procedure varies from situation to situation. Consequently, interpret the descriptions of the steps in the particular cycles only as one possible application.

STEP ONE: INTRODUCING THE RECORD. In introducing a new record to children, use words of a very innocuous nature. Try

not to influence their listening in any way. Use words something like: "I have a new record for you today. See if you like
it." Avoid any attempts to direct the children's reaction to the
music. Furthermore, avoid using terminology or giving information which might limit the way in which they listen to the
music. Specifically, do not give the title of the composition or
the story of the music. The children would try to hear the story
of the composition, and we have previously discussed the
limiting nature of that procedure. Also avoid giving the composer's name, since the status value which might adhere could
also serve to limit the children's reactions to the music.

In the introduction make no attempt to prepare the children
specifically for the composition or the record itself. The only
specific directions you might consider giving would be the
following: "When the record finishes, see if you can tell us
whether or not you liked it." This is enough direction for a
first hearing of any new composition. We are after the overt
reaction of the children expressed openly. Let the music speak
for itself, and avoid handicapping the children's free listening
by channeling it in specific directions.

STEP TWO: PLAYING THE RECORD. Wait before actually putting
the needle onto the record until you have silence in the room.
The children, over a period of time, need to learn that during
this type of listening session, they do nothing that might distract from the listening of another person in the room. They
do not move around; they do not talk; they do not shuffle books;
they do not tear paper. Although they do not have to listen,
they do nothing that would spoil the listening of someone else.
This atmosphere, though not difficult to achieve with a group
of children, must be worked for. If the children are too young
to maintain at least the silence that does not distract others,
they are not ready for this type of listening session. Do not
force and do not discipline. Wait for the readiness that will
come with more maturity.

The way the teacher listens to the record will influence the
way the children listen to the record. You will not, of course,
use the listening time to catch up on clerical work, or to fix

the bulletin board, or to do any one of the thousands of tasks with which teachers are overburdened. Teachers listen as carefully and as attentively to the music as they would like their children to.

When you have silence, start the record and adjust the volume properly. More errors are made in playing music too softly than too loudly. Try to arrive at a good balance. Then sit quietly and listen with your children.

You may have misjudged the length of time that your children can listen to a particular composition if it is a new one. If after about five minutes you notice many of the children becoming quite restless, listen for a place where you can lift the needle and stop the record. Consider that portion of the music enough for that session.

STEP THREE: THE DISCUSSION. When you have ended the playing of the record, start the discussion with a simple question. "How many of you liked it?" is as good as any. Look around and observe the number of hands which have been raised. Follow with another question: "How many of you did not like it?" Look around again with no change of expression to observe the hands which go up. Whether the children like or dislike the composition is immaterial to you. You are mainly concerned that they react to it. If a sizable group of your children did not respond to the first two, you may feel a third question to be in order. "How many of you cannot tell yet whether or not you like it? Some people want to hear a composition more than once before they decide."

The second major approach during the discussion period is to bring out the reasons for liking or disliking the composition. This can be sparked by another question from you, such as: "Who can tell us *why* he liked it or why he did not like it?" There is no way to predict the reaction that you may get to this question for any particular composition. The responses will depend primarily on the particular group of children that you have, the composition that you played, and the interaction that takes place between the music and the children.

Various children may say, "It seemed like happy music." "It

made me feel like dancing." "It made me think of something I did last week." "I heard music like that in a movie I saw."

You may get reactions like, "I don't like this kind of stuff. I like jazz or rock and roll."

Accept the children's honest responses willingly. There may be some children who will try to "get your goat." Do not let them upset you by any of their reactions. Your objective is to convince the children that the way they really feel about the music is the way you want them to respond to your question. Obviously silly or "wise-guy" responses can be eliminated and dealt with as you would deal with them in any circumstances. Do not confuse an honest negative reaction to the music with a "wise-guy" reaction. You know your children and will be able to distinguish among them.

The initial responses of children that they like the composition or do not like it and a beginning exploration of why they feel as they do might well terminate the first cycle.

Cycle Two

When you are ready for a second session and playing of the composition, probably on a different day, you might introduce it by saying something like: "We heard some music yesterday. I'm going to play it again for you. Some of you liked it and some of you did not like it. This time when I play it, see whether or not you feel the same way about it. After the record we'll talk more about why you liked it or why you did not like it." This type of comment serves as an adequate introduction to the second playing. You have still not given the title, the composer, or the story of the music. Avoid these three things until you have encouraged all the children who listen programmatically to develop their own programs or stories.

The time at which you will introduce the title of the composition, the name of the composer, and the story of the music, if there is one, will vary with the group. The precise moment cannot be analyzed in advance. The proper time is the point at which you feel that the children react freely, when they have come to realize that their stories are legitimate reactions to the music and that they may respond with their own stories just as much as to the given story of the music. After the class has reached that point, taking also into account those children who, not listening programmatically, must feel comfortable in not hearing any stories in the music, it is safe for you to tell them the story of the music when it has one.

Step two is similar to the corresponding step of the preceding cycle. Wait until you have the children's complete attention before playing the record. If necessary, you might comment that although you do not care if they do not listen to the music, the children must be careful not to disturb the listening of other children. Then play the record again.

During step three of the second cycle pick up the discussion wherever you left off during the first cycle. During this discussion period some children may respond with a story they heard in the music, a story they made up as the music played. You react to this with as much encouragement as you would to any creative effort on the children's part during any other kind of discussion: with interest, with encouragement, and with a kind of nodding agreement that this is a possible story that could be heard in the music. Ordinarily, when the first story is given, you might react in some fashion such as this: "Yes, that is a very interesting and possible story. There are many stories which different people hear in this music. Did anyone hear a different story?" You help the children who did not hear this particular story feel that it is perfectly all right for them not to have heard that story. In case some of them heard different stories encourage them to relate the stories that they heard. You will get a wide variety of stories about the same composition.

After you have listened to a story or two in this discussion period, you might introduce some words of encouragement for the children who do not hear any particular story in the music. Avoid leaving any children with the impression that they must hear some story in the music.

Cycle Three

During the introduction of the third cycle you might ask a more specific question: "After we play the record, see if you can tell us how you listened. What did you hear while the music played?" You may get more stories from the children describing what they heard in the music. Some children may describe different scenes or pictures that are not connected in any story. Continue to accept all reactions that the children have as perfectly legitimate reactions. Be sure to include the reactions of children who do not hear particular stories in the music. To spark this part of the discussion, you might ask a question like: "Some people do not hear particular stories in music. Could any of you who did not hear a story tell us what you heard while you listened? Or tell us what you liked or didn't like in the music."

You may get responses such as: "I like the sound of the different instruments." "I like the melody; I wanted to sing it." "I liked the way the melody was played first by one instrument and then by another one." There is no limit to the types of responses which you may get. The section of this chapter on "Ways of Listening" describes some typical responses. You may find, however, that your children may react in ways not included in that section. Your basic purpose is to elicit children's free, frank, and open discussion of the music.

Succeeding Cycles

During succeeding cycles you will have two objectives. One of them will be to continue to encourage all the children to react freely to the music as they feel it. Maintain an atmosphere of freedom in which children feel they can change their minds about the composition. Those who liked it may come to dislike it, or those who disliked it may come to like it with the familiarity that comes from repeated hearings.

An additional objective will be to share various ways of listening of different children. You might pick the reaction of one particular child and play the music with this kind of an introduction: "Let's see if we can hear what Joan heard in the music." Then play the record and get the children's reactions. Try this for several different cycles, utilizing various stories the children tell and various reactions of children who do not hear stories in the music. You will thereby broaden the listening horizons of all the children to include the ways of listening of the others.

We cannot specify the number of cycles which may be applied to any particular composition. We do not recommend the continual playing of one composition only until it is exhausted. You might go through several cycles with one composition, then turn to another composition and even a third before returning to the first or second. Use your own sense of discrimination and your own judgment concerning your children to decide when to go on to other compositions and when to return to previously played ones.

You recognize, of course, that there is no way to specify the limits of any one cycle. The cyclic approach is a general one which you can apply in your own situation. While part of the stimulus, scope, and depth of development within the total number of cycles may depend in part on your own background in music, one of the major points to be emphasized in this instance, as it has been emphasized throughout the book, is that the teacher completely untrained in music can carry this kind of active approach to listening quite far with children without getting in over his depth on technical elements.

If your own background has included some specific knowledge of form in music, you may want to encourage the reactions of children along those lines, at least to the extent of your own knowledge. It is true, however, that many children hear elements of form in music without specific teaching when they hear the return of a melody that was presented earlier in the composition.

You may also have reached the point in your own development where you recognize the sounds of various instruments and will want to encourage the further identification of those instruments by your children. Some of the children in your

class may have more skill in this kind of identification than
your training has brought you. In such cases tap their knowledge so that what they know can spread throughout the entire
group.

Be ready and willing to learn with your children. They will
learn from each other and from you. You will in turn learn
much from them. An experimental and questioning frame of
mind will be an invaluable aid to you. If you have resources in
your parent group or in the community, be sure to tap those
resources. A visit from an instrumentalist who can demonstrate an instrument and answer the children's questions about
it can be an exciting and very meaningful experience both to
your children and to you. Explore such possibilities carefully.

A visiting string quartet plays close to children.

Clover Drive School, Great Neck, New York. Photo by Harriet Arnold.
Courtesy of Perkins & Will, Architects.

KEEP IN MIND

The following items summarize the major content of this chapter. Individual items may be used for debate, discussion, report, or research topics.

1. Only as an active process does listening provide an important contribution to individual growth and development.
2. What a composition means can only be what it means to human beings, as individuals, regardless of their previous musical training.
3. "Good" and "not good" referring to music can mean only music that is liked or not liked by individuals.
4. Since music takes place in time, we hear only a single tone or tonal cluster at any one instant. Memory of what has gone before and what will come next requires some familiarity with the music.
5. Introduction of new elements in music has continually been attacked by some contemporary critics and musicians throughout the history of music.
6. Program music is music which attempts to depict a story in musical terms.
7. Abstract music has no definite story to tell.
8. Even with music written to tell a story, many possible stories are just as legitimate as the one the composer had in mind.
9. Some people listen to music storywise and others do not. Listening is an individual matter, and all ways of listening may be proper for various individuals.
10. Despite the contentions of some musicians, there is no innately superior mode of listening. Different ways of listening are purely matters of individual differences among people.
11. Music is organized sound.
12. We hear music with our whole beings, including our ears, our minds, our bodies, our experiences, our feelings, our emotions, and our intelligence.

13. The process of organizing sound is an activity. Composers organize sounds and so do listeners.

14. Selective hearing is the mechanism by which we listen only to the particular sounds that we want to hear.

15. The organization of sounds into music depends on the experiences of the listener for differentiation.

16. In schools the listening program encompasses all the musical activities which we undertake.

17. The music used in school programs should not be limited to "children's" music. The great music of all eras may be entirely suitable.

18. Extending a child's listening horizons depends on the individual child's ability to express openly his own reactions and his ability to learn from the reactions of others.

19. For free, frank, and open discussion, children need to have confidence that we as teachers want their true reactions and not a reflection of our opinions.

20. The developmental approach to listening consists of a series of cycles, each one of which contains an introduction by the teacher, a playing of the music itself, and subsequent discussion by the children.

21. In the initial cycle following the introduction of a composition new to the children, the major objectives are to have the children determine whether or not they like the composition and to begin to elicit reasons why they liked it or not.

22. In the second cycle we continue to determine the "whys" and discuss some of the stories individual children heard in the music.

23. The third cycle develops more deeply what it was the children heard while the music was playing, both programmatically and abstractly.

24. Subsequent cycles consist of sharing ways of listening and further exploration of individual reactions in greater depth.

CHAPTER EIGHT

Creative Music

CREATIVE MUSIC cannot be limited merely to a specific type of activity. It must be recognized rather as the underlying philosophical foundation for the whole of our music program. Creative music is not only a way of helping children construct songs and melodies. The growth and development of creativeness, part of the natural inheritance of every individual, is the primary reason for the existence of the music program and for the particular approach used in our schools to help children understand and thereby love music.

WHAT IS CREATIVE?

Every human being is born with a potential for creating. As an individual human personality he has within him the power to create new things or ideas. Individual humans vary very widely in their skills, their accomplishments, their understandings, their abilities, their achievements. In every facet of human accomplishment and endeavor it is natural to expect individual differences and variation. Correspondingly, we expect individual differences in creative powers. To expect and con-

227

cede differences in innate creative capacities does not mean, however, that powers of creativeness might be limited to only those comparatively few people able to produce great creative works.

Certainly, to write a symphony is a tremendous creative act. To concoct a new sauce or dish, however, is also a creative act. To design a dress, to write a book, to furnish a home, to write a play, to mold a piece of clay, to choreograph a ballet, to carve a piece of wood, to raise a child, to plan and cultivate a garden are all creative acts. All of these acts, as varied as they may apparently seem, have certain aspects in common. In each case we find an act of personal expression in which already existing elements have been combined in forms which were new to the individual ordering them. Creation does not imply developing something new and original starting from nothing at all. The elements, the building blocks, used in the creative act are inevitably present in the culture, the environment, the experience of the individual creator. These elements are utilized by the individual creator for an expressive purpose of his own. When an individual reorders, reconstructs, reorganizes these existing elements into patterns new and satisfying to himself as expresser, as the individual creator, we have a creative act.

The scientist in this sense may also be a creator. He does not work with brand-new elements. He builds on the foundations of the discoveries of other scientists. In his search for the new, he may reorganize already existing and known kernels of knowledge, information, and fact into a new pattern established by his own intelligent guesses, which he calls hypotheses. When he is satisfied with the pattern of organization he established, which he calls testing his hypothesis, we say that he has discovered a scientific fact. In actuality the scientific fact which he has discovered is the outcome of a creative act: the reordering of known elements into new and satisfying patterns.

The artist works in a similar fashion, although the nature of his medium and the objective of his search differ. The artist, too, uses already existing elements and reorders, reconstructs, reorganizes those elements into new and satisfying patterns. His search, although not for new scientific fact, is for the proper expression of his own idea just as much as the scientist searches for a proper mode of expression of his own idea. The artist's objective is an expressive one. He expresses his own emotional feeling, his own insights, resulting from his own experiences when he creates a work of art.

The writer of a novel uses those commonly existing elements —words—in order to make his personal expression in his effort to communicate his feelings with others.

In each of these cases we find a reordering, a reconstructing, a reorganizing of known elements by a person bent on self-expression, in order to communicate perhaps, or in order to satisfy his own personal need, or simply because he must. It is merely a difference in degree, not in kind, when a housewife creates a new sauce for a meal. She utilizes known elements; the condiments are there. It is her selection of them, her choice from among them which determines the outcome. She reorganizes, reconstructs, reorders these condiments in patterns she selects. A person designing a dress, whether it be a professional designer or a mother creating a garment for her child, utilizes materials already existing, selects from among them, and orders them, sews them, puts them together in a way which expresses her intent. These, too, may be creative acts. The choice from among materials and the expression of personal wish, desire, purpose, emotion determine the specific mode of ordering, constructing, organizing those materials.

Accessible to all human beings, the creative act is not limited to the great artist, the great composer, the great writer. Since each human personality has within him the ability to utilize elements already existing in his environment, choose from among them, organize them as he sees fit for purposes of his own, this power is present as a natural birthright in all human beings.

You may ask then, why do not more people utilize this power? We may answer in two ways. First, more people utilize their creativeness than recognize that they use it. Secondly, this

is a capacity comparatively easily hemmed in or blocked off
from use. That so many people are creative despite the tremendous blocks placed in the way of free, creative, personal
expression is a tribute to the tremendous power of the creative
act as a necessity of human growth.

Interpretation as Creation

The interpreter, whether one who reads a selection to others
or plays an instrument or acts upon the stage, must be considered essentially as a creator. He, too, takes known elements
and reorganizes, reorders, reconstructs those known elements
into new and satisfying patterns. But, you ask, how can that be?
Does not the pianist playing a Beethoven sonata read the score?
Is not the music the same for all who play it? Did not Beethoven express his intention on paper for all who read it to
play the same way? Of course, Beethoven has. His intentions
are there. But our musical notation system for all its exactitude
and precision about what notes to play is still very imprecise
musically. In matters of dynamics, feeling, flow of the musical
line, shaping of the musical phrase, and the small differences
in loudness and softness which we call nuance, much is implied
rather than stated on the music page. A purely straightforward
rendition of the actual notes on the printed page would surely
be a most unmusical performance. The shaping of the phrase,
the dynamic range and perspective, the nuance mentioned
above, the various contrasts and balances, the feeling for the
whole—all are determined by the individual instrumentalist.
There are variations in the interpretations of the same work
by individual pianists. These interpretations may very well
fall within certain broad limits of style determined by the era
during which Beethoven wrote and the over-all feeling for his
music which might be common to many, many different inter-
preters. Nevertheless, the personal interpretation of different
musicians of the same composition varies considerably.

In each of the individual interpretations we find a creative
act: the interpreter has created toward the intent of the composer. He has taken those notes, the material as it was written

on paper, and reordered, reconstructed, reorganized it to make his own personal act of expression. In so doing he does not do violence to the intent of the composer; he fulfills that intent.[1]

Listening as Creation

The listener, too, creates toward the intent of the composer. It is fruitless to expect music to convey specific meaning and content. If specific words could adequately express the meaning of music, then music would cease to exist as a separate art form.[2] The very reason for the continued popularity of music is its ability to evoke emotions and create feelings in us which words cannot emulate. The listener, therefore, should not be expected to get the precise meaning intended by a composer from any composition. Indeed, the composer never intended the listener to get any such single precise interpretation. As the listener utilizes the music of the composer, reconstructs, reorders, reorganizes it in the framework of his own experiential background in living, he is engaged in the creative process itself.

THE ROLE OF THE IMAGINATION

Essential to any creative act is the presence of imagination, the power of fantasy, the world of make-believe. The development of imagination and creativeness in our schools depends on far more than just the music program, but the nature of the art of music and, therefore, the music program in our schools will determine in part the full development of the imaginative powers of children.

The Real and the Unreal

Young children face among their many problems of development the problem of actual differentiation between what is

[1] See Aaron Copland, *Music and Imagination*, "The Creative Mind and the Interpretative Mind," Harvard University Press, Cambridge, Mass., 1952, Chap. 3, pp. 40–57.

[2] See John Dewey, *Art as Experience*, Minton, Balch & Co., New York, 1934, p. 74.

real in our lives and what is not real. The young child frequently asks, "Is it real?" The world in which we live is a very
astonishing place in many respects. Those of us who have
grown up with many of the changes which have taken place
rarely stop to think of the vast differences between this contemporary world and the world of as recent a time as a hundred years ago.

Within the lifetime of even the youngest reader of this book,
we have seen changes taking place in the ordinary lives of
people which in the not-too-far-distant past would have been
thought of as miraculous. Some of these changes have made it
even more difficult to draw the line between what is real and
what is unreal for our children. Not many generations ago it
would have been easy to say to a young child, "That's impossible. It cannot be." In the present stage of society's development it is not so easy. Many of the things impossible when we
were youngsters are now in existence. Think how confusing an
understanding of television really is to a child. Think how many
children in the earlier days of radio had difficulty understanding how voices were snatched out of the air. Some adults still
remember secretly thinking when they were youngsters that
the voices from the radio were really of little people "inside the
box." We can speculate about the number of our children who
perhaps think that there are little people within our television
sets.

Not many years ago the lifetime of most people was spent
within a comparatively small geographical radius from the
place in which they were born. Such a situation still exists in
many areas of the world. In our country, however, the mobility
of vast numbers of the population has become very apparent,
particularly since World War II. Our children are used to the
sensation of movement. Automobiles have become almost
second nature to them. Things such as automobiles, jet planes,
rocket ships, high-speed elevators, television, plastics, mechanical refrigeration, to mention just a few of the modern "mir-
acles" which we take so much for granted, are all of them of
such a nature as to heighten the confusion of the young child
in his efforts to grasp what is real and what is unreal.

The child watching a television program can very easily assume that he sees something that is really happening, that he has a ringside seat. The element of presence is one of the major factors in the fascination of both moving pictures and television. It is sometimes difficult to convince young children that in a television program people are merely playing different parts of a story, that it is all make-believe.

Children, in their dramatic play, frequently enact their confusion between what is real and what is unreal. Every teacher of young children has undoubtedly had an experience of the kind in which, while she was reading a story to a class, some child would ask plaintively, "Did it really happen?" or "Is it real?"

As adults we conceive it as our task to help young children make the differentiation between what is real and what is unreal. In making the differentiation we should not attempt to eliminate all consideration of the unreal from the life of the child. Our objective is not to make him a hard-headed realist. Indeed, this could be disastrous to our purposes of developing creativeness. What is necessary is the establishment of a clear understanding of and differentiation between actual and imaginary worlds.

The child who makes up imaginative stories for one reason or another may be confused in differentiating between what is real and unreal. The show-and-tell period that many teachers use as a teaching tool has many real values. That it also may have some dangers is exemplified by the case of a little girl who was rarely taken any place by anyone in her family. She came to school one day and shared the experience she had had the previous day on a trip to an amusement park, describing in vivid detail the marvelous time she had had. She described it in such detail that the teacher became quite suspicious. It turned out that the trip had never really taken place.

Circular Recognition of the Unreal

Was this child lying? Should she have been reprimanded? Certainly not. The problem for this youngster is far more important than the labeling of the incident. A reprimand could easily have worsened the difficulty. Psychologically, one of the problems to determine in a case of this kind is whether the child knew that the trip had not taken place or whether she had convinced herself that it really did.

An overemphasis on sticking strictly to the real can do much to hamper the development of the imagination, and we recommend that children never be pushed to eliminate consideration of the unreal from their lives. What is imperative, however, is a kind of circular recognition of the state of the unreal. A child needs to know that the supposed happening is unreal; he needs to know that *you* know that it is unreal; and he needs to know that *you* know that *he* knows that it is unreal. Under those circumstances, with circular recognition of the actuality of the situation, the full development of imaginative living and make-believe can be encouraged safely. This imaginative play with the unreal should continue, since the development of such make-believe is part of the development of imagination. It must have no loaded function, however; its psychological charge should be neutral through the circular recognition of the true state of the unreal. The use of the unreal in this way, leading to the development of creativeness, is quite different from a departure from reality which might reflect personality disorder.

We need, then, to help children develop their ability to differentiate between what is real and what is unreal. Rather than stamp out their utilization of the unreal, we must help them develop the circular recognition of the unreal so that it can be used as an expressive tool rather than an emotional necessity.

This kind of imaginative thinking can enforce and reinforce the creative approach to the music program and also can be reinforced by the creative approach of the music program.

CREATIVENESS IN SINGING

Three essentials have been suggested as descriptive of the act of creation: it is (1) an act of personal expression, (2) in which the individual in terms of his own previous experiences reorders, reconstructs, or reorganizes known elements, (3) resulting in patterns new and satisfying to him.

These essentials in the act of creation apply generally to the creation of music, but also apply specifically to the various facets of the music program which have been described in previous chapters. We now reexamine some of the suggestions made previously for their specific relation to creativeness, and also make some further suggestions for specific creative possibilities.

In order for a singing program to be creative, the three essentials must be present. Singing is certainly one of the most naturally expressive musical acts, involving as it does the human body as the instrument for making music. However, expressing implies an act of will on the part of the expresser. The attitude and feeling tone in the classroom must be such as to encourage children to want to make a personal act of expression in singing. If children do not want to sing, if the element of pleasure and enjoyment are absent from the singing program, there can be no real personal act of expression by them.

Ordinarily, expression must be of something. Musically speaking, such expressions have an emotional basis. The enjoyment of singing itself is also reflected in the expression of the emotion conveyed by the song itself. If the children do not feel the expressive nature of the song, they can have no part in expressing any feelings conveyed by it. Consequently, the initial impetus toward creativeness in singing is the attitude that the children have about singing in general, and specifically their attitude about singing a particular song. In Chapter 3 we have gone into much detail about ways of creating this attitude on the part of the children.

Since the creative act involves reordering, reconstructing, or reorganizing known elements, how may singing reflect a creative act? In singing, the known elements consist of the actual tones which together make the melody of the song itself. In spontaneous singing, children order the succession of tones which make the song. In the singing of songs of others, the element of reorganizing or reconstructing has to do with the order of tones determined by the composer of the song. In this instance the child in his singing fulfills the creative act as interpreter. The building of critical listening and the development of children's own standards for singing as they feel these standards emerging determine the degree of actual creativeness that may be involved. When adult standards are imposed upon children, the element of creativeness is eliminated. Consequently, it is through the development of children's own standards about their own singing and the encouragement of the sharing of those standards among the different children in the group that we help them develop singing as a creative activity.

The uniqueness or new and satisfying pattern which is the outcome of the creative act occurs as the song becomes the child's song, no matter who composed it. Every piece of music is recreated by the interpreter of that music as he creates toward the intent of the composer. As the child enjoys singing, applies his own standards of singing to the development of a song, thereby making it his own, and comes to feel that the song is a new and satisfying experience for him, he fulfills the three characteristics of the creative act.

In this way singing in the classroom helps to encourage the development of basic creativeness on the part of children.

The selection of a song because the teacher feels that the

Figure 19. TOWARD CREATIVENESS IN SINGING

	AIDS	HINDRANCES
Children's attitudes	Joyous participation involving the personal act of expressing.	Selection of songs without regard to whether or not children like them.
Standards	Development and application of children's standards about singing.	Imposition of adult standards about singing.
Caliber of participation	The song becomes the child's own and its interpretation a unique experience.	The song reflects the feelings of the adult. The child is not a vibrant participant, merely a vocal instrument manipulated by teacher.

children *should* enjoy it can in itself not be an intimate part of the creative act, unless in so doing he has not negated consideration of the actuality of children's own enjoyment of the song. Children do not reject a song that teachers suggest necessarily, but if they do reject it, drop that song and search for others that more nearly reach the children.

CREATING SONGS

The usual pattern suggested for helping children compose a melody or song leaves much to be desired in terms of actual creativeness. The pattern often recommended can in itself be a limiting rather than a broadening experience. Consequently, it is not surprising that the results achieved from these procedures fall into predictable patterns.

The Usual Procedure and Its Weakness

Ordinarily, the suggested routine recommends the selection of a suitable poem first. This poem is to be read rhythmically by the class, which is encouraged to emphasize and exaggerate the regularity of the scanning. The children chant the poem in unison, emphasizing the strong beats. Then, line by line, the children make up a melody for the poem. After they have chanted the entire poem several times, with the unpoetic and unmusical rhythmic emphasis, the children read the first line again. Then one child suggests a melody for the first line. Several other children may also suggest melodies for this line, and the class selects from among them. Then the entire group sings the melody selected for the first line and chants the words of the second line of the poem. Various children suggest melodies for the second line, and the class again chooses from among them. The entire group sings the two lines, the class chants the third, the children suggest possible melodies, and the choice is made. This procedure is followed until the entire poem is set to music.

We do not object to all of this procedure. The major difficulty and limiting factor comes in the very unmusical and, indeed, unpoetic rhythmic chanting of the poem. No poem is intended to be read aloud with emphasis on the strong beats or stresses in this artificial manner. The entire flow of the words and the feeling for the poem are ruined by this kind of false emphasis. The musical outcome of this kind of false emphasis is predictable in the sense that the music itself will reflect not the rhythmic flow of the words as the poet intended, but rather the exaggerated rhythmic flow of the words distorted by the scanning emphasis.

Melody consists of a variation both in tones and in the rhythmic sequence of the statement of those tones. The described procedure, unfortunately, seriously limits the possibilities for rhythmic variance and permits mainly only tonal variance. The result is a conforming type of dittylike melody which ordinarily reflects not the meaning of the words or the feeling of the poem, but the tyranny of the regular metrical unit. This is more akin to the regularity of metrical units dating to a previous era in the history of music and not a reflection of our own times.

Recommended Procedure

It would be far better, after the choice of a poem has been made, preferably by the children, to emphasize some of the various possible ways in which the poem might be read that best bring out its meaning and to help children recognize that the rhythmic flow has variation, that it does not demand an inflexible mold. Emphasize the expressive quality of the poem and have children read it in various ways. After discussion of the meaning content of the poem, after exploration of the various possibilities in the rhythmic statement of it, ask everyone to be quiet and suggest that the children sing melodies in their minds, without making a sound, that would be suitable for the poem. Wait, then, until a few children indicate to you that they have something to suggest and listen to them one by one.

The process of selecting one setting from among the various possibilities by group choice is satisfactory. It is quite possible, however, that more than one musical setting will be of interest. It is not necessary to select only one musical setting for any one poem. Poetry, just as music, conveys different feelings to different people. Consequently, there is no one specific musical setting that is most suitable for any one poem. There may be several and it would probably be wise for you to encourage variation in the settings.

Do not limit the procedure to a line-by-line approach only. Some children, conceiving a short poem in its entirety, may be able to sing an appropriate melody from beginning to end; some will do that better than they would be able to conceive of a melody chopped up into separate lines. Other children, however, will do better on the line-by-line approach. We recommend that you keep the possibilities open for either or both procedures.

Singing Mentally

In the procedure just described the recommendation was made that you have the children sing mentally, without making a sound. This requires, perhaps, some further exploration. The attribute of being able to sing mentally is not limited to trained musicians and composers. Everyone has the capacity for so doing. Mental singing differs from singing aloud—no actual aural phenomenon takes place. We can think a melody in our minds and think it just as specifically mentally as when we sing it aloud. Children learn to do this very readily. If you feel the necessity for explaining what you mean by mental singing to your children, it is very easy to do.

Pick some melody that they know very well. It might be some simple song, such as "Hot Cross Buns," "Yankee Doodle," or "Sweetly Sings the Donkey." Sing the song through with the class and then merely say to them something like, "Let's sing it again, but this time sing it only in your mind. We won't make a sound." Start the group with the same kind of cue that you use when they actually sing aloud. Watch their eyes as you use the same kind of simple conducting movements that you ordinarily use. Sing the song in your own mind as you conduct. At the end of the mental singing of that song, ask the children if they were able to hear it in their minds. You will find that they could.

Creating Songs and Words

We have described a process for creating songs using the poems of others and started with this procedure because it is one commonly recommended. However, it is frequently more desirable to develop songs with children from words of their own. The most commonly accepted procedure is to create a poem first. This might be a group or an individual project.

The development of creative writing is beyond the scope of this book. Be sure, however, as you develop any poems with your children that you differentiate between the writing of poetry and versification. Do not demand that all poems created by your children rhyme. Many will, because children enjoy rhyming. But all children do not rhyme, and all poetry does not necessarily rhyme. Therefore, try to have both types of poems created by your children, those which rhyme and those which do not.

After the group or the individual composes the poetry and you have the poem, the procedure is much the same as the one we have previously described in setting poems written by others to music.

Both words and music may be created simultaneously. While usually presumed to be somewhat more difficult, it is quite possible for children to do this. If the recommendations in Chapter 3 on singing have been followed, your children will have been encouraged to sing spontaneously. This will be an activity in your room that will continue informally and frequently. The spontaneous singing recommended is in actuality the creation of songs or snatches of song or song elements at the spur of the moment. Ordinarily, words and music are created simultaneously in the spontaneous song.

The impetus for spontaneous song, however, is ordinarily not preplanned. It comes, just as its label implies, spontaneously. Any incident may spark its development. It might be activity on the playground or classroom; it might be an impression of a particular event, the expression of a specific emotion about something that happened. Cherish these developments and encourage them. If you are able to help your children share their spontaneous songs with each other, you are helping the development of creativeness. Furthermore, you help the children develop facility in composing. The objective of creative singing is, of course, not the development of composers; it is the development of the creative powers in all children and the encouragement of the expressive-creative act.

There is an element of skill involved in creating music in that the more creating of songs that is done, the easier the very act itself becomes. Try to develop patterns in which children share their spontaneous songs with each other. Children learn to remember their spontaneous songs. Do not insist, however, on the sharing of spontaneous songs for fear of creating a restrictive aura about the activity. If children feel that they will always be asked to sing their own spontaneous songs for others, you may unwittingly limit their spontaneity as well as their desire to sing spontaneously. Some children, however, love to share experiences of this kind, and nothing would stop them from continuing with their spontaneous singing.

From time to time as you hear a particularly appropriate spontaneous song sung by one of your children, you might join her in singing it, or ask the child to repeat it to you. Try to sing it several times with the child to develop ease of remembrance. In much of spontaneous singing the child when asked to repeat the song will not repeat it the same way a second time. The difference between the spontaneous song and the composed song is the element of planning. A child may not be able to sing his spontaneous song a second time, because he does not remember it or because he has not planned it. A composer gets his inspiration from many places, and sometimes he improvises in order to spark his own creative feelings. He needs to remember the improvisation that he wants to develop, however, if it is to be of further value to him. The spontaneous singing of children falls into a category similar to the improvisation of the composer. Some of his improvisation he would want to remember, modify, improve, and utilize in his compositions. Similarly, with the spontaneous singing of children, much of it should be encouraged as the sparkle of the moment, to be sung, loved, enjoyed, and perhaps forgotten. Some of it, however, should be capitalized upon, made more specific, and held onto by repetition. If you ask a child to sing his spontaneous song again for you and his response is "I don't remember it," it would be wise to drop it and not insist. If you remember any part of it, you might sing that part of it with him, which might help him remember the rest of it. If it does not, there is no way you can recapture that spontaneous song itself.

It is also possible to use the spontaneous singing of a child which he remembers as the spark for the development of a song created by the group. It might be the start of a song. After the child sings it to the group, someone might well have an idea for continuing it. The song, therefore, could develop from the initial impetus given by the spontaneous singing of an individual child. Ordinarily, in such instances words and music will be composed simultaneously.

The Continuous Melodic Story

We have previously described the continuous melodic story, analogous to the continuous story using words. This continuous story is a melodic progression, however, and not a verbal one: the creation of melody without words. The use of a tape recorder to capture a continuous melodic story may also be a means of creating songs. Ordinarily, the continuous melodic line is a spontaneous effort, each person's contribution being sparked by those which have gone before. As such it is spontaneous creation or improvisation. After recording one or more of these, listen to them again and then modify them or retain them as the children feel their fitness. It is possible, then, to add words if desired by the children.

The development of words for a melody which has already been created is not a difficult task. Have the children sing the melody several times and ask them for suggestions for suitable words. The line of the melody and its rhythm will inevitably suggest some suitable words to the children. Once those words are started, the creative stimulus will flow among all the children.

CREATIVENESS IN BODILY MOVEMENT

Chapter 4 describes the program of rhythmic bodily motion and includes a discussion of the three various types of rhythmic activity possible in the classroom: formal rhythms, informal rhythms, and creative rhythms.

While both formal and informal rhythms have certain values which are discussed in that chapter, the most fruitful of the rhythmic activities as aids to the growth and development of children are the creative rhythmic activities. The expression of feeling is possible in each of the three types of movement, but the most expressive potentiality is through the creative rhythms. Formal rhythms are bound by the stereotype created by the teacher in her request for specific movements. Informal rhythms are bound by the type, stereotype, or verbal context of the composition. In creative rhythms children's expression becomes free bodily movement that reaches the highest level of expression of emotion through motion.

In the type of creative bodily movement based on music heard without label or context, the child becomes a combination of interpreter and original creator. He is interpreter in the sense that the music heard is interpreted through his body motion. He organizes, constructs, and orders the body movement appropriate to the music he hears without external limiting factors. In the type of creative rhythms based on children's feelings, with improvised accompaniment, the generalized expressive bodily motion is that felt by the child with no external stimulus. In this sense he is involved in original creation. In the pantomime activity his body motion is also original creation stimulated by the story which is being portrayed.

The expressive nature of rhythmic movement involves construction, organization, and ordering according to feeling. In its imaginative originality each moving statement offers a new and satisfying experience unique to each child.

CREATIVENESS IN PLAYING INSTRUMENTS

The instrumentalist creates music in two ways: as interpreter and as composer. When he performs a composition of others, he is involved as interpreter. The order of tones has been determined by the composer. The instrumentalist's task is to create toward the intent of the composer and, therefore, the aspect of creativeness involved is the element of interpretation, in a manner similar to one of the ways creativeness is involved in singing. Through the development of critical standards at the child's own level, through his participation in reproducing the order of tones intended by the composer and by making the composition an expressive creation of his own, the instrumentalist is clearly involved in the creative act.

The instrumentalist, however, may also partake of the creative act by ordering the very progression of tones which he plays. So, he is involved in the creative act from another perspective.

As in the singing program the process we describe in Chapter 5 on developing the rhythm orchestra places a premium on the actual creative process. The development of the orchestra depends on the expressive acts of the children. The initial impetus may come from the phonograph record, but the specific instrumentation and choice among the various rhythms to be played are made by the children. The act of expression, the reorganization of the musical material, and the development of new and satisfying patterns have all been part of the procedure by which the rhythm orchestra developed. Again creativeness is not only a specific activity in itself; it permeates all of the musical activities.

The development of the rhythmic continuous story and the rhythmic improvisation, or jam session, are also very clearly creative activities. No musical composition provides the initial impetus. No determining control is preestablished for the children. Both the continuous rhythm story and the jam session would be classified as spontaneous creations or improvisations.

Rhythmic Compositions

The development of a rhythmic composition involves the creative act, including preplanning and a conception of the whole as well as the ordering of materials, the act of expression, and the development of new and satisfying patterns. The procedure used for both the rhythmic improvisation, or jam session, and the continuous rhythm story can be developed to include the element of preplanning by the children. After a number of experiences in both of these activities, you will be able to help your children create a rhythmic composition. Several procedures might be followed. Utilize one which comes naturally in your situation. It might be easier to start with a development of the continuous rhythm story, since in that procedure only one instrument plays at a time. The objective now, however, is slightly different. In the continuous rhythm story the development of individual rhythmic reactions on the instruments by individual children is spontaneous. Now, however, you want to move from this spontaneous reaction into specifically planned ones.

Ask your children for suggestions for the initial rhythmic statement. Different children suggest a variety of rhythmic patterns which might start the composition. The class then selects from among the suggested beginnings the one which they would like to develop. Ask for ideas about a rhythm and an instrument suitable to follow this initial statement. Various suggestions will be made by the children. In each case have the first rhythm played and then followed by each of the various suggested second statements. The class selects from among the suggestions the one they consider most appropriate. Ask for suggestions, then for the next statement. Have the first two selected rhythms played and followed by each of the various suggestions for the third statement. The class again selects from among those suggested the one most appropriate. Continue in this manner until the children feel that the composition is complete. Note that there are no predetermined metrical units, there is no specific time value, there are no limiting factors other than the choices of the children. What is appropriate is in every case determined by the group.

We have suggested a total class procedure. You might want to try some variants on it. Select a group of children playing varying sounding instruments, or, better yet, have the children themselves form small groups of four or five playing a variety of types of rhythm instruments. Have each group work out a rhythm composition in some way similar to the procedure suggested above or in any manner in which they want to work.

The rhythm composition based on rhythmic improvisation differs from the procedure described above only in that more than one instrument plays at a time. Since this may be a somewhat more difficult procedure for the children to conceive, it may be more suitable for older than younger children. You will have to make the decision based on your knowledge of your own children. Naturally, the complexity of the resulting composition will vary with the age of the children, their experiences in music, and their feelings and attitudes. Expect simpler compositions from younger children if you try this procedure with them.

The generalized procedure is similar to the one previously used. Ask for an initial suggested rhythmic statement and ask the group to decide on the one that they would like to develop. Ask for suggestions about rhythmic patterns and instruments which might follow. If the children have been involved in improvising over a period of time, they will be full of ideas. It is never wise to start this creative activity without a background of experience in spontaneous creative activity, specifically with rhythmic improvisation. From the suggestions made, have the group decide together which would be most appropriate to follow the initial statement. Proceed then by playing the first statement and each of the suggestions for a second statement. Remember that combinations of instruments will be playing both similar and different rhythms simultaneously. The suggestions for continuation come from the children, who evaluate the suggestions and make the decisions. In this way your class creates an entire rhythmic composition.

You might also want to select one of the improvised rhythmic compositions to work on and develop. If so, you will depend on the children's memory of what they played while improvising. The procedure is quite simple. At the end of an improvisation, merely ask the children to evaluate what they have just played and to make suggestions for improving it. The questions to keep in mind are: (1) How did you like it? (2) How can we make it better? Try the various suggestions with the class and get their decision about the most appropriate suggestion. By a process of trial, modification, planning, reorganizing, reconstructing, a planned rhythmic composition emerges from the initial rhythmic improvisation.

CREATIVENESS IN LISTENING

The listening program detailed in Chapter 7 is based almost completely on the creative process. It places maximum emphasis on the direct interaction of children with music and relies for its development on the expression of children's feelings about the music which they hear, on their ability to reorganize, reconstruct, and reorder the basic elements of music with which they are familiar in new and satisfying patterns to them. Therefore, it fulfills our description of the creative act.

Creation is an active and not a passive process, and it is this activity aspect of the listening program that has received so much emphasis. We try to help children create toward the intention of the composer, and in so doing we help them make the individual composition a part of their own unique experience. The sharing of modes of listening provides the basis for an extension of the musical horizons of all children as they hear ways in which each of them listens differently from all the others. This imaginative process, with its focus on individual

"—and it comes out here?"

New York Philharmonic; Columbia Records.

248

expression of feeling and understanding, applies both to children who listen programmatically and those who listen abstractly.

As teachers we encourage the development of the imagination of children and the expression of feeling. The listening process becomes a highly individual matter, an active and a creative process with a maximum of interaction between the child and the music directly and a minimum of interference with this interactive process.

CREATIVENESS IN TEACHING MUSIC

The materials in this book have been compiled with the problems of the classroom teacher in mind. The creative music program suggested is based on a desire to build the best kind of music program we can conceive based on what we know of children, their growth and development, and the learning process. Fortunately, the major aspects of such a program can be carried on by the classroom teacher who has no specific technical training in music. Certain attributes other than the technical background are needed, however. In order to teach music successfully, the classroom teacher does not have to know the techniques of music, as helpful as these might be. What he does need is a certain attitude and spirit. The classroom teacher needs to be the kind of person willing to learn with children. He needs to be experimental in approach and willing to try new things. With his knowledge of children growing from living together with them in the classroom, the classroom teacher has many assets to capitalize upon. Since he needs no technical training to try out the various procedures recommended, there will be no block toward his efforts to develop a successful music program unless he creates one for himself.

Most of the procedures suggested in this book are not radically new or different. They do depart from some old practices which have long been tried, examined, and found wanting. The procedures suggested have all been tried and tested. They have all worked for some teachers. All of them may not necessarily work for you, and you do not have to feel that you must use all or none. Your task as the classroom teacher is to do the very best you can with the equipment you have. Do not wait until you feel that you can master all of the five kinds of musical activities detailed through the book. Every classroom teacher does not have to develop all five aspects of the program, although naturally, children will benefit if you can. Pick one aspect of the program which seems to hold for you the most promise and try it out. Do not expect to know all of the answers before you begin. Your attitude about music and your knowledge of your children will be two important assets upon which you can build. With all the different approaches facing you as new and untried experiences, the total weight may be frightening. Remember to evaluate your progress primarily on the basis of whether or not your children are having an enjoyable experience with music. If they are not, question yourself. Ask yourself, "What did I do that I should not have done?" "What could I have done that I did not do?" Plan your sessions carefully, but hold yourself flexible and ready to modify your plans as the exigencies of the moment demand. Set your plans for succeeding sessions in terms of the children's reactions to what took place in the preceding ones and in terms of your over-all objectives.

It takes a creative teacher to develop a creative program. Try different approaches. Music is so powerful in its appeal to people that the major asset on your side will be its direct appeal to children.

Try to develop a joyous singing program using songs that children love. Try making and playing rhythm instruments and the development of a rhythm orchestra. Try some improvisations. Try the continuous music story, both with the voices and with instruments. Try some bodily movement. If you feel timorous about stepping immediately into creative bodily movement, do not hesitate to start with formal or informal rhythms. Play much music for your children and encourage free, frank, and open discussion of it. Try a variety of activities and continue the development of those which you find most successful. Success encourages and failure discourages teachers as well as children. You will find that your successes will far exceed any minor failures. Try one new thing at a time rather than scatter your efforts over many different new and untried activities. Utilize your successes as the basis for your succeeding steps. As you develop these, your confidence will grow, and you will be more successful with those activities that perhaps previously did not work out so well.

It is sometimes helpful for more than one teacher in a school to try a similar kind of activity at one time. Mutual discussion after the experience can sometimes be very helpful in exploring additional possibilities.

In the knowledge that you have of your children, of your

Radio and television offer many opportunities to expand children's musical horizons.

New York Philharmonic's Young People's Concert, Leonard Bernstein conducting: Columbia Records.

community, of your children's background, and of yourself you must seek the specific answers to the problem of how to make the choice of activities by which you get started. Once you do get started, you will find that your successes will increase and that you will be able to help your children to an exciting music program that will aid their total growth and development and which will be an asset to them not only today but through their entire lives.

Teaching of this kind is a creative undertaking in its own right. You will be utilizing elements already existing—the needs of the children in your group and various possibilities among the different aspects of the music program. You will select from among these according to your view and will reorder, reconstruct, and reorganize the experience that children have. In the outcome you will discover that most satisfying of all achievements, the fulfillment of the original dedication which led you to teaching in the first place: the growth and development of children to the optimum degree.

KEEP IN MIND

The following items summarize the major content of this chapter. Individual items may be used for debate, discussion, report, or research topics.

1. Creative music is not merely a specific type of activity, but is the underlying philosophical foundation and approach to the whole music program.
2. Every human being is born with potential for creation.
3. In the creative act an individual reorders, reconstructs, and reorganizes existing and known elements into patterns new and satisfying to himself as expresser.
4. Creativeness, not confined solely to the great creative acts of genius, may be applied to all aspects of living.
5. The interpreter creates when he takes known elements, reorganizes, reorders, and reconstructs those into new and satisfying patterns. The instrumentalist, as interpreter, thereby creates toward the intention of the composer.

6. The listener engages in the creative process when he utilizes the music of the composer, reconstructs, reorders, and reorganizes it in the framework of his own experiential background in living.
7. Imagination is essential to any creative act.
8. In helping young children differentiate between the real and the unreal we must not kill the spark of imagination.
9. Imagination depends upon the development of power to use the unreal.
10. The development of the unreal comes under control with the circular recognition of its state. The child needs to know that something is unreal; he needs to know that you know it is unreal; and he needs to know that you know that he knows that it is unreal.
11. Singing becomes a creative activity when children who enjoy the activity apply their own standards to the development of a song, thereby making it their own. They then come to feel the expression of the song as a new and satisfying experience.
12. In the procedure often recommended for creating a song, exaggeration and false emphasis on the regularity of scanning frequently results in very unmusical and unpoetic songs.
13. In creating a song it would be better to emphasize the expressive content of a poem so as to stimulate the suggestion of melodies that express the meaning of the poem rather than the exaggerated metrical scanning.
14. We can think a melody in our minds and think it just as specifically mentally as when we sing it aloud.
15. Spontaneous singing of children may be an additional stimulus to creating songs.
16. The continuous melodic story may also stimulate the creation of songs.
17. An instrumentalist creates music both as interpreter and as composer.
18. The development of the rhythm orchestra and the rhythmic continuous story are both creative processes.

19. Rhythmic improvisation can be developed into a planned rhythm composition.

20. The listening program is based almost completely on the creative process when it places maximum emphasis on the direct interaction of children with music, when it relies for its development on the expression of children's feelings about the music they hear, and on their ability to reorganize, reconstruct, reorder the basic elements of music with which they are familiar in new and satisfying patterns to them.

21. Creative bodily movement becomes creative in both the sense of interpretation and original creation.

22. While the development of a creative music program does not require the classroom teacher to be specifically trained technically in music, it does require creative teaching.

23. The classroom teacher needs to be a person willing to learn with children, experimental in approach, and willing to try new things.

24. The classroom teacher should start his music program with that aspect of it with which he feels most comfortable.

25. The creative teaching of a creative music program helps fulfill an objective of all teachers by providing a means of stimulating the growth and development of children to their greatest potential.

♫ CHAPTER NINE

Reaching Our Objectives

CHAPTER 1 PRESENTED many specific values of the music program under the heading "Why Teach Music?" These values implied many objectives which were further developed throughout the book. We can now systematically state our objectives in the light of the background you have acquired and then examine ways in which you can determine for yourself how close you have come to accomplishing them.

OBJECTIVES

The objectives of the music program have been formulated in many ways by various people, just as the objectives of general education have been often and variously stated. The difference between the stated aims of any program and the real aims as reflected in current practice presents an acute problem. Too often the statement of aims and objectives is a high-level policy statement, philosophical in nature, that, unfortunately, shows little reflection in actual practice. We have reserved the statement of objectives of the music program until the last chapter so that the background of experiences and understandings came first. With this background, we can organize our

255

objectives reasonably and with greater expectations that the rationale of their development will provide better assurance of their accomplishment—a closer identity of practice to purpose.

The real objectives of the music program in our schools must relate to the growth and developmental needs of children. The general objectives of education apply to the music program as well as to the other aspects of the classroom program. It is unnecessary, however, to reformulate the general objectives of education, and this section will devote itself to the objectives unique to the music program.

Let us examine, now, our objectives, and then see how we can utilize these objectives for purposes of evaluation. Since the rationale behind these statements has already been explored, we shall do no more than list them here in organized form.

Guiding Principles

Behind each recommended musical activity, underlying every suggested experience in music, supporting, defining, and limiting the whole approach to the music program have been certain guiding principles which serve as a kind of frame of reference. They may be considered as testing or proving principles—standards by which all ideas for the music program must be tested.

1. The music program should help fulfill the developmental and growth needs of children.
2. The music program should release the music that is within children.
3. The music program should develop children's aesthetic sensitivity and creative potential.
4. The music program should provide each child with rich, joyous, and successful musical experiences that will be satisfying and fulfilling to him.

GENERAL OBJECTIVES

The music program has many general objectives that apply to various aspects of the program.

The music program should *help each child*

... develop positive and favorable attitudes about music.

... develop confidence in his own reaction to music.

... develop knowledge of and familiarity with a wide range of types of music—a repertoire of well-loved music, including all forms of musical expression.

... feel at home with music—listening, producing, and reacting to it.

... develop standards of judgment about music—sufficient to his own purposes and at his own level.

... develop a variety of ways of responding to music.

... develop an understanding of and feeling for the power of music.

... develop various musical means through which he can significantly express his feelings.

... understand how man has used music in different ways to communicate feelings.

... produce music through many mediums: his voice, his body, instruments.

SPECIFIC OBJECTIVES

Each facet of the music program, singing, movement and music, playing music, listening to music, and creating music also has specific objectives in addition to the general objectives.

Singing

To help each child

... develop confidence and pleasure in the use of his singing voice.

... develop facility in spontaneous singing.

... grow in his capacity to enjoy singing many different types of songs.

... learn to listen critically to the singing of the group.

... develop standards for judging the group's singing.

... have opportunities to conduct the group singing.

... compose songs.

... express his own feelings through song.

... gradually develop control over his singing voice.

Movement and Music

To help each child

... express emotion through motion.

... develop confidence in the use of his body as a medium of musical expression.

... use his body in expressive movement independently of any external stimuli.

... free himself from the necessity of stereotyped body responses to music.

... use his whole body for expressive purposes.

... interpret his feelings about music with his body freely.

... explore, examine, and understand his environment and his feelings about this environment and himself through creative body movement.

... interpret dramatic or descriptive content—to communicate feeling with his body.

Playing Music

To help each child

... feel at ease in playing rhythmic, melodic, and harmonic instruments.

... experiment with producing sounds.

... improvise with instruments.

... express his own feelings through playing instruments.

... participate in determining the orchestrations to be played.

... listen critically to his own and the group's playing.

... develop standards for judging his own and the group's playing.

... compose instrumental compositions.

... play instruments in ensemble.

... develop sufficient control over at least one mode of playing music to provide long-lasting satisfactions.

Listening to Music

To help each child

... listen to and become familiar with a wide variety of types of music.

... develop his powers of selective hearing.

... express his judgments and feelings about music openly, freely, and frankly.

... participate in listening as an active process.

... describe the way he listened to specific compositions.

... respect the feelings of others about the music regardless of his own judgment.

... try to hear in music what others heard.

... understand different ways of listening to music.

... differentiate and distinguish among various instrumental sounds.

Creating Music

To help each child

... have opportunities to create new things and ideas in various musical mediums.

... develop his creative powers.

... grow in his comfortable use of the expressive-creative act.

... develop facility in creating music.

... recognize, appreciate, and utilize the creative potential in all mediums of musical expression: singing, playing, listening, moving.

EVALUATION

To determine the value of any program for children, we must clearly have in mind just what we want to accomplish. Evaluation clearly must relate to purposes. Classroom teachers constantly evaluate their effectiveness. In various ways they try to determine how well they accomplish what they intended to accomplish. Elaborate evaluative instruments are not essential. In its essence evaluation is the act of determining the worth and effectiveness of what we do.

We can look, then, to the objectives already stated for real and specific aid as we attempt to evaluate our program. The objectives can be applied to serve three purposes:

1. To aid in arriving at the specific decisions about which musical activities to utilize in the individual classroom
2. To aid in determining the effectiveness of the music program for a specific class, group of classes, or school
3. To aid in determining the musical growth of individual children

Let us consider these three points as three levels of operation—equal in importance, but different from each other. Every statement in the objectives, both general and specific, may be reformulated as a question which could be applied to each of these three levels. The first of the general objectives reads: "The music program should help each child develop positive and favorable attitudes about music." We now reword this objective to apply to each of the three levels indicated above.

1. If our purpose is to determine the suitability of a specific activity in the classroom, we rephrase the objective as a question to read: "Will this specific activity help my children develop positive and favorable attitudes about music?"
2. If our purpose is to determine how effective our music program has been, we rephrase the objective as a question to read: "Has my class been developing positive and favorable attitudes about music?"
3. If our purpose is to arrive at some judgment about Johnny Smith's musical growth, we rephrase the objective as a question to read: "Has Johnny been developing positive and favorable attitudes about music?"

Naturally, all of the objectives would not necessarily apply in any given instance. The evaluative purpose would determine the selection of those applicable objectives to be rephrased as questions. Many teachers will want to apply evaluative criteria on level two in order to check their effectiveness. On level two, most of the objectives would be applicable for rephrasing. However, on level one, to determine the suitability of an activity, only those objectives applicable to the specific activity would be used.

In practical usage, on level two particularly, do not expect all of your questions to be answerable on a "yes" or "no" basis. Some questions will fall into these categories, but others will not. You may want to consider a kind of continuum represented by a line, with "yes" at one end and "no" at the opposite extreme. Your answers, then, would tend to fall somewhere along this line.

As an example of how you might proceed to construct an evaluation device of your own, we offer a chart, derived from questions based on the objectives, for the purpose of determining the effectiveness of a singing program.

	Yes				No
	1	2	3	4	5
1. Are my children developing confidence and pleasure in using their singing voices?					
2. Are my children developing facility in spontaneous singing?					
3. Do my children enjoy singing many different types of songs?					
4. Are my children listening critically to the singing of the group?					
5. Are my children developing good standards for judging the group's singing?					
6. Does each child have opportunities to conduct the group singing?					
7. Does each child participate in composing songs?					
8. Has each child grown in his ability to express his own feelings through song?					
9. Are my children growing in their control over their singing voices?					

Even these questions may have to be modified to meet the exigencies of the existing situation. If you have concluded that there is no abstract measure of precisely what a good music program is, you have concluded correctly. Nor is there a specific standard, measurable according to years or grades, by which the music program can be evaluated. Evaluation must always be in terms of purposes. Evaluation devices, therefore, must be geared to the function to be served. You may prefer to eliminate the specific procedure suggested and embark on developing a series of questions for yourself in which you embody the spirit of the objectives and frame them to reflect the specific purpose of the evaluation.

Here is a group of possible questions, based on the spirit and intent of the objectives, that might be developed in lieu of rephrasing the objectives as questions. The purpose is the same —to evaluate the effectiveness of the singing program.

1. Do my children enjoy singing?
2. Do they look forward to the music sessions with eager anticipation?
3. Do my children freely ask to sing?
4. Do they ask for favorite songs readily?
5. Do they sing spontaneously?
6. Do they respond easily to the continuous music story?
7. Are their standards for their own singing growing?
8. Is their sensitivity to the meaning of various songs growing?
9. Are they able to express their feeling for a song through their singing?
10. Is their repertoire of various types of songs increasing?

The purpose of evaluation ultimately must be to improve current practice. Improvement can come only as teachers feel the importance of improving, feel secure in trying new procedures, and feel comfortable about their potential for success in those new procedures. Consequently, the most significant evaluative devices are those which encourage teachers to proceed with self-evaluation. Evaluation by outsiders may give them some basis for their own judgment about any program.

But their judgment may influence teachers to change their practices very little. As a group, teachers are among the most sincere and hard-working people around. This book has been written for them.

This final chapter on objectives and evaluation will have completely missed its point if it is used as a basis for change based on administrative decree or fiat. Evaluation as intended here is meant solely for the use of teachers, individually or collectively, classroom and specialist, in their constant efforts to improve themselves and their effectiveness with children. Teachers can function admirably in this manner, and administrators would do well to encourage this development.

Teaching, an art as well as a science, has no magical formulas. There is no one right way to teach music or anything else. In teaching music you will have to feel your way, experiment, try, challenge, and change. And you will have to evaluate as you proceed. Learn with your children. The power of music to reach people and the feeling for music within children can be your greatest resources—the foundations of your music program. The genie of successful experiences in music is here. You have but to release it.

Appendix

ॐ APPENDIX A

Suggested Readings

Adams, Fay: *Educating America's Children,* 2d ed., The Ronald Press Company, New York, 1954, pp. 517–558.

Andrews, Gladys: *Creative Rhythmic Movement for Children,* Prentice-Hall, Inc., Englewood Cliffs, N.J., 1954.

Burrows, Alvina Treut: *Teaching Children in the Middle Grades,* D. C. Heath and Company, Boston, 1952, pp. 252–262.

Caswell, Hollis L., and Arthur W. Foshay: *Education in the Elementary School,* 3d ed., American Book Company, New York, 1957, pp. 200–218.

Coleman, Satis: *Creative Music in the Home,* The John Day Company, Inc., New York, 1939.

Copland, Aaron: *Music and Imagination,* Harvard University Press, Cambridge, Mass., 1952.

————: *What to Listen for in Music,* rev. ed., McGraw-Hill Book Company, Inc., New York, 1957.

Culkin, Mabel Louise: *Teaching the Youngest,* The Macmillan Company, New York, 1950, pp. 163–179.

Dewey, John: *Art as Experience,* Minton, Balch & Co., New York, 1934.

Fox, Lillian Mohr, and L. Thomas Hopkins: *Creative School Music,* Silver Burdett Company, Morristown, N.J., 1936.

Gans, Roma, Celia Burns Stendler, and Millie Almy: *Teaching Young Children,* World Book Company, Yonkers, N.Y., 1952, pp. 285–313.

Hartley, Ruth E., Lawrence K. Frank, and Robert M. Goldenson: *Under-*

267

standing Children's Play, Columbia University Press, New York, 1952, pp. 298–338.

Hurley, Beatrice Davis: *Curriculum for Elementary School Children,* The Ronald Press Company, New York, 1957, pp. 355–380.

Lee, J. Murray, and Dorris May Lee: *The Child and His Curriculum,* 2d ed., Appleton-Century-Crofts, Inc., New York, 1950, pp. 595–610.

Macomber, Freeman Glenn: *Principles of Teaching in the Elementary School,* American Book Company, New York, 1954, pp. 259–278.

Mursell, James L.: *Music and the Classroom Teacher,* Silver Burdett Company, Morristown, N.J., 1951.

New York State Education Department: Bureau of Elementary Curriculum Development: *Children, the Music Makers,* The Bureau, Albany, N.Y., 1953.

Ragan, William B.: *Modern Elementary Curriculum,* The Dryden Press, Inc., New York, 1953, pp. 444–454.

Rudolph, Marguerita: *Living and Learning in the Nursery School,* Harper & Brothers, New York, 1954, pp. 75–99.

Saucier, W. A.: *Theory and Practice in the Elementary School,* rev. ed., The Macmillan Company, New York, 1951, pp. 399–425.

Sheehy, Emma Dickson: *There's Music in Children,* rev. ed., Henry Holt and Company, Inc., New York, 1952.

Tooze, Ruth, and Beatrice Perham Krone: *Literature and Music as Resources for Social Studies,* Prentice-Hall, Inc., Englewood Cliffs, N.J., 1955.

℘ APPENDIX B

Song Collections

MANY SONG COLLECTIONS are available in addition to the music series usually used in schools. Although intended for adults, teachers and parents will find many songs in them very suitable for use with children. Of course, some songs in the adult books have no place in schools and selection will depend on adult judgment.

A number of these collections, included in the cross index of the Song List in Appendix C, are indicated with an asterisk. The books are listed according to the author, major editor, or collector.

*Boni, Margaret Bradford: *The Fireside Book of Folk Songs,* Simon and Schuster, Inc., New York, 1947.

*————: *The Fireside Book of Favorite American Songs,* Simon and Schuster, Inc., New York, 1952.

Botsford, Florence Hudson: *Botsford Collection of Folk Songs,* G. Schirmer, Inc., New York. Vol. I, *Songs from the Americas, Asia, and Africa,* 1930; Vol. II, *Northern Europe,* 1931; Vol. III, *Southern Europe,* 1933.

Coleman, Satis N., and Alice G. Thorn: *Another Singing Time (Songs for Nursery and School),* The John Day Company, Inc., New York, 1937.

269

Coleman, Satis N., and Alice G. Thorn: *Singing Time (Songs for Nursery and School)*, The John Day Company, Inc., New York, 1929.

Crowninshield, Ethel: *The Sing and Play Book*, The Boston Music Company, Boston, 1938.

Deutsch, Leonhard: *A Treasury of the World's Finest Folk Songs*, Howell, Soskin, Publishers, Inc., New York, 1942.

*Heller, Ruth: *Our Singing Nation*, Hall and McCreary Company, Chicago, 1955, (paper).

Hunt, Evelyn H.: *Music Time*, The Viking Press, Inc., New York, 1947.

*Ives, Burl: *The Burl Ives Song Book*, Ballantine Books, New York, 1953, (paper).

*Kolb, Sylvia, and John Kolb: *A Treasury of Folk Songs*, rev. ed., Bantam Books, New York, 1955, (paper).

*Landeck, Beatrice: *Git on Board*, rev. ed., Edward B. Marks Music Company, New York, 1950, (paper).

*————: *Songs to Grow On*, Edward B. Marks Music Company, and William Sloane Associates, New York, 1950.

Lloyd, Norman: *The New Golden Song Book*, Simon and Schuster, Inc., New York, 1955.

Lomax, John A., and Alan Lomax: *American Ballads and Folk Songs*, The Macmillan Company, New York, 1934.

————: *Folk Song USA*, Duell, Sloan & Pearce, Inc., New York, 1947.

————: *Our Singing Country*, The Macmillan Company, New York, 1941.

MacCarteney, Laura Pendeiton: *Songs for the Nursery School*, The Willis Music Company, Cincinnati, Ohio, 1937.

*Martin, Florence, and Margaret Rose White: *Songs Children Sing*, Hall and McCreary Company, Chicago, 1943, (paper).

Sandburg, Carl: *The American Songbag*, Harcourt, Brace and Company, Inc., New York, 1927.

*Seeger, Ruth Crawford: *American Folk Songs for Children (in Home, School, and Nursery School)*, Doubleday & Company, Inc., New York, 1948.

*Smith, Fowler, Harry Robert Wilson, and Glenn H. Woods: *Songs We Sing*, Hall and McCreary Company, Chicago, 1940, (paper).

Woodgate, Leslie: *The Penguin Song Book*, Penguin Books, Inc., Baltimore, 1951, (paper).

Song List, with Sources

THE FOLLOWING LIST of songs is meant to be neither all inclusive nor representative. It is merely a list to help you explore additional possibilities. You will probably find many old favorites you have not thought of for years. You may also find some new songs destined to become favorites. The major criteria for including songs in this list have been that they be easily accessible and that children have liked them.

Since the name of a song with no indication of where to find it can be more of a teaser than a help, each song is located in one or more of the song collections listed in Appendix B, where you will find the complete citation. The source books used in this index are listed below. In the song list the first number of each set following the title refers to the book in this list; the second number, after the colon, gives the page.

1. Boni: *The Fireside Book of Folk Songs*
2. Boni: *The Fireside Book of Favorite American Songs*
3. Heller: *Our Singing Nation*
4. Ives: *The Burl Ives Song Book*
5. Kolb: *A Treasury of Folk Songs*
6. Landeck: *Git on Board*

Abdullah Bulbul Ameer   10:15
All through the Night   2:337, 3:45
Alouette   1:124, 10:113
America   3:70, 8:151, 10:53
America, the Beautiful   3:167, 8:149, 10:58
Anatomical Song   7:118
Annie Laurie   1:110, 3:44
Arkansas Traveler   1:58
Auld Lang Syne   1:76, 3:5, 10:118

Barnyard Song   7:76
Believe Me, If All Those Endearing Young Charms   2:280, 3:47, 10:16
Billy Boy   3:46, 4:168, 8:71
Black Is the Color   3:52
Blow the Man Down   1:152, 3:31, 4:130, 5:122, 10:20
Blue Tail Fly   1:72, 3:65, 4:206, 5:140, 7:42
The Boll Weevil   2:81, 5:60, 6:24, 10:49
Bought Me a Cat   9:104
Buffalo Girls   3:64, 4:208, 9:32
Built My Lady a Fine Brick House   9:170

Camptown Races   1:64, 3:76, 10:37
Captain Kidd   2:332, 3:10, 4:44, 5:116
Casey Jones   1:142
Cielito Lindo   3:48, 5:202, 10:38
Cindy   5:182, 6:20
Clementine   1:82, 3:155
Coasts of High Barbary   1:166

Dixie   1:192, 3:90, 10:39
Dona Nobis Pacem   6:80
The Donkey   10:100
Down in the Valley   1:99, 4:168, 5:148, 7:9, 10:55
Drink to Me Only with Thine Eyes   1:90, 3:18, 10:3

Eency, Weency Spider   9:126
Erie Canal   1:37, 3:74, 4:228, 6:32, 10:99
Every Monday Morning   9:156

℘ APPENDIX D

Record Suggestions

THE QUANTITY of phonograph records produced in recent years has increased tremendously. Unfortunately, the volume does not always reflect high quality; even the best-intentioned companies feel impelled to appeal to various markets. Never before, however, has so much music of high quality been so accessible to so many people as through the medium of modern phonograph recordings.

This list of suggested recordings is intended to be neither complete nor representative; its purpose is to get you started. You will find many old favorites, perhaps, and some new suggestions. Although some of the selections you want will be recorded by one company only, you will find that in many cases you will have a choice. Where possible, listen to the record before you purchase it, so that you can better decide on its suitability for your purpose. Many of the records suggested are just as suitable for adults as for children, and you may find some suggestions to add to your own personal collection.

The types of records have been combined into a single alphabetical arrangement. Music by a single composer is listed under his name; collections of music by different composers

276

and music unidentified by composer are listed by title. Where possible, the recording musicians are identified. The speed of the recording is abbreviated at the end of the listing as (33) for 33 and ⅓ revolutions per minute, or (45) or (78) for those two speeds respectively.

All around the Mulberry Bush, sung by Florence Calder, Allegro Junior 306 (78)

America Marches, The Goldman Band, Camden CAL 125 (33)

American Folk Songs, sung by John Jacob Niles, Victor CAL 245 (33)

American Folk Songs for Children, sung by Pete Seeger, Folkways FP 701 (33)

Animal Fair, sung by Burl Ives, Columbia JL-8013 (33)

Bach, Johann Sebastian, *Air on G String,* Toscanini conducting the NBC Symphony Orchestra, Victor V7103 (78)

———, *Passacaglia and Fugue in C Minor,* Ormandy conducting the Philadelphia Orchestra, Columbia ML 2058 (33); or E. Power Biggs, organist, Columbia ML 4500, vol. 3 (33)

———, *Toccata and Fugue in D Minor,* Ormandy conducting the Philadelphia Orchestra, Columbia ML 2058 (33); or E. Power Biggs, organist, Columbia ML 4500, vol. 3 (33)

Barber, Samuel, *Adagio for Strings,* Musical Sound Books MSB 78158 (78)

Bartók, Béla, *Concerto No. 3 for Piano and Orchestra,* Gyorgy Sandor, pianist, with Ormandy conducting the Philadelphia Orchestra, Columbia ML 4239 (33)

———, *Concerto for Orchestra,* Reiner conducting the Pittsburgh Symphony Orchestra, Columbia ML 4102 (33)

Beethoven, Ludwig van, *Symphony No. 5,* Toscanini conducting the NBC Symphony Orchestra, Victor LM 1757 (33)

———, *Symphony No. 9,* Toscanini conducting the NBC Symphony Orchestra, Victor LM 6009 (33)

Blue Tail Fly, Shoo Fly, Paw Paw Patch, sung by Burl Ives with children's chorus, Decca K-107 (78)

Bozo at the Circus, Capitol DBX-114 (78)

Brahms, Johannes, *Symphony No. 1,* Toscanini conducting the NBC Symphony Orchestra, Victor LM 1702 (33)

———, *Symphony No. 3,* Koussevitzky conducting the Boston Symphony Orchestra, Victor LM 1025 (33)

Britten, Benjamin, *Young Person's Guide to the Orchestra,* Peter Pears, narrator, with Markevitch conducting the Philharmonia Orchestra, Angel 35135 (33)

Building a City, told and sung by Tom Glazer, Young People's Records YPR 711 (78)

Children's Favorites, (folk songs) sung by Burl Ives, Columbia CL 2570 (33)

Coates, Eric, *The Three Bears,* Musical Sound Books MSB 78038 (78)

Copland, Aaron, *Appalachian Spring,* Koussevitzky conducting the Boston Symphony Orchestra, Victor LCT 1134 (33)

———, *Billy the Kid,* Bernstein conducting the RCA Victor Symphony Orchestra, Victor LM 1031 (33)

———, *El Salon Mexico,* Bernstein conducting the Columbia Chamber and Symphony Orchestra, Columbia ML 2203 (33)

———, *Lincoln Portrait,* Rodzinski conducting the New York Philharmonic Orchestra, Columbia ML 2042 (33)

The Music of Aaron Copland, written by Raymond Abrashkin, conducted by Hendl, Young People's Records YPR 408 (78)

Copland, Aaron, *Rodeo Suite,* Levine conducting the Ballet Theatre Orchestra, Capitol P-8196 (33)

Debussy, Claude, *La Mer,* Toscanini conducting the NBC Symphony Orchestra, Victor LM 1833 (33)

———, *Afternoon of a Faun,* Ormandy conducting the Philadelphia Orchestra, Columbia ML 5112 (33)

Dukas, Paul, *The Sorcerer's Apprentice,* Ormandy conducting the Philadelphia Orchestra, Columbia AAL-26 (33)

Dvořák, Antonin, *Symphony No. 5 in E Minor (New World),* Toscanini conducting the NBC Symphony Orchestra, Victor LM 1778 (33)

Folk Songs for Singing and Dancing, sung by Tom Glazer, Young People's Records YPR 8005–6 (78)

Franck, César, *Symphony in D Minor,* Ormandy conducting the Philadelphia Orchestra, Columbia ML 4939 (33)

French Folk Songs for Children, sung by Martial Singher, Decca K-67

Gershwin, George, *An American in Paris,* Bernstein conducting the RCA Victor Symphony Orchestra, Victor LM 1031 (33)

———, *Rhapsody in Blue,* Oscar Levant, pianist, with Ormandy conducting the Philadelphia Orchestra, Columbia CL 700 (33)

Gounod, Charles, *Funeral March of a Marionette,* Fiedler conducting the Boston Pops Orchestra, Victor ERA-27 (45)

Grieg, Edvard, *Concerto in A Minor,* Guiomar Novaes, pianist, with Swarowsky conducting the Pro Musica Symphony Orchestra, Vox 8520 (33)

———, *Peer Gynt, Suite No. 1, Op. 46, and Suite No. 2, Op. 55,* Cameron conducting the London Philharmonic Orchestra, London LLP 153 (33)

Grofé, Ferde, *Grand Canyon Suite,* Toscanini conducting the NBC Symphony Orchestra, Victor LM 1004 (33)

Harmon, L. N., and F. N. Carter, *Harvest Time,* sung by Eugene Lowell Singers (folk songs from France, England, Japan, South America, Bohemia, and the United States), Young People's Records YPR 9001 (78)

Haufrecht, Herbert, *Little Hawk—the Indian Boy,* by Jay Williams and Raymond Abrashkin; sung by Arthur Malvin and chorus, Young People's Records YPR 435 (78)

———, *A Walk in the Forest,* from the book *In the Forest* by Marie Hall Ets, narrated by David Pfeffer, conducted by Lichter, Young People's Records YPR 805 (78)

Haydn, Franz Joseph, *Symphony No. 94 (Surprise),* Koussevitzky conducting the Boston Symphony Orchestra, Victor LM 9034 (33)

———, *Toy Symphony,* conducted by Goberman, Young People's Records YPR 1001 (78)

Honegger, Arthur, *Concertino for Piano and Orchestra,* Oscar Levant, pianist, with Reiner conducting the Columbia Symphony Orchestra, Columbia ML 2156 (33)

———, *Pacific 231,* Music Sound Books MSB 78156 (78)

Hughes, Langston, *The Rhythms of the World,* narrated by Langston Hughes, based on the *First Book of Rhythms* by the same author, Folkways FP 740 (33)

Hunter's Horn, Young People's Records YPR 421 (78)

Kabalevsky, Dmitri, *The Comedians,* Fiedler conducting the Boston Pops Orchestra, Victor LM 1106 (33)

Kleinsinger, George, *Pan the Piper,* narrated by Paul Wing, with Russ Case and his orchestra, Victor Y-2023 (78)

——— and Paul Tripp, *Happy Instruments,* Columbia CL 2587 (78)

———, *The Story of Celeste,* narrated by Victor Jory, Coral 9–2300 (45)

———, *Tubby the Tuba,* story and lyrics by Paul Tripp, narrated by Victor Jory, Columbia JL 8013; told and sung by Danny Kaye, Decca, CU 106 (78)

Lentil, based on the story by Robert McCloskey, harmonica played by Eddy Manson, Young People's Records YPR 1–309 (78)

Liadow, Anatol, *Folk Songs for Orchestra,* conducted by Goberman, Young People's Records YPR 405 (78)

Little Brass Band, by Hendl-Brown, told by Frank Gallop, Young People's Records YPR 703 (78)

Lockwood, Norman, *Riddle Me This,* lyrics by T. Niles, told and sung by Lee Sweetland, Children's Record Guild CRG 5015 (78)

May, Billy, *Rusty in Orchestraville,* story by Alan W. Livingston, instrument voices by Sonovox, performed by Henry Blair and Billy Bletcher, Capitol L 3007 (33)

Mendelssohn, Felix, *Concerto in E Minor,* Jascha Heifetz, violinist, with

Beecham conducting the Royal Philharmonic Orchestra, Victor LM 18 (33)

Milhaud, Darius, *La Création du Monde,* Bernstein conducting the Columbia Symphony Orchestra, Columbia ML 2203 (33)

Moore, Douglas, *The Emperor's New Clothes,* libretto by Raymond Abrashkin, conducted by Goberman, Young People's Records YPR 1007–8 (78)

———, *Puss in Boots,* libretto by Raymond Abrashkin, conducted by Lowell, Young People's Records YPR 8003–4 (78)

———, *Said the Piano to the Harpsichord,* told by David Allen and Gilbert Mack, Young People's Records YPR 411 (78)

———, *The Wonderful Violin,* played by Mischa Mischakoff, Young People's Records YPR 311 (78)

Moussorgsky, Modest, *Night on Bare Mountain,* Stokowski conducting his symphony orchestra, Victor LM 1816 (33)

———, *Pictures at an Exhibition,* Ravel orchestration, Toscanini conducting the NBC Symphony Orchestra, Victor LM 1838 (33)

Mozart, Wolfgang Amadeus, *Symphony No. 40, G Minor, K.550,* Toscanini conducting the NBC Symphony Orchestra, Victor LM 1789 (33)

Muffin in the City, from the story by Margaret Wise Brown, told by Norman Rose, Young People's Records YPR 601 (78)

North, Alex, *Little Indian Drum,* story by Thelma Field and Margaret Wise Brown, told and sung by David Brooks, Young People's Records YPR 619 (78)

Prokofieff, Serge, *Cinderella,* adapted by Leo Israel, told by Norman Rose, conducted by Mohaupt, Children's Record Guild CRG 201 (78)

———, *Classical Symphony,* Koussevitzky conducting the Boston Symphony Orchestra, Victor LM 1215 (33)

———, *The Love for Three Oranges, March from,* Ansermet conducting the Orchestre de la Suisse Romande, London LS 503 (33)

———, *Peter and the Wolf,* narrated by Alec Guiness, with Fiedler conducting the Boston Pops Orchestra, Victor LM 1761 (33); or narrated by Frank Phillips, with Malko conducting the London Philharmonic Orchestra, London FFRR LPS 151 (33)

———, *Symphony No. 5, Op. 100,* Koussevitzky conducting the Boston Symphony Orchestra, Victor LM 1045 (33)

Ravel, Maurice, *Bolero,* Ormandy conducting the Philadelphia Orchestra, Columbia AL-51 (33)

———, *Mother Goose Suite,* Koussevitzky conducting the Boston Symphony Orchestra, Victor LM 1012 (33)

Rimsky-Korsakoff, Nicolas, *Scheherezade,* Monteux conducting the San Francisco Symphony Orchestra, Victor LM 1002 (33)

Saint-Saëns, Camille, *The Carnival of the Animals,* Markevitch conducting the Philharmonia Orchestra, Angel 35135 (33)

———, *Danse Macabre,* Toscanini conducting the NBC Symphony Orchestra, Victor LM 1118 (33)

Sandoval, Miguel, *Little Pedro,* Latin American Folk Songs, English lyrics by Leo Paris, sung by David Pfeffer, et al., Children's Record Guild CRG 5025 (78)

———, *Little Pedro and the Street Singers,* Children's Record Guild CRG 5028 (78)

Schwartz, Tony, *1, 2, 3, and a Zing Zing Zing,* street games and songs of children of New York City, recorded and edited by Tony Schwartz, Folkways FP 703 (33)

———, *Millions of Musicians,* a documentary of musical expression in everyday life, conceived, recorded, and narrated by Tony Schwartz, Folkways FP 60 (33)

Sing a Song with Charity Bailey, Vols. I and II, Decca K-155 and K-156 (78)

Smetana, Bedrich, *The Moldau,* Toscanini conducting the NBC Symphony Orchestra, Victor LM 1118 (33)

Songs in French for Children, sung by Lucienne Vernay, Columbia CL 675 (33)

Songs of the South African Veld, sung by Josef Marais and his Bushveld Band, Decca 5014 LP (33)

Songs to Grow On, Vol. 2, School Days, with Pete Seeger, Charity Bailey, Lead Belly, Adelaid Van Way, Cisco Houston, Folkways FP 20 (33)

Spirituals, sung by Marian Anderson, Victor LRM 7006 and LM 110 (33)

Square Dances for Children, Columbia J-147 (78)

Strauss, Richard, *Till Eulenspiegel's Merry Pranks,* Reiner conducting the RCA Victor Symphony Orchestra, Victor LM 1180 (33)

Stravinsky, Igor, *Capriccio for Piano,* Monique Haas, pianist, with Friscay conducting the Rias Symphony Orchestra, Decca DL 9515 (33)

———, *The Firebird Suite,* Stravinsky conducting the New York Philharmonic Orchestra, Columbia 4ML 4882 (33)

———, *Petrouchka,* Ansermet conducting the Orchestre de la Suisse Romande, London LLP-130 (33)

Tchaikovsky, Peter Ilyich, *Nutcracker Suite,* Stokowski conducting his symphony orchestra, Victor LM 9023 (33)

Train to the Farm, told by Norman Rose, sung by Eugene Lowell Singers, Children's Record Guild CRG 1011 (78)

Train to the Zoo, told by Norman Rose, sung by Eugene Lowell Singers, Children's Record Guild CRG 1001 (78)

Weber, Carl Maria von, *Rondo for Bassoon and Orchestra,* Eli Carmen, soloist, Young People's Records YPR 1009 (78)

Index